WHO ARE THE "G[...]
MODERN AMERIC[...]

They are our society's [...]
Gifted, educated, ambitious, they are ready at
a moment's notice to sell their homes and move
thousands of miles away in search of power,
prestige, higher salary. Forty-two million
Americans change their home addresses at
least once every year.

Such constant uprooting robs the individual of
his sense of identity. It leads to gnawing loneliness and moral bankruptcy. And, as Vance
Packard shows in this compelling study, it is
destroying the social fabric of cities and towns
across the nation.

"Astonishing revelations...a thoughtful, well-
documented, informative book which should
be read and pondered by all."
—*Nashville Tennessean*

"Thoughtful, highly readable...Packard is at
his best." —*Saturday Review*

"Touching live nerves in this society...he has
been able to popularize social research which
in the hands of most of his colleagues would
have turned to methodological mud."
—*Kirkus Reviews*

"Eye-opening, incisively written, totally compelling...will help us all to rediscover the lost
sense of community and continuity in our
lives." —*Book-of-the-Month Club News*

A NATION OF STRANGERS
was originally published by
David McKay Company, Inc.

VANCE PACKARD

A
NATION
OF
STRANGERS

PUBLISHED BY POCKET BOOKS NEW YORK

To Jane, Prudy, and Harvey

A NATION OF STRANGERS

David McKay edition published 1972

POCKET BOOK edition published February 1974

L

Standard Book Number: 671-78662-8.
Library of Congress Catalog Card Number: 72-85755.
This POCKET BOOK edition is published by arrangement with David McKay Company, Inc. Copyright, ©, 1972, by Vance Packard. All rights reserved. This book, or portions thereof, may not be reproduced by any means without permission of the original publisher: David McKay Company, Inc., 750 Third Avenue, New York, N.Y. 10017.

Front cover photograph by ESI Graphics.
Printed in the U.S.A.

Personal
Note

To the best of my knowledge, all my aunts, uncles, and grandparents spent most of their lives within thirty miles of Troy, Pennsylvania. They were farmers, horse traders, merchants, mailmen. One uncle was a local telephone tycoon. My parents' 105-acre dairy farm was in a hilly area seven miles from Troy. As a boy I believe I knew everyone living within four miles of our farm. And I guess Dad knew just about everyone in the county. He enjoyed talking. We met people as families at Grange Hall suppers on Saturday nights. Mother played the organ. We met at church festivities, at cattle auctions, at the milk station, at the icehouse pond, and at the contests on the steep road leading to Granville Summit on Sunday afternoons. The contest was to see who could drive his car the farthest up the hill in high gear.

When I was nine my parents made a radical decision. They aspired for my sixteen-year-old brother and my nineteen-year-old sister (and for me) to have college educations. The only way they could finance this, they felt, was to move a hundred and fifteen miles from our rural community to Penn State College (now University) where Dad became supervisor of the college farms. It seemed a thousand miles away geographically and psychologically.

The change in worlds hit my father most vividly. For five months—soon after the move—he was acutely ill with a well-known psychosomatic disorder. We all suffered considerable homesickness. In the long run the move probably was beneficial, at least for the children: it assured us college educations at a nominal cost. Since Mother took in college students as roomers to help with family finances, I had college students as roommates during most of my years from eighth grade through senior high school, which may or may not have had a beneficial influence on me.

Today a number of my relatives still live near Troy, but several of my cousins, my nieces, my brother, and my sister are scattered in many states. The nearest relative to my home in New Canaan, Connecticut, is a niece who lives about a hundred and ten miles away. My two sons live in Wisconsin and Pennsylvania; my mother-in-law, until her recent death, lived much of the time in Florida. I have no idea where my daughter will be living by the time this is published because her husband has just returned from Vietnam to re-establish himself in civilian life. As for myself, I now am away from New Canaan overnight a great many days each year.

When my wife Virginia and I moved to New Canaan twenty-four years ago it was a semi-rural town and I soon knew most of the people living within a mile of us. In recent years almost all the old neighbors have moved and many dozens of new houses have sprung up near us, many of them occupied by high-mobile managerial and professional families. One house very close by, for example, has been occupied by four families in five years. My wife and I make stabs at inviting newcomers in, and there are still a few old standbys left in the neighborhood, but today I wouldn't even recognize half of the people living within five hundred yards of our house. Virginia and I feel increasingly isolated.

Our experience of mounting isolation and family fragmentation is mild indeed compared with the experiences of many people I have met. We at least have a home base, and we don't have to keep moving.

Personal isolation is becoming a major social fact of our time. A great many people are disturbed by the feeling that they are rootless or increasingly anonymous, that they are living in a continually changing environment where there is little sense of community. The phrase "home town" may well fade from our language in this century. Already half of all U.S. heads of families live more than a hundred miles from where they were born—and one out of five lives more than a thousand miles from his birthplace.[1]

I will seek in this report to inspect this rootlessness as it exists in many places, primarily in America but also abroad. What are its causes, what are the new institutions it is creating, and what is its impact on our values, our behavior, our emotional well-being, and the functioning of our communities? How are people adjusting to rootlessness? And what are some of the better remedies being advanced and devised to ameliorate it?

In four of my earlier books I presented evidence that increased rootlessness was an important cause of some of the curious behavior I was then describing. It gradually dawned on me that this increasing rootlessness of people was such a pervasive phenomenon that it has a lot to do with what ails America as a society. This conclusion led me, in 1968, to undertake the analysis which is presented here.

I have sought in all my previous books of social comment, including the four just mentioned, to put the focus on what is happening to the individual as the result of pressures created by social and technological change. Here my primary concern may seem to be on what is happening to "community" and what is needed to restore it. In my view, however, I am still talking about the individual. There is normally a certain tension between the individual's yearning for freedom and the community's need for cooperation and rules. But the individual needs a sense of community. This is a point that has often been overlooked in recent years. He needs it for the shaping of his own sense of identity. He needs it if he is to achieve a sense of self-esteem and well-being. The challenge is to achieve a congenial balance between the individual's yearning for freedom and his current urgent need for community and continuity. Ways must be evolved to slow down the accelerating social fragmentation.

I have imposed on so many people in this research that I won't attempt any proper acknowledgment. A number who helped will be mentioned at appropriate places. I really must, however, specifically express my indebtedness to officials of the American Telephone and Telegraph Company and the General Telephone and Electronics Corporation in many parts of the country who provided me with mobility rates in their towns, as reflected in main residential telephone disconnects. And I likewise must thank officials and hostesses of Welcome Wagon International for briefing me on newcomers in many of the towns I visited. I also want to thank officials and several members of Firestone Local 7 of the United Rubber, Cork, Linoleum and Plastic Workers of America in Akron; numerous officials of the National Institute of Mental Health, of the U.S. Department of Labor, and of the Bureau of the Census. And I feel a very special indebtedness to sociologist Pierre de Vise of the Hospital Planning Council for Metropolitan Chicago for the hours he spent in briefing me on the shifting of ethnic groups in greater Chicago. Also for their repeated counsel and assistance I thank Henry Senber, Judith Chayes Neiman, Laura Howes, William Crotty, Douglas Werner, Arthur Gould, Jr., Simon Burrows, Kirkham Cornwell, Jr., Randall Packard, Vance P. Packard, Cynthia Richmond, Ann Bridgman, and Marion Fuller.

Contents

PART THREE: IMPACT ON THE WAY PEOPLE BEHAVE

PART FOUR: TOWARD REDUCING THE FRAGMENTATION

"One thing you see is how many lonely people there are. People pick us up and pour out their life stories to us."—KEN LUSSENDEN, UNIVERSITY OF MICHIGAN STUDENT, IN DESCRIBING HIS PRIMARY IMPRESSION AFTER HITCHHIKING ACROSS AMERICA.

"Pretty soon we are all going to be a metropolitan-type people in this country without ties or commitments to long-time friends and neighbors."—ELI GINZBERG, SPECIALIST IN HUMAN RESOURCES AND MOBILITY, COLUMBIA UNIVERSITY.

"Many people prefer moving to staying around and saying good-by to everyone else."—TWO WIVES IN HIGH-MOBILE BIRMINGHAM, MICHIGAN.

1.

A Society of Torn Roots

The increasingly rootless nature of Americans provides a fresh, and to me fascinating, perspective for assessing the drift of modern societies.

While the footlooseness of Americans as pioneers was a source of vitality and charm, several of the new forms that the accelerating rootlessness of Americans is taking should be a cause for alarm. Great numbers of inhabitants feel unconnected to either people and places and throughout much of the nation there is a breakdown in community living. In fact there is a general shattering of small-group life. A number of forces are promoting social fragmentation. We are confronted with a society that is coming apart at the seams. And in the process we appear to be breeding a legacy of coldness in many of the coming generation.

To explore this major phenomenon of our times I made a number of trips to towns and cities in the United States that had attracted my curiosity. And briefly for comparative information I visited cities in four countries abroad. Typically in America I would fly into the town or city to be visited, rent a car and drive around for a day

1

or two to get the feel of the area, and then begin talking with people about their life patterns. I would also talk with people who might have special knowledge such as local officials, reformers, professors, social workers, school officials, businessmen, realtors, and union officials to get their impressions. There were many group discussions.

And usually in the evening at my motel, with little else to do, I would read published or mimeographed reports of investigations I had assembled dealing with aspects of contemporary rootlessness: its prevalence, forms, causes, effects, and possible amelioration. Also in my research I conducted samplings involving a few hundred people in four communities.

The exploration led me to believe that at least 40 million Americans now lead feebly rooted lives. We are seeing so deep an upheaval of life patterns that we are becoming a nation of strangers.

In a broad sense this contemporary uprooting takes many forms. There is, for example, the uprooting of traditional male-female relationships, of traditional religious beliefs, of vocational stability because of rapid job obsolescence, and of onrushing technological and social changes in general. In this exploration I will focus only on five forms of uprooting that are *creating greater distances between people.*

First, there is the uprooting of people who move again and again and again into strange locations. Although there are often positive values in moderate mobility (and I will examine them), continually repeated mobility is another matter. This is especially unsettling when there is an element of compulsion in the moves, as is so frequently the case when transfers of business and governmental personnel are involved.

Then, there is the uprooting that occurs when once authentic communities undergo upheaval. This is caused partly by the accelerated population growth since World War II and partly by the disruptions created by vast skyways cutting through populous areas . . . by urban renewal . . . the in-and-out migration of industrial plants . . . ethnic groups competing for urban living space . . . the repeated desperate flight of urban families outward toward cleaner air, some greenery and, hopefully, less crime. With this turbulence, brand-new suburban areas that were created only fifteen or twenty years ago are already being viewed as obsolete. In such an environment millions of Americans who continue to live in one house might be called psychological nomads: they stay on but the turnover of people around them is so great that they can no longer enjoy a sense of place. They find themselves with few close ties to friends, kinfolk, or community.

Third, there can be a sense of uprooting even when one's neighbors remain. As people increasingly live in multiple-dwelling units made necessary by the imploding pressures of millions of rural and small-town people crowding into metropolitan areas, neighbors frequently live side by side in anonymity. Although it is not invariably true, dwellers in high-rise apartment houses tend to remain strangers. A large city's vast throngs—when not naturally subdivided into small-group affiliations—tend to become coldly impersonal and wary.

Fourth, there is the fact that even in smaller cities, where people live in their own homes on tree-lined streets, individuals may remain strangers to their neighbors if continuous-operation plants and offices dominate the area's economy. And this is increasingly the situation. With highly automated companies operating around the clock, the people working on various time shifts tend to look for sociability not to neighbors but to people living elsewhere who are geared to the same time shifts as their own.

Finally there is the accelerating fragmentation of our basic social unit, the family. This can be seen in the steady rise in broken families, in the increasing number of family members over sixty who move away (often great distances) to retirement "villages," and in the rapidly rising numbers of young people to leave their home localities permanently or for extended periods. Millions of young people now lead life patterns of near chronic movement. Some go with packs on their back, others go on two-wheeled vehicles. And in the early 1970s small live-in vans

replaced sports cars as the favorite four-wheeled vehicle
of sophisticated young Americans. Other millions of young
people travel far from their home communities to attend
college. And college for many turns out to be a vast multiversity where their principal source of personal identity
may be the ID card. Still other millions of young are
learning to be mobile through the courtesy of the Pentagon, which arranges involuntary tours to all parts of the
nation and globe.

In all this disruption of familiar patterns, some people
respond with a deepened sense of loneliness. James Ger-
aghty, who has been commissioning *The New Yorker's*
cartoons for three decades and tries to keep abreast of the
national mood, remarked some months ago, "Loneliness
is the name of the game." And another perceptive observer of the national mood, James Reston, wrote in *The
New York Times* in another context: "There is a sense of
loneliness in the country." He was speaking primarily of
the many people who no longer have confidence in their
leaders and have come to doubt the fidelity of numerous
U.S. institutions. Such doubt unquestionably was behind
much of the disgruntlement about the "system" or the
"establishment" noted in the support for the defiant
George Wallace, a genius at tapping disgruntlement, in
the 1972 primaries. George McGovern, in a different
way, also soared to national prominence by tapping disgruntlement.

A sense of loneliness also undoubtedly accounts for the
fact that many of the most popular songs of the past few
years have focused on the sense of hurt and yearning.
Carole King lamented in a smash hit that nobody seemed
to stay in one place any more. In another very popular
tune she exclaimed how good it was to know you had a
friend. And in the taverns of Northern industrial cities
former hillbillies for months sipped beer to the lament, "I
wanna go home, I wanna go home."

Other loosely rooted people react to the disruption of
familiar patterns by hyperactive sociability. On the Upper

West Side of Manhattan, at least one party-throwing social circle consists of people who all happened to meet while walking their dogs.

Still others react to uprootedness by doing their own thing and becoming indifferent to all but a few fellow citizens.

Whatever the individual reactions, we are rapidly losing several critical ingredients of a civilized, salutary society. We are seeing a sharp increase in people suffering alienation or just feeling adrift, which is having an impact on emotional and even physical health. We know there is a substantial increase of inhabitants suffering a loss of sense of community, identity, and continuity. These losses all contribute to a deteriorating sense of well-being, both for individuals and for society.

It is not reasonable, incidentally, to compare today's mobility of people with that of frontier days. Then, people typically traveled in wagon trains where they developed a deep sense of shared experience and companionship. At the end of their journey they usually located in villages small enough in scale so that they soon knew everyone. And they depended on one another for protection from Indians, outlaws, and marauding wolves or mountain lions. Today's mobility is likely to be a more solitary act that ends by putting the mover among a mass of disoriented neighbors. The only protection today's mover needs is from hoodlums and business gougers, and he usually can't expect much help from new neighbors.

The most disquieting aspect of today's uprootedness is that transients at the prime of life frequently come from the ranks of our more talented citizens, including many of our natural leaders. In frontier days it was working people and the losers seeking a second chance who most often migrated. Today the high-mobiles are more likely to be people of talent and leadership skills, the kind who ordinarily play the major role in holding a community together and giving it a source of pride. When these more talented citizens increasingly lead lives of near perpetual motion, the communities they move in and out of must improvise, must continually revise programs, and must settle for second or third best in leadership.

Although movement of people is only one element contributing to the social fragmentation we are witnessing it is a major and conspicuous element. And it is measurable. Therefore I'll sum up briefly the findings of two organizations that keep closest watch on the movement of Americans: the U.S. Bureau of the Census and the American Telephone and Telegraph Company.

Census experts have long felt that there is more geographic mobility within the United States than in almost any other country in the world. Recently, reasonably comparable census data from several countries have pointed to this higher velocity of Americans. U.S. Census Bureau expert Larry H. Long cites figures for the 1960s from Great Britain, Japan, and Canada.[1] When allowance is made for variations in life expectancy these findings emerge:

—The average American moves about 14 times in his lifetime.
—The average Briton moves about 8 times.
—The average Japanese moves about 5 times.

A population specialist in France, incidentally, estimates that changes of address each year in that country are at about one half the U.S. rate.

But mobility is now increasing in most countries affected by technological change. (For evidences of worldwide increases in mobility see Appendix A.)

Where technology is in a runaway stage, as in the United States, both mobility and general uprootedness tend to run highest.

About 40 million Americans change their home addresses at least once *each year*. And more than a third of these people move across a county or state line. In this twentieth century there has been a 25 percent increase in people living in a state other than the one in which they were born. That is only mildly suggestive of the amount of total movement that has actually been occurring. The massive leap in mobility that started with World War II can be seen by comparing the proportion of migrants moving across county lines in two five-year periods twenty years apart: 1935–40 and 1955–60. (The Census Bureau first began recording such moves in the 1940 Census.) During the twenty-year period from the 1940 Census to the 1960 Census there was a leap of 50 percent in such internal migration.[2]

Census figures indicate that the proportion of people changing their addresses each year plateaued out from the World War II peak and has been involving about 19 percent of all Americans each year.

Telephone company records on the other hand show a quite different picture. Telephone records show a steady and quite sharp rise in people on the move since 1945 when World War II ended.

The American Telephone and Telegraph Company keeps records, for the nation and for every town and state where it operates, of the percentage of main residential telephones in service that are disconnected within each year. Almost all disconnects represent moves by subscribers.

These records show that, while the disconnect rate was 17 percent in 1946, the first full postwar year, it rose gradually to 25 percent by 1971!

How can one account for these quite different pictures of recent mobility recorded by the two organizations? There seem to be two main explanations:

For one thing the Census figures do not reflect the *extra* moves of the many Americans who move more than once within a single year, whereas the phone company records catch every move of phone users.

Also with rising affluence many mobile college students have private telephones and have them disconnected between school years. Census officials acknowledge that in their annual mobility check they miss the movement of many of the millions of college students who now go away to college.

Both the Census and telephone records understate U.S.

mobility somewhat because many movers do not get counted by either organization. Neither organization, for example, records the moves of people who live in military barracks . . . nor the drifting movement of hundreds of thousands of young people on the road . . . nor the tens of thousands of Americans living in travel trailers or houseboats.

The picture that emerges, then, from the Census and telephone figures is this:

At least a fifth of all Americans move one or more times each year; and the pace of the movement of Americans is still increasing.

The Bell System records show dramatic variations in mobility rates by regions, states, and cities. Some areas are still highly stable, others highly volatile. Whereas the disconnect rate in 1971 for central Pennsylvania was 14 percent of all phones in service, in central Los Angeles it was more than 40 percent. The seven states with disconnect rates of less than 20 percent were all in the U.S. Northeast whereas the eight states with disconnect rates above 35 percent were all west of the Mississippi (see Appendix B). The disconnect rate of Canadians was virtually identical with that of Americans: 25 percent.

In all the shifting and growth of the U.S. population some states and some cities are growing or shrinking at sharply contrasting rates. The 1970 Census showed, for example, that while Nevada registered a 69 percent gain in population during the decade, West Virginia registered an 8 percent loss. A description of the big population gainers and losers among states and cities can be found in Appendix C.

Increasingly, population movement in the United States can be described as a milling around in response to organizational transfers or new job opportunities or as a search for a more salubrious climate. However there are four major flow patterns worth bearing in mind:

1. The movement of people from interior states to seacoast states or to states bordering the Great Lakes.
2. The flow of people to the West and Southwest. The

long rush to California, however, has slackened, and its outflow of people nearly matches its inflow.

3. The interchange between the South and the North. The South used to bemoan its population drain and its brain drain. Now both situations are reversed. For the first decade in a hundred years the South has gained more than it has lost. Northerners are tending to abandon their grimy old cities such as Erie, Pennsylvania, for the gleaming new cities of the South such as Memphis, Atlanta, and Tampa. From 1940 to 1970, with the mechanization of crop-picking and mining, many millions of relatively poor whites and blacks south of the Mason-Dixon Line came to Northern cities in search of employment. It is fair to say the South was exporting its unemployment, sometimes systematically. Meanwhile new industries such as aerospace that require large numbers of engineers, technicians, and skilled managers have been springing up in the South. Many of these have been sent or lured down from the North. Quite possibly this circulation of population has played some role in the dramatic cultural and political changes which have occurred in the deep South during the past decade.

4. And, most momentous, there has been the vast movement from rural areas to metropolitan areas. This represents the greatest migration and upheaval in the history of the United States. In just twenty years, from 1940 to 1960, 17.5 million people left farms—or more than half the 32 million people living on farms in 1940! By 1975, the Census Bureau estimates, 65 percent of all Americans will be living in metropolitan areas.

THE HIGH- AND LOW-MOBILES

In all the swirling of population, who are the chronic movers? Broadly speaking, Americans with a proneness to frequent moves are found most commonly in certain social classes, occupations, religions, age groups, and types of dwelling. This is particularly true of the people who move beyond their present localities. For example:

SOCIAL CLASSES. Measured by either income or education, it is the people with some college education or with substantial incomes who are most likely to move across county lines to new localities. About three quarters of all people who are moved by long-distance moving companies work for large organizations, either corporate or governmental. And they tend largely to be managerial, professional, or technical personnel. Of all occupational categories, people in these groups are the ones who most often move across county lines each year.

People who are unemployed tend to be above average in changing addresses, but mostly they move only short distances. The relative bulwarks of stability in U.S. society turn out now to be the working-class people, particularly those with salable skills and union affiliations.

There seem to be three principal reasons for this.

—Working-class people tend to build their lives more intensely on kinship ties, on ethnic ties, and on their local neighborhoods. If they move to different counties or states their explanation frequently is that they want to get closer to kinfolk from whom they had become separated.

—Working-class people tend to be more fearful of change and the unknown, to be less adept at coping with new neighbors, new employers, new surroundings.

—In three decades of generally affluent times blue-collar workers have generally not felt pressure to leave their local labor market.

Blacks now are substantially less likely to make long-distance moves than are whites. However, they change addresses somewhat more frequently than whites within the locality where they have been living.

OCCUPATIONS. It is harder for doctors with their own practices to move than it is for teachers or even architects. A doctor who moves faces the time-consuming task of establishing a new clientele, whereas teachers have readily transferable skills and no clientele. Most local storekeepers and entrepreneurs, like doctors, find moving a substantial distance a formidable challenge, unless they move just to set up another branch. On the other hand geologists, especially for oil companies, are a notoriously wandering group, as are aeronautical engineers, computer specialists, salesmen, and marketing managers. The Atlas Van Lines estimates that the corporate manager in marketing or engineering has, in recent years, been moving every two and a half years, as compared with every five years during the mid-1950s.

Among manual workers, "laborers" are considerably more mobile than what the Census calls "craftsmen, foremen and kindred workers."

AGE. Whatever the job category, the people in the work force between twenty-five and thirty-four are the most mobile, and mobility decreases with each decade that jobholders get older. Young people between eighteen and twenty-five constitute a fourth of all movers; and their mobility rate in recent years has been rising sharply.

RELIGION. The same kind of ties and external supports that tend to keep most craftsmen and other thriving working-class people close to their home neighborhoods include also the ties of religious affiliation. Working people, especially those whose ancestors came to the U.S. after 1890, are heavily represented in the Catholic Church. And among Catholics the Church to an unusual degree is likely to be seen as a community center and as a dominant force binding people to their neighborhoods.

TYPE OF DWELLING. People living in apartments and other multifamily dwellings tend to be more mobile than people living in single-family dwellings. And renters are about three times as mobile as homeowners. In Los Angeles, for example, 85 percent of all people renting their dwellings move each year. Often this move may be only a mile or so.

If present trends continue, the various forms of uprootedness I've cited will become more pervasive and social fragmentation will intensify, not only in the United States but in much of the rest of the Western world. We could reasonably surmise this from the fact that nomadic values and habits have become particularly evident among young adults. We could surmise it too from the current and projected upsurge in apartment living, especially in the suburbs. Another solid basis for surmising there will be increased uprootedness in the future is the fact that the nature of our technocratic society, as we are permitting it to evolve, seems to demand such an increase. The pressures are for short tenure in places.

Whatever the reasoning, social scientists are forecasting still greater rootlessness for the future. Harvard University's Daniel Bell, in looking to A.D. 2000, predicts our society will be considerably more mobile. Warren Bennis, president of the University of Cincinnati, sees us moving into an era of "temporary systems, non-permanent relationships, turbulence, uprootedness, unconnectedness, mobility, and above all, unexampled social change." And Brandeis University's Philip Slater, in observing that our society is already one of the most mobile ever known, predicts: "We will become increasingly a nation of itinerants, moving continually on an irregular . . . circuit of jobs."

On the other hand, resistance movements are beginning to emerge.

But let us get down to specifics.

PART ONE

Journeys
That
Explain
the
Uprooting

The following nine chapters describe my visits to a number of towns and cities to examine some of the strange new kinds of turbulent or truncated communities and pseudo communities emerging in the late twentieth century.

In the first four chapters I examine the distortion in several towns and cities (and in their life styles) that have been made to meet the needs of private enterprise.

Then, in Chapter 6, I offer some glimpses of the very great impact of the federal government in spawning restless and often ugly new kinds of towns and cities.

In Chapter 7 the focus is on the impact of college towns as breeding places for high-mobiles.

Chapter 8 describes some odd new kinds of communities for older people created largely by the fragmenting of families and the breakdown of intimate community life in many urban areas, especially in the North.

In Chapter 9, I try to comprehend the turbulence and reverberating effects created inside inner cities by the shifting and elbowing of ethnic groups.

And in Chapter 10, I examine the results of three novel forms of urban sprawl.

The question hanging over all these nine chapters is: What is happening to community life as a result of the uprooting, fragmenting, and disorientation described? I am not describing isolated types of situations. Tens of millions of people are involved. Community life is threatened, or at least being reoriented in ways that remain to be tested. And this is happening in face of the fact that participation in community is a fundamental human desire.

There have been dozens of definitions of "community"

15

with some consensus on the essential ingredients. Usually, for example, a specific geographic place is assumed.

My own view is that an authentic community is a social network of people of various kinds, ranks, and ages who encounter each other on the streets, in the stores, at sports parks, at communal gatherings. A good deal of personal interaction occurs. There are elected leaders or spokesmen whom almost all the people know at least by reputation. Some may not like their community but all recognize it as a special place with an ongoing character. It has a central core and well-understood limits. Most members base most of their daily activities in or near the community. And most are interested in cooperating to make it a place they can be proud of.

Readers might bear these characteristics in mind while pondering the nine chapters that follow.

"Men in managerial roles all get the company message. If you want to go up, be prepared to move—not just to Texas but Saudi Arabia. And don't tell us you have a problem with the wife. If you want to be static, okay, have roots."—A STANDARD OIL COMPANY MANAGER.

2.

Towns for Company Gypsies

The upheaval triggered by advanced technology and modern business practices is creating some brand-new types of communities—such as Darien, Connecticut—that bear little resemblance to traditional communities. Darien, once a typical New England town, has taken on its new, swollen form primarily because corporate managers and professional specialists have proliferated and they are largely a nomadic group. Darien is one of their hundreds of campaign grounds. A wife in Darien doesn't burst out laughing when someone says IBM means "I've Been Moved." She's heard it before, no matter what company her husband works for.

Corporate personnel with status ranging from supervisors and professionals to quite high managerial levels move either because they are transferred or because they are jumping to another company. And even if the corporate officials move only infrequently they may be highmobile because their jobs require a great deal of traveling. Or they travel long distances to work because their life styles usually impel them to seek out homes in distant suburbs.

In Darien there is a very large concentration of men who have been transferred . . . who have to commute forty miles to their jobs . . . and who also take a great many long trips as part of their jobs. It is a transfer town, a bedroom town—and a traveling man's town. Thus it seems an especially fine prototype of the town for company gypsies.

Corporate officials and specialists are transferred for a variety of reasons presumed to promote corporate efficiency. It is believed to be good to have men who are as interchangeable as possible. When I say "men" I include the 2 or 3 percent of such personnel who are female. This tiny percentage is rising, however, and women's libbers are proposing that marriage contracts specify whether the husband will be willing to move if the wife gets an attractive job offer she wants to take.

It is also presumed by corporations that responsible personnel are broadened in their corporate viewpoint by serving time at a variety of the company's outposts. General Electric, to cite an example, has facilities in more than two hundred different places in the U.S., plus many abroad.

And then there is the fact that modern technology has created the need for hoards of specialists who can be sent to new plants or trouble spots for a day, a month, or a year. *Business Week,* in estimating that the average corporate official spends at least a third of his time traveling, mostly by jets, explained: "Not too long ago you put a good superintendent in charge of a distant plant and let him run the show." Today, it added, "the business is too big, too complex, too competitive. It takes constant shuttling by the specialists—safety men, labor-relations experts, purchasing agents, tax experts, attorneys, technicians—to keep things going."

And then there is the intensive traveling to and from district sales offices of national companies. The district offices of a great many companies operating in the Carolinas are in Charlotte, North Carolina. According to one estimate, about 10,000 sales people leave Charlotte every Monday morning to make the rounds of branch or local offices.

The recent great growth of mergers has also promoted the shuffling and uprooting of people as "deadwood" is eliminated and new managements for the absorbed companies are brought in. And then of course a man may be moved by a superior who wants to be rid of a potential rival.

For such reasons, in the past fifteen years there has been a sharp, and generally steady, increase in the mobility of corporate personnel above the foreman level, with dips in the upward curve during recessionary periods. Men near the top are less likely to be moved, but they may well be lured to another, larger company. United Van Lines found in a survey of corporate policies that during a recent four-year period there had been a steep increase in the proportion of companies reporting they had a systematic policy of periodically relocating their personnel. About a third of all companies queried acknowledged such a policy.

The University of Evansville conducted a "Forum on Moving" in 1969, at which reports on the policies of corporate traffic managers were read. One conspicuous trend cited was the increased frequency of transfer of corporate managers in the twenty-five- to forty-year-old age bracket. Two thirds of them had moved at least once every three years; and one in five was transferred at least once *every* year.

An official of Atlas Van Lines estimated that of the many million changes of address each year, more than half of the moves involve either a corporate transfer or a change of jobs. In 1972 a spokesman for United Van Lines, in commenting on the acceleration of long-distance moving in recent years, attributed the rise largely to the transfer by major companies of their top- and middle-management personnel.

The proliferation of enterprises abroad that are wholly or partly owned by American-based corporations has created a demand for really super-mobile families. Standard Oil Company of New Jersey has more than a hundred foreign affiliates; and many large U.S. companies such as the National Cash Register Company, Singer Company and the Colgate-Palmolive Company earn more than half of their profits from foreign operations.

Thus we have foreign enclaves of Americans spotted around the globe—2,000 in arid Dhahran, Saudi Arabia; 4,700 near turgid Tripoli, Libya. Some of these people make an effort to mix with nationals of the country where they reside; but the general pattern is for Americans to cling together around their backyard barbecue pits, often inside walled enclosures.

A wife who has served several tours of duty abroad with her husband confessed that her major problem is the "cultural shock" of coming back to the grubby business of cooking and house cleaning in the U.S.A. In India, she explained, she and her husband had five servants, company-paid club memberships, a chauffeur-driven car, and company-paid tuition for their son in a private school.

As for movement created by employees of all sorts who quit to take new jobs, an increase in job-jumping has recently pervaded American business at most levels from bottom to top. And similar increases are reported in much of Western Europe.

U.S. Government records show that the monthly "quit rate" in manufacturing rose 80 percent in the five years before 1970. (The 1970 recession may have slowed it a bit.) The National Foundry Association came up with the astounding finding that 141 foundries surveyed showed an average annual turnover of about 75 percent of their employees.

Some people quit because their job skills become obsolete in a period of frenetic technological change; others quit for more money or pleasanter jobs or just because they are restless. At the blue-collar or lower white-collar level, a change in jobs does not necessarily mean a change of residence, but the managers and professionals who change jobs are likely to have to pack up and move to a new area. One reason is that where key personnel are concerned many companies in an urban area have anti-raiding pacts with competitors in the same area.

Fortune magazine reports that among younger college-trained managers "restlessness shows every sign of being endemic." It suggests that "the compulsion to move along" may be the "central explanation" for the big increase in job-hopping among managers. Professor Eugene E. Jennings of Michigan State University found in a long-term study of 1,500 managers that their proneness to job-jumping increased 500 percent in fifteen years. He has concluded that, for many, movement for the sake of movement has become a "mind fix."

A major additional reason for the increase in job-jumping among managers and professionals is the emergence of dozens of large executive recruiting firms. In 1951 there were six such U.S. firms; today there are several hundred. As middlemen they not only actively recruit potential job-jumpers for their corporate clients but make it easier for men interested in moving to let their availability be known on a confidential basis. One leading recruiter, John Handy of New York, urges all young managers to re-examine their situation, with an eye to moving, at least once every four years. He states that it is a blessing if the ambitious junior manager "does not meet the right girl until he is twenty-eight, because he should hold himself free to move from one company or industry to another, and to any area of the country. . . ."

Another leading recruiter, Wardwell Howell of Ward Howell Associates, with offices in New York and London, compiled for me a list of the twenty-six most recent senior-level executives his office had moved. In only four moves could the executive conceivably have continued to live in the same home he had been living in. The other twenty-two moves required moving vans and a major uprooting of home life. Twenty were to another state or county, and the average distance involved was approximately 820 miles. Eight of the moves were to the New York area, so it is quite possible that at least one of these movers ended up living in Darien, Connecticut.

*   *   *

For such corporate movers Darien is a likely place to settle because about 95 percent of all managers whose families move to the New York area head for the suburbs to house-hunt. Towns along the north shore of Long Island Sound are among the attractive hunting grounds because there is a commuter railroad (creaky as it is) into midtown Manhattan. There are also some attractive bedroom towns in New Jersey but commuting to New York City from there is likely to be by bus or car.

Managers and their wives arriving to house-hunt usually say they want a nice suburb as close to New York as possible. And often they have been clued in by their superiors on where to look. They soon discover, however, that prices for what they have learned to consider an appropriate house are fantastic in the Westchester County towns such as Pelham and Larchmont. An appropriate house is one with four bedrooms and a touch of rural setting, near good public schools. Rural touches are hard to find in this area and real estate taxes are oppressively high. Many searchers continue exploring on out the shoreline railroad track into Connecticut, and find that prices in the first town across the border, Greenwich, which is a chairman-of-the-board type of town, are still fantastic. And so many explore farther out the railroad-expressway line till they reach Darien, about forty miles from Manhattan. Here they just may possibly be able to get that "appropriate" house within their means. The average selling price in Darien recently has been about $70,000. If the explorers can't afford Darien or nearby New Canaan and North Stamford, realtors refer them farther out and inland to places such as Wilton, Weston, or Easton—where rural touches are plentiful but daily commuting can take three to four hours out of each day.

Darien has a strong image in corporate circles as a good transfer town for middle- to upper-level managers because it has the kind of people and accouterments—including address—that go with the executive life. Some companies subsidize promising men being transferred to the New York area so that they can live there.

Managers or professionals and their families who choose

to settle in Darien usually have come a long way geographically. Mrs. William Lawrence, Jr., the local Welcome Wagon representative, drew up for me a list of the points of origin of the last fifty new families she had called upon in Darien. Forty-one had moved in from some other state or country. They came from such U.S. places as Winnetka, Illinois; Summit, New Jersey; Houston, Texas; Pasadena, California; Gates Mills, Ohio; and from posts in eleven foreign countries.

Not all the managerial types who settle in Darien will be moving on soon. Some are older men who have been tapped for executive suites at their company headquarters. New York and its immediate environs has more world headquarters of major corporations than any other area in the U.S.A. Thus, for many executives, Darien will be the last stop. After a few years of corner-office glory at international headquarters they may, perhaps, be able to afford to retire in Darien. But thousands of others who have settled there in recent years are younger hustlers who know they have been brought to the New York area for some temporary or special assignment before being transferred again.

They tend to settle in newer areas of Darien where they will also be among other high-mobiles and where they can get out fast, they hope, when the time comes to sell. Miles Road has become known as a high-mobile area, as have Wilson Ridge Road and Briar Brae Road. Some newcomers shun the more settled areas of town where mobility is often quite low. If, later, a manager discovers he is more or less permanently assigned to the New York area, he will usually get into a less transient neighborhood, such as Tokeneke or Ridge Acres, as fast as he can.

I contacted several dozen wives in Darien who had arrived within the preceding eighteen months, to inquire about their thoughts and experiences regarding moving. Several I tried to contact had already moved on to such places as Narberth, Pennsylvania, Sarasota, Florida, and Singapore. And two others said they were in the process of moving on again.

In describing past experiences in moving, one said she

had moved twenty-two times in the twenty-five years of her marriage . . . another had moved fifteen times in the thirty-one years of her marriage . . . another had moved eight times in nine years . . . still another had moved sixteen times in twenty-one years. And one woman I talked with mentioned that her son, now in the eighth grade, had already lived in seven towns.

Many of the new arrivals join the Newcomers Club, which is sponsored in Darien by the Young Women's Christian Association. The Newcomers can be members for only two years. In 1970 they had an organizational crisis because the president, elected after a year's residence, had to resign in mid-term. Her husband was being transferred to the West.

At first glance Darien seems an unlikely place for executives and would-be executives to settle. The center of the town is where the New Haven Railroad crosses over U.S. Route 1. And a couple of hundred yards away trucks and cars on the elevated Connecticut Thruway roar by. One local joke is that the least envied status in town is that of a person having a house caught between the tracks and the thruway.

Darien also has little in the way of tradition. Any family whose roots go back twenty-five years is Old Family. And while the town technically is in New England it has little resemblance to traditional New England towns. The best giveaway of this, as an informant noted, is that the Presbyterian church rather than the Congregational church, which dominates most true New England towns, is by far the town's biggest. Darien has a lot of transplanted Southerners and Midwesterners.

The fact that it is an enclave rather than a genuine community can also be seen in the fact that virtually all its hundreds of schoolteachers commute from elsewhere. They can't afford Darien's housing prices. A house costing less than $38,000 is a rarity, and the rule of thumb is that a family can't afford a house costing more than twice its annual income. One new school principal complained to the school board that he couldn't find a house in the town that he could afford. A woman who has been in Darien more than twenty-five years offered this succinct comment:

"Darien is a town where a child can grow up and never see a dinner pail." Also the child may never see a Jew. Darien first came into national prominence because of the novel and movie, *Gentleman's Agreement,* about a town that didn't sell houses to Jews. Today there are Jews in Darien—about one per 700 population. And almost the only Negroes a Darien child may see will be cleaning women coming in from nearby Stamford or Norwalk. But from the transferring manager's viewpoint, Darien has some strong appeals: it is on the water . . . it has a multitude of clubs . . . it has tight zoning . . . it has several handsome residential areas . . . and it has relatively tolerable railroad commuting service to New York City.

A Darien businessman who has lived there all his life said: "The town is divided between commuters and locals and they seldom cross paths except in the stores; and there is a certain amount of resentment." The wife of a transferee who had lived in Darien two years told me: "You feel you are not really accepted here because they expect you to move and so they don't care about getting acquainted."

A somewhat more precise picture of the divisions would show three major groups, with little interaction between them:

1. The locals—people who were raised in Darien and make their living there, as merchants, contractors, etc. Some are of old Irish-Yankee stock, many are of Italian ancestry.

2. The Darien people—families from somewhere else who have made it by living in Darien more than five years. They dominate the town socially.

3. The transients—who will be moving on after one to four years of residence.

Many of the newer houses in the Darien-New Canaan area are put up by builders on speculation for the transient market and are "box colonials." Most are so standardized that, as one broker put it: "You often don't really need to go look at a 'builder house' that is for sale, you just note the location, bedrooms, and price." At the lower price margin, new three-bedroom stock houses designed for transients can be got for $50,000; but the four-bedroom house designed for the in-and-out manager is easier to resell. Those now going up average about $78,000 in price. One broker said, "We like to have people from places like Birmingham, Michigan, or Lake Forest, Illinois, because they are already educated to high-priced property and are not shocked. People from the South or from the Boston area do a lot of moaning and groaning. Most are not well heeled and they want the maximum mortgage of 75 percent."

A counselor for the Darien office of Family and Children Services confirmed the anguish: "What we hear all the time is the cost of housing in Darien. Many people are overextended and find themselves carrying a mortgage of $500 a month, which they can't afford. We see these families who are overextended frequently."

Darien is still too young to have a tight social structure —but it is trying. Children's Aid is known as the "most exclusive sorority in town." It was started three decades ago by about six women to collect clothes for the poor and to offer social services. Today it has about 120 members. You can't be considered for membership unless you have three letters of introduction—even though you are an experienced social worker. Admission is based primarily on how long you have lived in Darien. As a practical matter a large proportion of new memberships are going to the daughters of early members. As one old-time resident observed tartly: "This is the first sign that we're finally getting a second generation here."

Another sign is the Cotillion, which stages coming-out parties for socialites in the area. At first it was a quite casual organization. Now the first criterion for acceptance is length of residence in Darien; and the proportion of girls accepted as legacies is getting longer. I asked an insider what would happen if a vice president of Union Carbide moved into town and wanted his daughter to come out at a Cotillion. Would he have a problem? The answer: "He would have to work awfully hard."

Darien, as indicated, is a conspicuously "clubby" town: riding clubs, curling clubs, garden clubs, beach clubs, and golf clubs. Some are expensive and have long waiting lists. Wee Burn is *the* golf club. A new member who gets accepted will have to pay nearly four thousand dollars in initiation fees, dues, bond purchase, assessments, etc. And he will lose most of it if his company soon transfers him somewhere else. The only consolation is that the company often pays much or all of the bill anyway.

Despite these efforts to build up an Old Guard system, Darien has several notable institutions for helping transients develop a social life. The Darien Community Association—which is open to any resident—houses under one handsome roof a variety of cultural, social, and hobby groups. The Newcomers Club is exceedingly active. And interestingly the Junior League Club is a route for induction into Darien for those incoming wives who were socially select enough—where they came from—to be Junior Leaguers. Transfers are permitted by the national organization from any of the 216 clubs that dot the country. The Junior League Club that includes Darien also has members in the three nearby towns of New Canaan, Wilton, and Westport, and the two nearby cities of Stamford and Norwalk. Altogether there are 1,000 members—and 500 of them are in Darien!

As mentioned, Darien is not only a transfer town but a bedroom town. This fact is seen around dawn any weekday morning at the railroad station. The platform is filled solid, five deep, for about a hundred yards with commuters to New York. Darien's 2,100 are a part of the 220,000 commuters who flood into New York via seven different train lines each morning. They are waiting for the five principal commuter trains that theoretically leave between 6:45 A.M. and 8 A.M. Since the trains frequently run twenty to fifty minutes late any train's arrival creates a scramble to get aboard. Some disgusted commuters form car pools and take the expressways to New York.

If the commuter returns that night he will probably arrive home, if lucky, around 7 P.M., but often later. If he has young children they may already be in bed or being prepared for bed.

But several times a month he will not return home at all. He will be jetting off to Minneapolis, Dallas, or Los Angeles, or all three, on business. As I mentioned, Darien is also a traveling man's town. The evidence of this extra dimension of our corporate gypsy's style of life is seen in the fact that the Darien railroad ticket office sells 4,000 ten-trip tickets to New York a month and only 200 monthly commutation tickets. The ten-trip tickets cost more than twice as much per daily round trip (about $4.50) as the monthly commutation tickets. But for the high-mobile managerial and professional man who has to travel a lot on his job, the monthly commuter ticket doesn't make sense.

What all this adds up to is that Darien is essentially a woman's town five days a week. One recently arrived wife said the hardest thing about feeling a part of the "community" was how "dead" it was during the week with so few men around. There is little weeknight social activity because the men are so tired and get home so late. Commuting husbands are badly underrepresented in community affairs and on town boards. Far more than in most communities, women are represented on the town's governing bodies. The wives of the transients, however, rarely get sufficiently involved to play such roles. They may plunge into parent-teacher groups or fund raising, but that is about it.

Most transient wives assume they will soon be moving on again, and view the prospect with varying degrees of equanimity. About three quarters of all major companies prefer to give an employee the option to refuse transfers, and he is rarely told he will be shelved or eased out if he declines the move, but in fact most companies take it for granted that an ambitious man will pick up his family and move if he is asked to do so. A brochure of the American Management Association a few years ago put the mandatory element quite bluntly. It said: "It always comes as something of a shock when we are asked to pull up stakes and move on to a new job in a new place. Actually 'asked' as used in this sense means 'ordered,' for implicit in the request is the understanding that refusal to accept the transfer will seriously impair the employee's effectiveness to the firm—and, consequently, his chances for further advancement."

Many corporate wives have been screened before the husband was hired for their "flexibility" and "adaptability" so that they are not a cross section of American womanhood. This is particularly likely to be the case if the husband got his job via an executive recruiting firm. The firm, as middleman, doesn't want to injure its own reputation with a client company by proposing a man who, it later turns out, has a balky wife.

Some wives, in any case, say they like the transient style of life. Others just accept the move as a fact of life. A manager's wife in Darien who had moved into sixteen different neighborhoods in the twenty-one years of her marriage said:

"I feel it is the wife's duty to go where the pay check is." She added that a man must know his company to get ahead, "and that means moving."

Another said: "I believe that if a move is coupled with more money or more responsibility a person should accept."

Still another viewpoint was expressed by a woman I wrote to who had already left Darien in her ninth move in sixteen years of marriage. She said:

"I cried when we left Florida; I cried when we left Darien. It is an emotional upheaval no matter what. But this is the way my husband's work takes him. No doubt we will be transferred again within another two or three years."

That would be about par. Of thirty-six recently arrived Darien wives I questioned on how often they had moved since marriage, the average length between moves turned out to be two and a half years.

DARIEN'S SISTER SUBURBS, U.S.A.

When a business executive moves, or is moved, from Darien to another major metropolitan area, with the usual bewildering array of municipalities ringing it, there is usually at least one Darien-type town to head for. These equivalent towns are known variously as mirror towns, transfer towns, or turnover towns. In the case of Darien's equivalents they are not usually the really rich or Old Money establishments, but they are heavily peopled with nomadic corporate executives and professionals. (A lower-level corporate nomad living in a $32,500 house in, say, Yorktown Heights, New York, would also have his suburban transfer towns to head for in every part of the country. These usually would be dominated by tract developments.)

There are both company relocation experts and independent consultants who can advise the transferee on how to find his transfer town with a minimum of town-prowling (see Chapter 13).

One of the most charming consultants I encountered was a young blond woman who talked swiftly and humorously about moving managers. She worked in "national sales" at Executive Homesearch, which is headquartered in New York City. She agreed that Darien "is as typical a town for high-mobile executives as we have." And she added, "I can take a transferring family from Darien, and in any metropolitan area of the United States I can put these people in approximately the same environment as far as schools, types of neighbors, same income bracket, same family background, same education, anywhere across the country. They will not be changing their environment, they will be just changing their address." She continued, "Most will want the standard managerial house. All brokers know what it is: four bedrooms, two and a half baths, large living room, dining room, eat-in kitchen, a family room, and two-car garage. When we talk about managers we say they want the standard house. They will go for ranch, split-level, or colonial as long as it has the standard requirements. There is no standard on acreage."

For the next couple of hours she showed me where she would put this family transferring from Darien. Here is the gist of what she would recommend:

CHICAGO: "Now if they are going to Chicago I'd expose them to the whole North Shore but their best bet for a duplicate environment would probably be Lake Forest. If they are tired of the long commute from Darien they'll like Lake Forest and will probably seek a fairly new house, from four to twelve years old. They will especially be attracted by the area's excellent school system. Glencoe would also be a good possibility for the more affluent corporate official. Going west, maybe Hinsdale, which is an older community. Not south. You really wouldn't go south unless the man's job is in south Chicago. If the people are willing to commute and want a rural feeling and are a bit horsy they might like Barrington."

LOS ANGELES: "This is a very difficult city. The only way I can guide a person is to find where the husband's business address is going to be. There is only one way you can commute; you drive. There are buses for certain areas but they take forever. If the man works in downtown L.A. the best bet probably is San Marino. You wouldn't go to Pasadena any more because of their school problems right now. That may be straightened out and there are lovely sections in Pasadena comparable to some of Darien's.

"You would also look in Pacific Palisades, Westwood, Brentwood, West L.A. And you can find some of the same kinds of people in Bel Air, which is huge, that you find in Darien. It still has some areas where you can still find a nice place for less than $100,000. Beverly Hills would be out. It is fantastically overpriced. If the man is working to the south in the area that has all the aerospace plants, the first choice is Palos Verdes Estates, near Long Beach."

Q.—"Isn't that where the houses have been sliding into the ocean?"

A.—"They don't talk about it, and not every house is hanging on a cliff. It's just a terrific community.

"Going out southeast, you get a lot for your money in the Friendly Hills section of Whittier. Tustin would have a lot of appeal. If the Darien family can afford to spend more than $100,000 they'll find that parts of Newport Beach remind them a lot of Darien."

SAN DIEGO: "The first place to look there is easy: La Jolla."

SAN FRANCISCO: "If you are moving from Darien and will be working downtown your big hope would be to try to find a place in Hillsborough or Burlingame; but you probably will end up buying in Woodside or Atherton near Palo Alto. Or if it is convenient to commute to the north over the Golden Gate Bridge into Marin County, the Darien family will look at Tiburon and Belvedere out on the peninsula. They are chic but foggy.

"Across the Bay a lot of nice new areas are developing. I could send the Darien buyer to Walnut Creek but he probably would not be happy because everything is so new. Orinda and Moraga are nice, and might appeal to him, especially if he is working on the east side of the Bay."

DETROIT: "I hate sending people to Detroit. I'd divorce my husband first. For the most part there is so much ugliness. But if you go, Grosse Pointe Farms is the newer suburb. The Darien person might also feel comfortable moving to Birmingham. If the Darien family has a good supply of money it might be able to find something suitable in Bloomfield Hills, next door and a little farther out. Dearborn might appeal to some Darien families but it is a funny place with a weird attitude toward life."

PHILADELPHIA: "The Main Line is still the first place to look."

BOSTON: "This has some great areas for the Darien transferee. I'd look first in Wellesley or Concord or Lexington or Lincoln. Also Milton and Weston are nice. Westwood and Dover are also lovely areas. In general, prices tend to take a really big jump outside Route 128 [Boston's circumferential highway]."

WASHINGTON, D.C.: "I'd love Washington if I was moving from Darien. If I was going to look in Maryland, which you can reach without having to fight the bridge traffic over the Potomac, I'd look in Bethesda and Potomac, which are in Montgomery County. Chevy Chase is not as rural as Bethesda. However, many people adore Virginia and think Maryland is awful. If I was in Virginia, I'd either head toward Mount Vernon or toward Fairfax County; and I'd be sure to look at McLean."

CLEVELAND: "The Darien equivalent there definitely would be to the east, and most obviously Chagrin Falls. Euclid is more like Bronxville. To the west, Bay Village is very nice and has rural touches, but it tends to developments."

ST. LOUIS: "The place for the Darien person to look is Ladue. It has a marvelous school system. Next, I would recommend Clayton, also comparable to Darien."

KANSAS CITY: "A Darien person will find Mission Hills very nice, and it is old, established, exclusive. He might also look in the Wycklow area."

ATLANTA: "This is one of the few major metropolitan areas where the Darien person should look inside the city itself—in the northwest section. Some of the nicer new homes are going up out in DeKalb County."

MINNEAPOLIS: "You would go to Edina or Wayzata."

PITTSBURGH: "You would go to Sewickley or Fox Chapel."

DALLAS: "The Darien person will feel at home in almost any suburb in this city. Most have highly transient populations."

HOUSTON: "The nicer areas are Memorial Drive or the Tanglewood area, west of downtown Houston. Houston is funny. You can spend a fortune to get a house or you can find a real bargain. A lot of big companies are coming there."

How true this last comment is—and how "funny" Houston is—can perhaps be seen in the next chapter.

"A real turmoil was going on in my mind. For a month I got very little sleep and my stomach could not hold food."
—A BLACK, MIDDLE-MANAGEMENT OFFI-
CIAL OF THE SHELL OIL COMPANY, RECALL-
ING HIS REACTIONS UPON LEARNING THAT
HIS ORGANIZATION WAS BEING TRANS-
FERRED 1,742 MILES SOUTHWESTWARD
FROM NEW YORK CITY TO HOUSTON, TEXAS.

3.

Migrating Firms— and the Towns They Invade

While talking with realtors in Darien, I discovered that 35 families who were about to leave town all worked for the same company and were all going to the same place—Houston, Texas. Further inquiry revealed that at least 125 Shell Oil Company families from Fairfield County, where Darien is located, were being transplanted to Houston; and several hundred families from New Jersey were Houston-bound.

Altogether about 1,400 families—involving at least 4,500 people—were, because of a corporate decision, moving far southwestward into a dramatically different climate and life style. The company was moving its operating departments and its headquarters from New York City to Houston, more than seventeen hundred miles away.

Shell is just one of many dozens of corporations that have recently made massive transplants of personnel. General Dynamics Corporation in 1971 moved its headquarters from New York to the St. Louis area. Almost simultaneously UMC Industries, Inc., a conglomerate, moved its headquarters from St. Louis to New York. Corn Products Company recently moved from Chicago to New Jersey. . . . Atlantic Richfield Company moved a number of departments from Philadelphia to New York. . . . Xerox Corporation moved its headquarters from Rochester, New York, to Stamford, Connecticut. . . . Allied Chemical Corporation moved 1,000 employees from New York to Morris Township near the middle of New Jersey.

And then there is the Blair Corporation, a sales promotion firm specializing in coupon mailing, that moved most of its operations from America's largest city, New York, to the small town of Blair, Nebraska, whose principal industry has been the manufacture of manure spreaders. Blair Corporation liked the name of the town.

As U.S. industries become increasingly "light" and thus less dependent upon heavy raw materials than upon personnel, their companies feel increasingly free to be mobile. Some of the recent moving has been to get into areas where living or operating costs are lower. Living costs in several Southern cities run 15 to 25 percent lower than in some Northeastern cities. For one thing, in the mild, sometimes hot climate of the South, houses can be built cheaper.

Many corporations also are moving to the suburbs— partly to escape urban pains and partly to get closer to housewives with white-collar skills. Movements to the suburbs have been conspicuous not only in New York but in Detroit, St. Louis, Atlanta, and Chicago.

Some of the massive moves apparently have been made at least partly for personal, almost whimsical reasons. Ken Patton, the Economic Development Director for New York City, noticed in every significant case he had analyzed that companies moving to the suburbs went in the direction of the president's suburban home. In short, the boss saw a way to cut down his commuting.

Even in the long-distance move of General Dynamics from New York to the St. Louis suburb of Clayton, Mr. Patton points out, the company's new chairman was getting nearer home. He had been living near Clayton before joining General Dynamics and didn't move his family East. Whatever the technical factors, one result of moving General Dynamics a thousand miles westward was that the new chairman was able to get home to his family in several minutes rather than the several hours it took jetting from New York.

Mass transplants by big organizations can jolt the towns being invaded. Aiken, South Carolina, was a favorite watering place of America's entrenched Old Money society until the 1950s, renowned as a center for fox hunting, polo, and horse racing. Then abruptly the federal government announced that an enormous atomic energy facility would be built nearby. In a matter of months Aiken was inundated by DuPont and Atomic Energy Commission scientists and managers—and thousands of construction workers. Split-levels appeared near the gracious mansions. As the population trebled, the technocrats developed their own social hierarchy, helped to build golf courses, which they preferred to riding. Aiken became a bustling town with only touches of the old grandeur remaining, and its reputation as a gathering place for the Old Money elite has faded.

From a family's viewpoint, being part of a mass transplant by a company is both better and worse than being transferred individually. It is better because the husband at least has many acquaintances among the people being moved; and there is a sense of all being in the same boat. The U.S. Army learned during World War II that individual morale remained higher when soldiers being sent into strange, new situations were sent by units rather than individually. This has become harder to implement with increased specialization even of G.I.s. (The same evidence of undisturbed morale might be deduced from the experiences of nomadic tribes that travel as a close-knit group.)

Mass moving of corporate personnel is worse, however, because the transfer is not likely to be linked to either a promotion or a raise; and there is even more of an element of compulsion. Mass moves affect not just managers and professionals but clerks and maintenance people as well. And for the latter, who have had less experience with moving into new areas, the thought of moving is more likely to create a sense of dread. A large proportion of them say they will quit rather than make the move.

In the case of the Shell move to Houston, this difference in willingness to move showed up vividly. Richard Bauer, in charge of coordinating the transfer, recalls:

"We invited all the people in our New York office whose jobs would be transferred to come to Houston if they wanted to, including stenographers, typists, and mail girls. Among the professionals and managerials, in excess of 90 percent were willing to make the move. Many in fact had been in Houston before." Among non-professionals, about one third were willing to make the move, Mr. Bauer reports. Some were married women whose husbands had jobs in New York. In a few cases husbands of such married employees gave up their New York jobs and moved with their career wives to Houston.

Shell's official explanations for the move, made on rather short notice for many, were that it was seeking more efficient operations and that it was becoming harder to transfer good people into New York City. (In 1971, however, more corporations moved their headquarters to the New York area than left.) Shell stated that a number of American cities had been scrutinized before the decision went to Houston. There is at least one status-related reason for suspecting that Houston was the overwhelming favorite almost from the start. Long before the announcement was made New York employees heard rumors that a skyscraper was growing in downtown Houston. It was to be the highest skyscraper west of the Mississippi. And it was going to have Shell's name on it. Anyone who has visited downtown Houston knows that its skyline has a host of buildings reaching into the sky erected by the great names of oil and gas such as Gulf, Humble, Sunoco, and Tennoco. Now, mighty Shell's skyscraper would be towering far above them all.

Soon after the announcement, Shell's official house

organs began running laudatory articles about Houston; and the New York house organ carried an interview with a family who had recently moved from New York to Houston. The interview ran under the headline: "WE LIKE IT DOWN HERE!"

As the center of the petrochemical industry, Houston has been America's fastest-growing major city: in just one decade during the sixties it leaped from fourteenth to sixth among the largest cities of America. It is forty miles across at one point. In a sense Houston itself is largely the product of migrating industries.

As noted earlier, Houston is a "funny" city: vulgar and yet in some ways appealing. It is a kind of place you can like a lot or loathe intensely. Few people are neutral. Houstonites like to call it "Baghdad on the Bayou." With all its new wealth on display, it is quite possibly the most gauche, virulently suspicious, politically reactionary city in the country. One oil man of some sophistication from New York who served time at a Houston post for a year called the experience, for him, one of being sent to a warm-weather Siberia. A top European official of the international parent company, Royal Dutch Shell, spent some time in Houston and reportedly refers to it as a ghastly interlude in his life.

In summer the climate is sizzling and muggy, a fact which inspired entrepreneurs to build America's first air-conditioned baseball field there.

These are some of the possibly disagreeable aspects of Houston that a transferee will face:

—Houston is a city of violence. It has the highest murder rate of any of the nation's dozen largest cities. Its rate is four times that of Boston. Much of the violence arises from extreme right-wing groups such as the Ku Klux Klan and Minutemen trying to bomb or burn out people they consider to be peace-loving radicals. The house of a business professor at the University of Houston was set afire because he belonged to the American Civil Liberties Union, which seeks to uphold the constitutional rights of Americans. In Houston it is not uncommon to see well-dressed residents driving pickup trucks with large rear windows. In the windows can be seen gun racks holding rifles, shotguns, or carbines. Some have such gun-laden trucks for functional reasons but for other Houstonites it's said to be a form of status display. Houstonites assert good-naturedly that more people die there of shotgun wounds than from auto accidents.

—Much of Houston is untidy, cluttered, smog-ridden. It has grown so fast that neon-lit loan shops and gas stations nestle close to downtown oil skyscrapers. The city's center is strangled by looping skyways. Less than a quarter mile from City Hall one can walk under a tangle of eight overpasses in a space of thirty yards. Fumes, mainly from the petrochemical plants, were hospitalizing an average of 50 residents a month in mid-1971. Most of Houston's fashionable shops are located several miles from downtown.

—Houston has a penny-pinching government, despite the city's fabled wealth. Its annual school expenditure per pupil is about $300 below the national average.

—Houston, most conspicuously of all, is pretentious. Its airport is not just an "international" airport; it is the Houston Intercontinental Airport, with some of its signs repeated in three languages. A six-lane highway runs through the middle of the city's Convention Hall.

The pervasive pretentiousness is most conspicuous perhaps in the homes, especially in the newer sections southwest and northwest, which are largely populated by corporate managers. (The astronauts and scientists working for the NASA space program mostly live southeast of Houston near their facilities.)

The newer areas to the west overwhelmingly offer newcomers tract houses. Handsome, maybe, but still tract. Thousands upon thousands of the newer houses feature half-timbered styles of Merrie England, or columned houses, the columns often square and made of brick. Others have great stained-glass windows reaching two stories high. Still others have extremely peaked roofs. Many of the tracts at first glance remind one of a pasteboard Hollywood set for a Disney fantasy.

The straining to offer tracts suggesting opulence shows up in their names. Since River Oaks on the southwest side is one of the older, most prestigious areas, the word "oaks" appears in a great many of the newer developments. A transferee can choose from Enchanted Oaks, Whispering Oaks, Rustling Oaks, Candlelight Oaks, Garden Oaks, Nottingham Oaks, Knob Oaks, Shadow Oaks, Southern Oaks, West Oaks, Afton Oaks, White Oak Acres, and Forest Oaks. If a transferee drives from Enchanted Oaks in search of Candlelight Oaks he will pass through miles of disheveled treeless urban sprawl and past mobile-home parks and numerous junkyards.

Since the better homes are supposed to be where the trees begin—much of the land around Houston is flat and treeless—the word "forest" also has great appeal to the poets who invent names of developments. The transferee can choose from Inverness Forest, Sherwood Forest, Ponderosa Forest, and Chateau Forest. And then there is just plain Tall Timbers.

"Estate" is another word that seems to have a nice ring to the kinds of people who sell tract housing in the Houston area. There are Lakeside Country Club Estates, Humble Estates, Sequoia Estates, River Woods Estates, Memorial Park Estates, South Main Estates. Finally the transferee may be advised to look in one of the "manor" developments: Post Oak Manor, Braes Manor, Meredith Manor, Shamrock Manor.

The newcomer wishing to play golf will find that getting into a club is both difficult and expensive, especially in the established areas. Three thousand dollars would be a relatively cheap price for gaining entry in the better areas, with the really exclusive ones requiring a payment of more than $15,000. Many of the new housing developers selling to transients now start by building a golf course as the lure and then build their houses around it.

As indicated, Houston does offer transferees some appealing features. Its claim to being a "friendly" town is apparently justified. At least Houstonites tend to be friendly to people like themselves or those who think as they do.

Perhaps this "friendly" air is cultivated because so many Houstonites are relative newcomers from someplace else. I heard a number of comments by Shell people indicating their neighbors were friendly. For example, William Kuhlke, who has been with Shell for seventeen years and has four children, mentioned that within a week of his arrival children on the block had baked a cake for his daughter's birthday. The Kuhlkes, within that week, knew five of their neighbors. Two had come to call; and his wife met the other three while walking the baby.

Houston's low cost of living also can be very appealing to someone transferring from the New York area. The U.S. Bureau of Labor Statistics finds that it costs about 25 percent more to maintain a "good standard of living" in New York City than in Houston. At Enchanted Oaks, north of Houston, I told one of the sales representatives that I was scouting for a house for a neighbor who was being transferred from Connecticut. The salesman asked what price range he was interested in. Unprepared, I looked around and said, "Oh, about $55,000." The salesman replied, "We don't have anything above $39,500."

At the new Candlelight Oaks development northwest of Houston I inspected a number of houses that had been purchased by Shell Oil personnel but had not yet been occupied. The houses, to me, a New Englander, seemed stacked unnecessarily and uncomfortably close together; but the buyer was getting a lot of house—about 3,100 square feet—for $45,000 or less. He was getting not only most of the ingredients of the standard transferee house (four bedrooms and two and a half baths) but usually also a "family room." All the houses had posh touches. Houston houses don't require insulation and few have basements. However, a Shell official who ended up in Nottingham Forest felt he was getting about the same size house he had in New Jersey but on a smaller plot and without a basement.

Finally, for all its pretentiousness, Houston does have some genuine elegance. Houstonites have recently discovered culture and have built a fine new concert hall. And they have in their Memorial Drive, which winds westward from downtown, one of the world's longest, handsomest boulevards. It runs for about fifteen miles and while the houses along it are generally tract houses most are expensive and handsome. America's only possible comparable drives that I have seen would be Sunset Boulevard in the Los Angeles area and Sheridan Road along Chicago's North Shore. And also west of downtown is the recently built Galleria Complex that holds a special fascination for residents of often muggy Houston but dazzles out-of-towners too. It is a multi-level, covered, chic shopping mall shaped like a stadium that is built around an ice-skating rink.

Of the first 400 Shell families to make the move from the New York area to the Houston area, 55 percent went into the southwest section, which includes the Memorial Drive area. Thirty-five percent went into the newer tracts to the northwest, such as Candlelight Oaks, which generally are less expensive and less elite. Eight percent went to northeast, and only 2 percent southeast, where NASA is located.

The Shell relocation staff working with Mr. Bauer counsel the transferees on some of the pitfalls to watch out for in buying a house in the Houston area. Many houses are bought without a lawyer's advice since titles are insured. Shell's relocation staff, I gathered from talking to some of the tract salesmen, ride herd on the developers to see that the transferees are not saddled with such things as weak upstairs flooring or poor plastic sewer piping. With more than 1,400 prospective home buyers, Shell obviously has clout—or influence and persuasiveness—with the developers, and sometimes uses it on behalf of its personnel.

A special challenge to Shell in making the mass move to a Southern city was the fact it had a number of blacks at its New York headquarters, some in quite high positions. A few made the move south. One recalled his forebodings and indecision after reading the notice that his department was being shifted to Houston. For him it would not be a promotion—just a transfer. He was a soft-spoken middle manager with a sizable staff. He and his wife owned their own home in New York and had two children approaching adolescence who would have to be uprooted if he made the move.

"It was a hard decision," he said. "I had to ask myself whether, after working for Shell for five years, I would want to start all over again at another organization; and I did feel comfortable with the people I was working with for Shell in New York." As indicated earlier, he suffered a month of emotional turmoil.

"I finally took the option of saying I would at least go down and take a look at the Southern city," he continued. "I found we could get better accommodations than we had anticipated because the company had done its homework with the realtors. I was promptly introduced to a realtor who had been asked to consider my problem, and in a short time he helped me get a home. He was a white man and the house I got is bigger and better than the one we had back in New York. It is in southwest Houston about five minutes from the Astrodome, in a predominantly white area with a few Negroes. Shortly after we moved in, my next-door neighbors came by and introduced themselves, and my children have made friends and go to school on bicycles.

"But I would repeat, if the Shell Company had not done the groundwork of dealing with the realtors, a black man could never make the move without a great deal of pain. He could beat his head against the wall and never find comparable housing if he didn't have some help."

Even with the assistance Shell could offer—and it spent more than $8,000 per family moved—some of the people making the move found it a rough trip. A young analyst with a crew cut, who had been transferred to New York just a few months before the mass move to Houston was announced, was still looking for a house when I saw him in Houston. He thought he had a deal and had moved his wife and four children down, but the deal fell through because the FHA ruled that he had insufficient income for the mortgage that had been arranged. While looking for another house he, his wife, and four children were living in a motel, with help from Shell.

Maybe being with a firm that picks up and moves to a distant clime can be an adventure for some, especially if they have learned to be highly adaptable. But it can be traumatic for a great many others.

4.

The Three-Shift Towns

In using the word "early," young Mr. Zelenka was describing a state of mind rather than the time people in Akron actually go to bed. The fact is that they go to bed at all hours. A greater proportion of Akron's labor force in manufacturing has been working between midnight and dawn than in any other U.S. city.

Some of Akron's boosters like to call it the City of the Future. Perhaps it is, because more and more Americans are working at night. If it is, then the "future" looks pretty dark to this observer, despite Akron's publicized bowling and golf tournaments.

Although Akron has only a moderate rate of residential mobility, its populace is one of the most disoriented of any city in the country. The disorientation and the uprooting of both living patterns and neighborhood life are due to two elements in the economy of Akron:

—Akron is the rubber center of America. A half dozen giant tire and rubber companies (Firestone, B.F. Goodrich, Goodyear, General Tire and Rubber, Mohawk, and Seiberling) have their home offices and plants there. With the introduction of expensive automated machinery the plants have increasingly gone to continuous operation around the clock. Most of the plants operate with three eight-hour shifts, the personnel working five days a week. Until very recently Firestone had operated most departments around the clock with four shifts of six hours each. In these cases the personnel worked six days a week. It has now gone over to the three-shift system. At this writing Goodyear is the only major plant that breaks most of its round-the-clock operations into four shifts.

On the four-shift day predominating at Firestone, when I was there, the first shift began at 6 A.M., the second at noon, the third at 6 P.M., and the fourth at midnight. The townspeople referred to the two night shifts as the Back Shifts and to the two daylight shifts as the Front Shifts. Nearly 20 percent of Akron's rubber workers are working between midnight and dawn; and about 40 percent are working sometime during the night.

This segmenting of life into shifts not only dictates patterns of daily living for the families geared to them but largely determines socializing patterns. It can leave one feeling he is a stranger on his own street, if his neighbors are geared to different shifts.

—Akron's next biggest industry, which doesn't involve manufacturing, is nevertheless a producer of disorientation and unstable living patterns. The city is one of the nation's leading trucking centers. Nearly 100 trucking firms have their headquarters in Akron and at least 70 other trucking firms operate out of the city. Trucking is largely a continuous-operation industry and it too demands a great deal of night work from its drivers and loaders. Furthermore the men often don't know when they will be called to make a trip or how long they will be gone.

At a round-table discussion I attended with social workers of the county's Family and Children's Service, a number of the social workers expressed a conviction that trucking in Akron was more disruptive of family life, at least, than the staggered shifts of the rubber industry. The trucker is mobile and may get mixed up with women; his wife is lonely and she may get mixed up with men. In any case the father is often away from his family for many days at a stretch; and the women are often forced by necessity to take over the job of being the man of the house, a move which seems threatening to many of them.

Akron has other industries. It makes books, toys, matches, and automobile rims, for example. Analysts for the U.S. Department of Labor estimated a couple of years ago that in Akron about 16 percent of *all* employees in manufacturing go to work *late* at night—the highest proportion they found in any large metropolitan area in the U.S.A.

Following very closely behind Akron in proportion of late-night workers is Canton, twenty miles away, which is heavily oriented to steel processing. Here are the other U.S. metropolitan areas where more than 9 percent of all manufacturing employees were working a graveyard shift which ends at dawn, in descending order, after Canton, with the important industries causing the night work cited:

Portland, Maine	(*paper*)
Savannah, Georgia	(*paper bags*)
Chattanooga, Tennessee	(*textiles, chemicals*)
Pittsburgh, Pennsylvania	(*steel*)
Spokane, Washington	(*steel*)
Green Bay, Wisconsin	(*paper*)
Midland-Odessa, Texas	(*oil, chemicals*)
Des Moines, Iowa	(*farm machinery*)
Charleston, West Virginia	(*chemicals*)
Phoenix, Arizona	(*electric machinery*)
Beaumont, Texas	(*oil, chemicals*)
Baltimore, Maryland	(*steel, electric machinery*)
Albany, New York	(*machinery*)
Houston, Texas	(*chemicals, oil*)

All these cities involve industries that have turned increasingly to continuous operation because of high equipment costs.

In some smaller towns and cities largely dependent

upon one plant for employment—such as Sparrow's Point, Maryland, outside Baltimore, which has the world's largest steel plant—the percentage of people working after midnight would run extremely high.

Businesses heavily dependent upon computers—such as brokerage houses, banks, and insurance offices—also have recently gone more heavily into demanding night people as employees. With several million dollars tied up in computers which, unlike humans, don't need to sleep, eat, or relax, the company managers feel guilty if the machines are idle.

Night people also are in growing demand to man the thousands of motel desks, the stores staying open later and later at night, the flight control centers and—with soaring crime rates—the police beats. An indication of the growth in numbers of night workers can be seen in the fact that at Tas-Tee Catering, Inc., which provides food services to Cleveland industries, food sales to night workers jumped 50 percent in three recent years.

Some companies making heavy use of night people try to spread the graveyard shift around by having employees rotate their shifts every few weeks. But this merely increases the personal disorientation of eating, sleeping, bathroom, and other habits.

In a few rare spots such as Las Vegas people operate around the clock with little awareness of whether it is dawn or dusk; but more commonly night people keep trying to live as they always did. However, they are often plagued by drowsiness and feelings of discomfort.

At night, Akron and Canton are very definitely not cities of bright lights and socializing in public places. Downtown Akron is absolutely dead at night. In one and a half hours of driving around the city between 11:30 P.M. and 1 A.M. I found no evidence of night life, such as you would see in abundance in San Francisco, Boston, or New York. A number of neon-lit bars near rubber factories were well patronized. I later learned that a few bowling alleys, mostly on the outskirts, stay open after midnight. Aside from the factories and bars, the only sign of activity I saw was at an occasional car wash. The vast Midway shopping plaza with its great variety of emporiums was totally closed down at 12:15 A.M. (Wives of course can obtain such items as groceries during the day—if they themselves aren't working.)

The Goodyear Company has a large bowling center for employees but that too was closed down at twelve-fifteen. As midnight approached at the main Goodyear plant many wives with their children were waiting in cars near the gate. The men leaving at the midnight change of shift seemed mainly to be about thirty to forty years old and were amiable. The younger men going in to replace them seemed less amiable.

Canton, before midnight, seemed even more deserted except for a few children under twelve seen on the streets. At ten-thirty I sat in one of the largest downtown theaters killing time watching the movie *Bob and Carol and Ted and Alice*. There were never more than three or four other people in the theater. At one point it got down to one other person. Around 11:30 P.M. I began driving around the downtown area and the maze of streets in the flatland mill areas where steel product companies such as Hercules Engine, Timken, and U.S. Steel and many of their employees' homes are located. It was eerie, in a light rain, to see the brightly lit mills against the darkened houses and stores. Suddenly at about eleven forty-five there was a torrent of cars heading for the mills, almost every one occupied by a lone driver. By twelve-fifteen the reverse flow of cars with lone drivers was at full tide. Many of the drivers stopped off at the Classic Bowling Alley where the parking lot was jammed by twelve-thirty and every lane was full.

But let's return to my main night city of interest, nearby Akron. It is a splotchy confusing city for the most part, with a few pleasant residential areas. Railroad trains roar through the center of the city. Various skyways ring much of the downtown area but none will get you downtown in any direct fashion. This is an oversight the city fathers hope to correct. Much of downtown—which is basically one prosaic street—is under renovation.

An official of the rubber workers' union said, "Actually, America's cities haven't recognized night working as a social problem." Aside from the bars and bowling alleys and a few small grocery stores in Akron, adjustment to the night people has been minimal. The University of Akron operates from 7 A.M. to 11 P.M. A number of banks have night depositories. Montgomery Ward has been experimenting with Sunday openings. Even the workers still seem to continue to think in conventional terms. Earl Rhodes, a young machinist at Firestone who works from 10 P.M. till dawn, said, "Our lunch break starts at 2 A.M."

Some late-night-to-dawn workers expressed uneasiness about leaving their wives at home unprotected late at night. One said his wife sleeps with a loaded gun nearby. Many also felt they were forcing a more lonely than normal life on their wives by their different sleeping patterns.

Efficiency engineers during World War II concluded that night workers would thrive best if they led lives just like ordinary nine-to-five workers. That is, after finishing work, go home to a full dinner, pursue hobbies, watch TV, call on friends, etc., till bedtime (around 1 P.M.); sleep till time to get up and have breakfast in the evening before driving off to work.

That is not, however, the way it works in Akron. People are still stuck with the idea that one eats dinner mainly in the evening. And any male adult quickly discovers that watching TV in the morning and midday hours, before the theoretical "bedtime," is not much fun because the shows are mainly geared to housewives.

The way people actually function in Akron varies with each person. A union official commented: "Some of the hardest drinking starts at six o'clock in the morning. Everything is all turned around for them. Some drink all morning and get home about noon."

Earl Rhodes, a machinist, lives in a village south of Akron but usually stops off at a bar that has go-go girls as dancers when he gets off work at 6 A.M. The girls are not topless but they are skimpily clad and they dance on a little platform with juke box music. After sipping a couple of beers he goes home at about 8 A.M. and feeds the riding horses in his small barn. (With overtime he has been making about $260 a week.) Then he goes to bed at about 9 A.M. and stays there until about 3 P.M. He added, "I hate it. You never get to see many people. It seems contrary to human nature."

On the other hand David Zelenka, who lives on a shady street on the west side of Akron, likes the late night shift. (He has been making $14,000 a year, by piling up overtime.) He pointed out that there is a six-cent-an-hour bonus, and you have fewer supervisors running around making demands. And since your wife is sleeping, you don't need a second car. He goes directly home at 6 A.M. to greet his wife and two children as they are waking up. "It's the closest time we have together," he said. "I take the children to school and then come back and go to bed." Or, in the warm months, he may go directly from his job to the golf course at 6 A.M. "I get there before the course opens. You have the course to yourself and pay greens fees when you finish." Mostly he plays with fellows from his shift.

Louis Cerbellino worked the third shift at Firestone, from 6 P.M. to midnight. He dropped by the Firestone local's headquarters while I was there. Holding his young daughter by the hand, he explained that since she had a cold that day and didn't go to school it gave him a rare opportunity to spend several hours with her.

Akron working people enjoy arguing about which is the worst shift. (If there are only three shifts the breaks usually are at 6 A.M., 2 P.M., and 10 P.M.) There is little argument—whether there are three shifts or four—that the best starts at dawn. In some Firestone departments it takes twenty years of seniority to get on it. If there are shifts around the clock the argument is whether it is worse to work the shift that runs into the evening or the late shift that goes into dawn.

All but one of the dozen union members I talked with disliked "Back Shift" or night work. And it may take you ten years of seniority to get off night work. The only argument was whether early night work or late night work was more upsetting. A top union official said that early night work was the most disliked, especially by the younger men. At first glance the late night shift ending at dawn would seem more repellent. Psychologically it is harder to go home at dawn than it is at midnight. Late night work is also more disorienting. As one union official said: "A man doesn't even know when his bowels are supposed to move regularly!"

The most frequent complaint expressed about late night work was the difficulty in trying to sleep during the day. A time-study expert from the union said, "You can be in bed ten hours and only get six hours' sleep. I lay in bed most of the day, get up at 4:30 P.M. for supper, and I'm still tired and lie back down again." Others said they split up their sleep: two or three hours in the morning and then three or four more before they go back to work.

The upstairs window shades of thousands of Akron homes are pulled down most of the day, but there is still the problem of trying to keep preschool children quiet because Daddy is asleep.

Several of the men also complained that late night work raises havoc with one's sex life. The husband and wife rarely sleep together. As for pre- or post-sleep intimacies, one union leader explained: "During the day the wife doesn't feel like scampering around. Matinee sex is not the best for women. And the kids are often in the house. The late night shift is hell on your sex life."

Those who like the shift that ends around dawn tend to be older men who have become oriented and have a second source of income. Several have little machine shops they enjoy and profit from. And a number of farmers like this shift because it gets them home just in time to milk their cows.

The most disliked shift—and the one that the experts at the Family and Children's Service say is most disrupting—is the one requiring people to be on the job in the early evening. It is even more disrupting to family life. A union official recalls: "When I was on the early night shift I only saw my school-age children for any enjoyable period of time on weekends." And then there is the disruption of social and recreational life. Another official said that the third shift ruins your chance of seeing any of your old friends in a socializing way. "You just can't go out on Friday night and socialize. And you can't be involved in football, basketball, baseball, and other sports activities at the company. Most start at 7 P.M."

Almost all of the rubber workers I encountered said they did not know much about the people living near them on their block. One said that out of sixteen neighbors on his block only two worked his time shift. Dr. Alexis Anikeeff, industrial psychologist at the University of Akron, explained: "What happens in these situations is that the people become accustomed to making friends with other people who are compatible in terms of shifts and hours." Gerald Gelvin, head of the Firestone local of the rubber workers' union, said he didn't know most of the people living near him and explained, "People in neighborhoods today really don't socialize much anyhow. I don't say that this is caused entirely by the shift pattern. It's a trend of the times, but the shift patterns certainly add to it. You may be working first shift and your really good friends are on the third shift. No matter how much you may want to, it's discouraging to try to get together." A union member explained: "Most of the people in the apartment where we live are working on other shifts. The only thing I say to the neighbors is 'Hi.' I have no contact with them at all. My wife is different. She does talk to some of the other wives."

Earl Rhodes, the machinist, related: "All our new friends work the same hours I do. For social life my wife and I mostly associate with people I work with on the late night shift." On the street where he lives he socializes with only one neighbor, who also happens to be on the late night shift. He occasionally chats with, and theoretically could socialize with, a neighbor who works the early morning shift but since it takes so long to get onto this first shift the other man's family is so much older that the two families don't have much in common. Louis Cerbellino, who, as noted, works the early night shift, commented: "Most of the people living around us work in the rubber shop. All have different shifts. I see during the day some of the people who work the late night shift. But most of our neighbors work during the day and are just getting home when I am leaving for work."

And David Zelenka, the young machinist, said: "Almost all the friends that we socialize with are on my late night shift. A few are on the first shift in the morning. It seems to work out better that way. The second shift is almost impossible to socialize with and the third is hardest of all."

As for the neighbors on his street, he doesn't socialize with any of them regularly, partly because the men work a different shift. But he also mentioned another attitude I encountered frequently in my research. He wasn't sure it was a good idea to get too close to one's neighbors. They might turn out to have irritating habits you might become intolerant of. To many people like him the word "neighbors" now has a negative connotation.

The shift workers I talked with in Akron did not show much enthusiasm or interest in their neighborhood or express any pride in it. They didn't identify with it in any unifying sense. They didn't even seem aware it was a neighborhood. It was just a place where they lived.

> *"We hope to be back here for Christmas."*—JOSÉ DE LA FUENTE OF MCALLEN, TEXAS, IN DESCRIBING HIS PLAN TO TAKE THIRTY-FIVE MIGRATORY WORKERS AND THEIR CHILDREN ON A 5,100-MILE JOURNEY NORTHWARD IN A DILAPIDATED BUS.

5.

Staging Areas for Modern Nomads

McAllen, Texas (pop. 38,000), is about as mobile as a town can get. At first glance McAllen might be mistaken for a typical, stable town in Kansas. On very flat land, its main street is dominated by stores with such names as Sweeneys, McRay's, The Parisienne, Klinck Drugs, and The Coed Shop. The vast majority of its city officials have Kansas-sounding names and most of the police look like the police you might see in a typical Kansas town.

One clue that McAllen is not really in Kansas is that two thirds of the faces you see in McAllen have a Mexican caste. Another clue is that you see an awful lot of out-of-state licenses on cars. A third is the occasional rows of palm trees. Years ago someone managed to grow palm trees there—and McAllen now calls itself "The City of Palms." It is seven miles back from the Rio Grande (partly to avoid its floods) and it faces, across the plains and the river, the much larger Mexican city of Reynosa.

One reason McAllen rates as a super-mobile town is that it is the staging area for caravans of camper trailers that frequently take off for excursions deep into Mexico.

When a Wally Byam Tour, limited to people who can afford Airstream trailers, calls for a rendezvous in Mc-Allen, 400 trailers are likely to start assembling—from many states—in the vast parking lot surrounding the McAllen Civic Center. The Chamber of Commerce energetically encourages the assembling of these caravans.

It also welcomes the 5,000 people from about forty states who take refuge on McAllen's semitropical flatland till the frost or snow leaves their native states farther north. Two large tourist centers help winter people meet each other and kill time till winter goes away.

But of the forty-seven pieces of promotional literature I examined at the Chamber of Commerce not one made any reference to McAllen's only real claim to national fame: it is the number one staging ground for migratory farm workers in America.

McAllen is the largest town in Hidalgo County and, according to officials of the U.S. Department of Labor, Hidalgo County provides more migratory farm workers than any other county in the United States. It supplies, for example, three times as many migrants as the next three highest counties in Texas combined. Since McAllen is the largest town and has the principal employment center in Hidalgo County, it is the country's primary staging center for workers moving north.

It is estimated that about 30,000 migratory workers from McAllen and other areas of the county start the trek northward each spring and return in the fall. Since most take unemployable children and mothers of infants with them, this means that nearly one fourth of the entire population of the county joins the migrant stream each year. Most are Americans of Mexican ancestry.

In the United States of the 1970s there are many kinds of migratory workers besides those working for large farm organizations. There are, for example, many thousands of professional athletes such as baseball, football, basketball, golf, hockey, tennis players, and bowlers who are on the road much of the year. There are the thousands of jockeys and trainers; the thousands of racing-car drivers and mechanics; and the thousands of actors on circuits or in summer stock companies.

Outside the world of entertainment, there are nearly 100,000 long-distance truck or bus drivers . . . the many thousands of airline pilots and hostesses . . . the tens of thousands of bridge and other mobile construction workers . . . the hundreds of thousands of traveling salesmen . . . and the thousands of oil well specialists such as cappers who move as their jobs move.

But the biggest demand for migratory employees is to harvest—and often nurture—the large-scale crops of business entrepreneurs in farming.

For some crops, the whole harvesting industry moves on a northern sweep. The strawberry industry, for example, is largely mobile. In the early spring entrepreneurs assemble a great deal of equipment and workers near Hammond, Louisiana. The caravan starts north as the crop ripens. At each stop the crews pick, sort, pack, or process and often truck the crop to wholesalers. By midsummer the crews have fanned out—but usually have traveled at least a thousand miles northward.

Farther west, the crews of "custom cutters" of wheat, rye, and barley start northward from north Texas or Oklahoma at about the same time. The entrepreneurs of these crews often have a quarter million dollars invested in equipment. A single combine that will cut a twenty-foot swath of grain and separate the grain from the husks costs at least $17,000.

These grain crews move northward in a belt about three hundred miles wide and a thousand miles long until they reach North Dakota. The crew boss gets bulletins from state and federal agencies which help him arrive at a customer's farm within twenty-four hours of prime cutting time. If he has several combines he can cut 60 acres a day, or if rain threatens he can turn on the combine lights at night and, by working a twenty-hour day, harvest 350 acres in three days—a feat which helps make his services attractive to grain growers.

The crews of these "custom cutters" are, among migratory workers, an elite group. Usually all-male, they often drive their own cars and live in motels. Most are of "Anglo" background. Some are husky college students picking up summer work. Pay ranges from about two dollars an hour for unskilled to four dollars for skilled crewmen, and food is usually included.

About 95 percent of all the nation's 300,000 migratory farm workers, however, lead a rougher life for less pay. As harvesters of the nation's vegetable, fruit, and Christmas tree crops, their mobility has made them subject to exploitation; and only in recent years have they managed to develop some organized resistance to exploitation and to win some government supervision over their relations with employers.

There appear to be four main status levels among migratory farm laborers:

—The lowest status is assigned to "stoop labor," which requires continual bending over to pick tomatoes, beans, cucumbers, sugar beets, asparagus, cantaloupes, etc.

—The next status is assigned to work that requires climbing ladders in fruit trees. Apparently it is the strain of reaching, the lifting of ladders, and the risk of falling that make such work relatively unpopular.

—For those in manual work, top status goes to those who pick from fruit bushes and vegetable stalks that can mostly be done standing fairly upright. Hoeing also would be included here.

—The highest status goes to the person who is given the responsibility of driving or running a machine. He or she becomes a person apart in terms of dignity, and is especially esteemed by Americans of minority backgrounds. The economist Peter Drucker quotes a manager of a Latin-American sugar plantation as saying: "I can always tell an Indian who has driven a truck or a tractor. He stands straight and talks back to me."

The hundreds of thousands of migratory people who help to harvest the nation's fruits and vegetables follow three main streams.

First, there is a strictly East Coast stream that has its

main staging area in the spring around Belle Glade, Florida. Consisting mainly of blacks, with a mixture of whites out of the Appalachian country coming in farther north, this human stream flows up to New Jersey and to the Long Island potato growers.

Second is a strictly West Coast stream that operates mainly within California but reaches also into Oregon and Washington. Its main staging ground is at El Centro in the Imperial Valley opposite the Mexican border town of Mexicali. This stream is mainly Mexican-American with an increased mixture of itinerant Anglos as you get north of Fresno.

Finally, there is the main stream, whose staging ground is south Texas, and particularly Hidalgo County's town of McAllen. As it moves north this stream fans out into tributaries reaching all the way to New Jersey in the East and to the state of Washington in the West.

The U.S. state attracting the greatest number of interstate migratory workers is Michigan, with its large crops of apples, cherries, and cucumbers. About 40,000 migratory workers, mostly from Texas, a thousand or more miles away, reach Michigan each year. Ohio, Indiana, Illinois, and Wisconsin, in that order, attract the rest of the 150,000 migratory Texas farm workers.

The migrants flowing up out of Texas have developed stop-over places based on a long day's drive. By far the largest in the United States is Hope, Arkansas (pop. 9,000), which boasts it is on "Main Street in Southwest U.S.A." The northeast-bound Routes 67 and 30 intersect there.

The industries of the town include making mattresses, garments, and vinyl floor coverings; and nearby, for a fee, visitors can dig for diamonds. Like McAllen, its boosters are shy about mentioning its only real claim to national distinction. In *This Is Hope,* a 70-odd-page brochure, there is no mention of the fact that 50,000 migratory workers stop there each year. Most are coming from, or heading for, south Texas. Often in early June nearly a thousand migrants stop over each day. Since they were stopping there anyway the residents of Hope decided to get the stopping-over organized; and the federal government came in with a grant to the Arkansas State Employment Service. Now there are a number of trailer houses, divided into two sections, that can sleep a total of eight persons. Clean sheets can be obtained for twenty-five cents a person. There are picnic tables, shower and toilet facilities, a place to wash clothes, and a nurse on duty twenty-four hours a day.

In contrast to Hope, Malhoun County, isolated in eastern Oregon, actively promotes the fact it has fine housing facilities for migrants. Although it is in an isolated area about 12,000 migrants pass through it each year. The authorities hope its permanent camps will be used as a sort of home base for migratory workers who have commitments to go on to The Dalles area on the Columbia River and into Washington and Idaho. Malhoun County, with the advent of irrigation, has an intermittent need for large crews of workers to handle crop harvesting. As a further move to lure migrants Treasure Valley Community College has an extensive program of education for migrants' children.

Back in Texas, McAllen's school system has established a special migrant school with an accelerated program to help migrants' children go north without falling hopelessly behind. Its school year, forty-four days shorter than the regular school year, runs from October 20 to May 8. Still, many children arrive late and leave early. Many families start moving north around April 15.

The median number of years that migratory workers in Texas have spent in school is about six. They mostly speak a special Mex-Tex language, which mixes Spanish, Indian, and English, and on the road most let the crew boss, who is often a relative, speak for them. He also negotiates terms of employment. The average crew of workers is about twenty, plus children; but some caravans have more than a hundred persons. Usually the crew leader, working with the Texas Employment Commission's office in McAllen, maps an itinerary that will provide as many job orders as possible. These written itineraries, which are now required by law if more than ten workers are involved, are filed with the federal government, which seeks to get migrants where the jobs are.

While I was at the barracklike Farm Labor Office on the eastern edge of McAllen, a tall, staid Michigan businessman, accompanied by a wisecracking Mexican-American lad to serve as interpreter, entered and began earnestly consulting crew leaders. The businessman produced pickles and was trying to line up five hundred pickers for his summer cucumber crop.

The kind of life migrants lead was matter-of-factly described to me by a crew chief, José de la Fuente, a man of great dignity, who had an ambitious program planned. His plump twenty-three-year-old son Ranulfo and his daughter Juana acted as translators, although later in our talk it became clear that their father could speak English reasonably well.

José de la Fuente was planning to embark with thirty-five workers and five children on April 15 for Delaware, a trip of 2,400 miles, to work for asparagus growers. The growers were giving him a $20 allowance per worker for travel costs, or something less than a penny a mile. The trip would be made in a bus he had bought in poor condition for $500. He had been working to get it in better shape—but as a precaution, in case the bus broke down, he was going to follow it in a car. The migrants would sleep in the bus at roadside parks and buy groceries along the way. After Delaware they would go to Maryland for a while, then work westward and arrive in Wisconsin by mid-October to cut, trim, and separate Christmas trees.

The pay per worker would average $1.60 an hour, about the same as he and his son had earned during the winter in a packing plant near McAllen. But up north, he said, working conditions are better "and they treat you better." In some cases he had arranged piecework pay for his crew and some of his best workers should be able to earn $150 or more a week. Señor de la Fuente had been taking crews north for seven years. In general, he said, things are getting better.

After processing the Wisconsin trees the crew would return to McAllen in time for Christmas, and for a reunion with old friends and kinfolk on both sides of the border.

This is an important cautionary point to remember in considering migratory workers as seemingly the most uprooted members of our society. There are truly uprooted migratory workers in America, such as the Anglos who are simply drifters in central California, but the Mexican-Americans from south Texas do have significant roots.

All the time they are on the road they are amid kinfolk or people they have usually known for years, so that, like a nomadic tribe, they remain a cohesive group. Thus the adults have relatively little basis for being plagued by a sense of uprootedness or loneliness. However, their children are hard hit. They are torn from their schools and are moved from one bewildering town to another, where they often spend long stretches alone as their parents work, and they are often treated by local youngsters as aliens.

Another point to remember is the fact that the Mexican-American migrants attach enormous importance to returning annually to their homes in south Texas. Their homes are simple: small square bungalows mainly, but most have gardens and are colorfully painted.

The nation's leading authority on migratory workers, James Nix of the U.S. Department of Labor, relates:

"I was surprised at the number of these migratory workers who are homeowners back in Texas or wherever their home base is. One of our studies showed that 48 percent owned their own home or were in the process of buying one. This means that they are higher in homeownership than the general population of the United States."

Quite probably this buying of homes reflects their extraordinary need for a sense of place.

"People ask me where I am from and I say nowhere."—AN AMERICAN AIRLINES HOSTESS, IN DESCRIBING HER EARLY LIFE AS A "MILITARY BRAT" LIVING AT ELEVEN MILITARY BASES IN THE UNITED STATES AND ABROAD.

6.

Life on the Nuclear Frontier

Thus far, in my visits to towns, I have focused primarily on business practices which are scattering Americans or fragmenting their communities. Here, the focus will be on the role of the federal government in uprooting the lives of many millions of families each year, with particular attention given to its defense and space activities.

The United States of the early 1970s has ten times as many men under arms as it had in 1940, three decades earlier. The total number now approaches 3.5 million. Many are married; many are draftees. And many, with or without families accompanying them, are transferred from base to base both within the United States and abroad. Senate Majority Leader Mike Mansfield in 1971 estimated that the U.S. has close to 2,000 bases of some sort abroad in thirty different countries. Other estimates indicate that approximately a half million dependents of Defense Department personnel are stationed overseas.

At European bases there is nearly one dependent for each military man. In 1969 the Military Airlift Command transported 81,000 Defense Department dependents to places outside the continental U.S.A. (i.e., 1,512 dependents to Goose Bay, Labrador; 1,469 to Lajes, Azores; 6,304 to the Panama Canal Zone; 3,807 to Bangkok, Thailand).

To supply all the nation's military personnel with everything from Polaris missiles and swing-wing planes to ping-pong balls, more than 100,000 plants, employing several million men and women, operate in thousands of U.S. towns and cities. Jobs open up or close down at the decision or whim of the Pentagon. Hundreds of towns and cities have become desperately dependent upon military orders, or upon nearby military installations.

The disruption of lives and communities of all this military-space-related activity is almost beyond the power of contemplation. It is easier to look at a few specifics.

A sample of the emotional chaos married couples go through as the thousands of anonymous military order cutters juggle their lives can be seen in the experience of a couple I'll call Joe and Dorie Whitten. (Joe is still in the military.) They were recently out of college in upstate New York. She had studied psychology; he had studied economics and had been in Air Force ROTC.

First they were shipped off to Laredo, Texas, for a year. When the end of that tour of duty was nearing, Joe got orders to go to Okinawa. He was advised that because of the housing shortage Dorie would not be able to join him for six months. A few weeks later, however, he got a new and different set of orders directing him to Topeka, Kansas. They had barely readjusted their plans when he got still different orders that he was being sent instead to Columbus, Ohio, for a year. But as it turned out the base in Columbus began being shut down five months after their arrival. In two of those five months Joe was sent off to South America. With the Columbus base shutting down they were reassigned to Hampton-Norfolk, Virginia. Then they were sent off to Europe; after two months they came back, and at last report he was back in Europe. All this upset happened to a couple who didn't have to cope with the added distress of a husband being sent into an area of military combat or tension, which has been the experience of hundreds of thousands of U.S. families.

Not only people but communities often experience trauma as a result of military and aerospace activities. A good place to look at the effect on communities is Great Falls, Montana, a very special kind of military-space town.

Flying east over the magnificent snow-capped Rockies, I saw for hundreds of miles great buttes jutting up from the high plain against a magnificent sunset. This is indeed the country of the Big Sky. And racing below was the great Missouri River, dropping 530 feet over five water-falls in the short span of twelve miles. These were the falls that caused the American explorer Meriwether Lewis a lot of trouble in June 1805. Nestled in a bend of the river is the city of Great Falls (pop. 60,000), laid out on a near perfect grid with a large civic center near the river. Obviously someone years ago had the vision to attempt to build a fine city.

Great Falls has a national distinction to match its setting. Just to the east of the city is the Malmstrom Air Force Base, nerve center for the largest intercontinental ballistic missile complex in the Western world.

In fifteen years the base has come to dominate Great Falls, to swell it preposterously, and to create a sloppy, confused, dreary civically listless metropolis that is just starting to attempt a comeback. In much of the fifteen years the city has been plagued by triple-shift schools and, when I was there, still had one junior high school on triple shift. A substantial proportion of Air Force personnel, especially those who are married, live with their families off base and are counted as residents of the town. The same applies to the base's many civilian employees.

Great Falls today is a city in which one of its top restaurants, Eddie's, is a cement block building where cowboys and Air Force captains rub shoulders while Eddie, in his lumberjack shirt, passes out salacious cartoons to his favorite male customers.

Thanks to the base, Great Falls now has an acute identity problem about where its "downtown" is. The original downtown, near the civic center and river, began deteriorating after the construction of the Air Force base. Businesses began moving out of the "downtown" area. Pawnshops, bait shops, and gas stations came to be conspicuous parts of "downtown." The town's businesses had been moving, or expanding, out to Tenth Avenue, ten blocks south. State highway officials had made it into a four-lane highway so that the traffic flowing from the city's airport to the Malmstrom Base would by-pass most of the city. The planner neglected to put any limitation on access to the highway.

Today Tenth Avenue is a five-mile stretch of neon-lit hamburger joints, pizza parlors, hot chicken stands, motels, a shopping center, trailer sales lots, etc. Rivalry is so great between downtown and Tenth Avenue that in a recent year the city's boosters couldn't get together on how to decorate the city for Christmas. A city planner explained to me: "Tenth Avenue is a monster. It got out of hand."

More than two hundred missile sites are near Great Falls. A helicopter hovered over my car much of the time while I tried to orient myself to the roads near the Air Force base. When I first checked in at my motel I saw a bull's-eye type map on the wall with dots on it and with Great Falls a great dot at the eye of all the rings. My first jumpy conclusion was that it must be a map such as the Russians surely have since the Great Falls base and silos would be top-priority targets in any nuclear war. Closer inspection revealed that it was a map showing where other motels of the same chain were located within several hundred miles of Great Falls.

Most residents I consulted had seen great vans with "explosives" posted all over them go by, accompanied by police escorts wailing their sirens. The only reaction of residents, beyond indifference, is annoyance that they have to move over to let the vans pass. All the people I questioned also had a pretty good idea where at least one missile silo is located. A psychology professor at the College of Great Falls said: "People see beautiful new roads going out into nowhere and assume they must lead to one or more silos. There is no apprehension or interest in the missile silos on the part of people in the area."

The existence of the base is not the only reason why Great Falls has a highly transient population. The city serves as district headquarters for a great many U.S. business firms. A district manager spends much of his time checking up on local offices within a couple of hundred miles, and reporting the results to his superior at regional headquarters.

Mrs. Rosemary Hingst, the Welcome Wagon hostess in Great Falls, reported that, out of four calls she had made the previous week on newcomers, three involved husbands who planned to take up their duties traveling out of town within a few days. Air Force men, too, it should be added, usually spend several days at a stretch away at a silo before returning to their homes in Great Falls.

From all this it should be no surprise that Great Falls has a transient population. Just how transient it is startled even me. Lee Robinson, manager of the Great Falls Bell Telephone Company, reported that about 44 percent of all residential telephone users have service to their homes disconnected each year. This almost always means they have moved. He said that the closer you got to residences near the Air Force base the higher the disconnect rate ran.

In the Air Force, in general, a majority of both officers and enlisted men are married; and motivational studies have revealed that the attitude of both groups toward making a career in the Air Force is less negative if their families are stationed near them.

Another indication of the high mobility of Air Force families was supplied to me by officials of the Loy School, about 99 percent of whose student body are children of Air Force personnel. It is not an Air Force school but a part of the city's school system. However it is located at a corner of the fenced-in Air Force base so that children living on base come through a special opening to the school. Children living off base walk or are bussed. Some of the teachers are wives of Air Force personnel. An official estimated that the school loses 70 percent of its students every year because their parents move; and it loses 30 percent of its teachers!

With all the transience and traveling on the job, Great Falls has become a rather lonely city. It is so lonely in fact that many wives are willing to spend much of their pay for adult baby sitters during the day so that they can work. It seems better than sitting home. A teacher's wife after living two months in Great Falls told me: "I have met very few of my neighbors. Most of the women around here work. You never see anyone. We have met the bachelor who lives next door. He is a retired man."

One wife told Mrs. Hingst that her three small children were lonesome and she wondered if Mrs. Hingst knew of any children they could play with. After some search Mrs. Hingst found some children a block or so away who said sure, they would like to play. A school official fairly new to Great Falls commented: "We have heard many people say they don't like Great Falls at all. It is windy —and it is not friendly."

Some of the unfriendliness is due to the alien ways of the military folks, as seen through the eyes of native Montanans. The fact that the military complex pumps more than $50 million a year into the local economy does not wipe out the edginess. One native, a professor at the college, said the local people see their area of Montana being "spoiled and uprooted by all the changes going on by the missile bases and resorts and Eastern interests taking over. The continual moving upsets them. They say, 'Why can't these people plant gardens and take care of lawns like we do?' "

The mobility plus the tensions have until very recently made it difficult for the people of Great Falls to do much about the acute problems arising from the city's transformation. Apathy has been the dominant mood. John Mooney, a city planner, said that until recently, at least, the attitude of residents was that "they couldn't care less." Most residents still don't want to become involved in government or community affairs and are not aware of what the City Council or the Planning Board is doing.

Mooney pointed out that under the law 40 percent of

the voters must participate for a school election to be valid. At a time when the schools were groaning under triple and double sessions it still took three elections to get out enough voters to put through a bond issue.

The churches too find their high-mobile congregations vexing. Two ministers reported it was very difficult to achieve any leadership or continuity or program planning. Mrs. Hingst, who is the wife of a minister, said that if an incoming family is a strong church family it will usually get its former minister to write a letter of transfer. But she added, "People who move around a great deal are less likely to transfer in. They seem to feel, 'Why get started, when you'll be moving out?' "

While I was visiting Great Falls a group of citizens called the Great Falls Movement was trying, with some apparent success, to focus the attention of residents on the city's more acute problems. A driving force in the movement was a local minister, Robert K. Leland. Meetings had been held at which residents were invited to list the ten problems of the city that bugged them most. An over-all list of 105 major concerns emerged—such as getting a community youth center, doing something about the deplorable streets (some of them are still made of old wooden blocks), and dressing up the splotchy "drive" along the waterfront of the Missouri River out to Rainbow Falls. When I was there it was decorated by an untidy trailer camp. But the Great Falls Movement's leadership was beset by a typical disheartening problem in the town's transience. One of the strongest men on the steering committee had just been transferred to California.

U.S. towns dominated by the Army, the Navy, or by defense and aerospace contractors also dot the landscape. A book could and should be written about them. Here I will just try to indicate briefly how they relate to our main area of interest: how they are promoting uprootedness and social fragmentation in America.

THE ARMY TOWNS

There are many dozens of them near U.S. towns. The once puritanical sawmill village of Leesville, Louisiana, has for thirty years been dominated by nearby Fort Polk. At Fort Polk millions of infantry G.I.s have been trained whenever the demand for G.I.s was high. Leesville has become a neon-lit boom-and-bust honky-tonk town constantly battling the incursion of prostitutes.

A fair sample of brand-new "communities" created by Army posts can be seen in the 3,500 rented trailers that have sprung up, often in hodgepodge arrangement, near Fort Rucker, a few miles from Dothan, Alabama. Rucker mainly trains helicopter pilots and the roar of the choppers night and day keeps the trailer homes in almost constant vibration. Open sewers are a common sight and recreational facilities are negligible for the children, who are known as "trailer rats." *The New York Times* writer Joseph Lelyveld vividly captured what married life is like in these trailers when he interviewed Mr. and Mrs. Johnny Johnson after they had been living for the first four weeks of their marriage in one of these trailers perched on flat red Alabama earth. Mrs. Johnson made an ironic grimace as she referred to the rented trailer as "home." She said she and her husband would never dream of trying to entertain any friends there because of cramped, untidy conditions. Her days are numbing in their boredom. She dislikes the trailer too much to bother about much house cleaning, but there is nowhere to go. She did not know the names of any of the other young women stranded in her particular court. Some were worse off, she said, because their husbands were already in Southeast Asia.

THE NAVY TOWNS

Practically every aspect of social and municipal activity throughout the entire Tidewater area of Virginia is influenced by the U.S. Navy. An executive of the National Association of Government Employees advises that "Norfolk and its environs may well be the most extreme example of the impact of extensive federal activity." Not only is the Navy the largest employer in the region but the Army has two forts nearby. Also there is an Air Force base and the nation's largest private shipyard, which owes its growth largely to the Navy's presence.

My own hunch, however, is that, for sheer impact of U.S. defense spending on a major metropolitan area, Norfolk is surpassed by Charleston, South Carolina.

I had long heard of Charleston as one of America's most gracious and historic cities and I knew that a number of books had been written on "unchanging Charleston." But I also know that in the late 1950s and in the 1960s the area's congressman, L. Mendel Rivers, first as ranking Democrat and then chairman of the House Armed Services Committee, had been blatant and ruthless in pumping military spending into the Charleston area. His predecessor as chairman, Carl Vinson, reportedly cautioned him: "You put anything else down there in your district, Mendel, and it's gonna sink."

Rivers not only got an incredible variety of Navy and Marine installations into his district but also an Air Force base, a number of large defense plants—and even a Veterans Hospital. More than half of the payroll of the entire Charleston area today is military-related. This clout is felt in civic affairs. Much to the annoyance of natives, being a military man seems to give an office-seeker a big edge in getting a public appointment.

Today "unchanging Charleston" is an invaded city with one of the most transient population of any major metropolitan area in eastern United States. Southern Bell Telephone records indicate that about 37 percent of all the residential telephone users in the Charleston district disconnect their phones each year. There is one area of Charleston, however, where the telephone records show little movement. That is the small area south of Broad Street consisting entirely of glorious, serene old homes and public buildings and a bandstand amid trees hanging with moss—the heart of traditional Charleston. The area is a visual delight. Residents are mostly native. And there is a saying among the natives that Broad Street—where a number of old law firms are located—"is as far uptown as anyone would go."

Beyond Broad Street, and a few older blocks of renovated homes near the harbor, Charleston becomes more shabby and desecrated the farther you go inland. A slashing skyway makes dead ends of once handsome thoroughfares.

Rivers Avenue—named for guess who—runs for miles along many of the defense establishments that the late congressman brought to his city. It is an avenue of unrelieved visual mayhem—junkyards, three-minute car washes, used-car lots, shopping centers, fried chicken stands, and mobile-home emporiums.

THE BASES ABROAD

Experienced air travelers tend to shun the direct flights from New York to Frankfurt, Germany, because of a bulk-rate arrangement the military has with U.S. commercial airlines. Of the 65,000 dependents the Defense Department sends to and from Frankfurt each year, many go by commercial airline. A computer arrangement advises a military center in New Jersey how many unsold seats each plane in New York headed for Frankfurt has; and the military managers load into buses just enough dependent women and children and infants, and some fathers, to fill the unsold airplane seats and rush them to the New York terminal before flight time. Thus a full-fare-paying civilian is likely to find himself on a jam-packed plane with quite a few understandably fretful children.

Many of these dependents are headed ultimately for Heidelberg, near Frankfurt. Ancient Heidelberg with its medieval castle, its centuries-old hotels, and its historic university has a population of approximately 90,000 Germans and, now, about 30,000 Americans. The city is a major headquarters for the United States Army in Western Europe.

The American military men and their dependents live almost entirely in their own vast unwalled enclave at the edge of Heidelberg. The enclave is made up mainly of complexes of large, low apartment housing; streets have mainly American names; different areas have names such as Patrick Henry Village and Mark Twain Village.

A medical man stationed there told me: "There are usually twenty-five to thirty children to a stairwell. It is similar to ghetto living. Most of these families here have absolutely no friends in Heidelberg except among other military families. And these usually are families whose fathers are attached to the same military company."

THE AEROSPACE TOWNS

There are big military production towns that have nothing to do with aerospace. For example Groton, Connecticut, builds submarines; Springfield, Massachusetts, builds guns, and Oakland, California, builds jeeps. But planes, missiles, and spacecraft, and their launch areas, have created some of the more spectacular and volatile late twentieth-century military towns. Technically, much of the space exploration program is not supposed to be related to defense, but whenever Congress threatens to cut back space spending, the argument is heard that manned space flights are crucial if the U.S. is to maintain its "defense capability."

One thing the aerospace towns all have in common is a considerable amount of turbulence and transience in their living environment. People working for aerospace companies are a mobile breed; and if they move it may well be to an entirely different region of the United States. When the cutbacks in the aerospace program began in 1969–1970 tens of thousands of scientists, engineers, and technicians found themselves priced out of their job market. To support their families many took up jobs, they hoped temporarily, pumping gas and selling encyclopedias.

Aerospace dominates many areas including Seattle, Washington, Wichita, Kansas, and a dozen towns on Long Island. But there are significant configurations. There is the "aerospace crescent" stretching from the launching center at Cape Kennedy in Florida to Houston's NASA Manned Spacecraft Center. Along the crescent there are aerospace towns not only in Florida and Texas but in Louisiana, Mississippi, and Alabama, with the greatest concentration of installations near the peak of the crescent at Huntsville, Alabama. In the two decades from 1950 to 1970 Huntsville has grown from 16,500 people to about 160,000, thanks almost entirely to the location there of the Marshall Space Flight Center and the Redstone Arsenal, with associated aerospace industries. Then with federal contract changes it shrank to 138,000. Even the Chamber of Commerce acknowledges that the city's population is transient.

The other notable configuration is the immense concentration of aerospace industries in restless California. Greater Los Angeles is peppered with aerospace plants, most of them associated with its four giants: McDonnell-Douglas, Hughes Aircraft, the ailing Lockheed Aircraft, and North American Rockwell. At one point North American Rockwell had over 100,000 employees. Its headquarters is in El Segundo, which calls itself "The Aerospace Center of the World." The town, engulfed by Greater Los Angeles, has a population of 16,000. Most of the employees of North American Rockwell and the other aerospace companies near Los Angeles live somewhere else. Their residences are, on average, twenty miles away from the place of work. Even before the big cutbacks in aerospace began, 27 percent of North American Rockwell's employees were leaving each year to work elsewhere.

But perhaps Sunnyvale, California, is the best prototype of an aerospace town.

Sunnyvale is in central California, northwest of San Jose. Before World War II it was a sleepy prune-raising village. During the war it began making airplane landing gear and has been mostly in the munitions business ever since. Today it has a population which, while fluctuating abruptly, averages around 100,000. And it can justly boast that it is the missile-rocket-producing capital of the Western world. It makes Polaris and Poseidon missiles and Agena rockets; and it has a variety of electronics and other defense contractors. Altogether the city's economy is almost totally dependent on U.S. defense spending.

Its residents move at a frenetic rate. Pacific Telephone and Telegraph Company records indicate that about 37 percent of the residents move every year. Sunnyvale's city manager explains that "change has become almost a tradition." And an editor of the Sunnyvale *Standard* adds: "We're used to seeing people come and go."

As a city, Sunnyvale is confusing. Its old main street is long gone. There is a sort of civic complex but also there are twenty-odd shopping areas. The city government, which in recent years has had an executive of one of its major electronics industries as mayor, is computer crazy. All public records on individuals—including lawsuits, arrests, and welfare acceptance—are being put into computers for instant retrieval by interested officials. The library is substantially computerized. Future plans call for an almost entirely computer-run city.

Meanwhile the residents are listless about civic matters. Less than a fourth of the voters bothered to come out for a City Council election; and an even smaller proportion came out for a school board election.

Residents complain about the sameness, blandness, tidiness, and brand-newness of the city. It seems remote from real life. There are few old people, few ethnic minorities, few Jews, no ghettos, few local charities, few really rich or poor. Some residents complain about what they view as an abnormal amount of mate-swapping. The town's trees look like trees on drawing boards. There are virtually no buses and few sidewalks; it is assumed that if you want to go anywhere you will drive.

The impact on the lives of families involved in continual relocation in aerospace towns will be discussed in more detail in Part Three.

GOVERNMENTAL PEOPLE-MOVING ACTIVITIES, GENERAL

As a sort of postscript I should note a few of the ways that government in America, both federal and state, promotes mobility, and often rootlessness:

—The construction of superhighways through urban areas has, as indicated, uprooted tens of thousands of families and created dislocation and division of established neighborhoods. The same is true of the urban renewal projects in hundreds of cities. The renewal program was idealistic in concept but has often been used in ways not anticipated by its creators. Under the U.S. law establishing the program, the federal government puts up most of the money and enables local governments to use their power of eminent domain not only to evict for a public *use* but also for a public *purpose*. Ostensibly this purpose was to eliminate slums and urban blight. As a practical matter it is often used—as in Chicago—in such a way that poor are shoved out and replaced by apartments for the well-to-do near downtown department stores, or so that blacks are ejected from white neighborhoods.[1] The urban renewal program in Chicago has torn down about three times as many dwelling units as it has constructed. In New York City, because of urban renewal, several thousand families must relocate each year. The impact of renewal on inhabitants of a Boston area will be reported in Chapter 17.

—The Manpower Administration of the U.S. Department of Labor has in the past few years gotten itself broadly involved in moving people from one part of the country to another. An official observed to me: "Five years ago no one would have dreamed of the government helping people move." Now it has spent several million dollars helping several thousand people move from depressed areas or areas of widespread job layoffs to areas of relative labor shortage. Some people from Long Island, New York, were moved to California. And the government moved several hundred south Texas people to Dallas and helped them get jobs in aerospace plants there. On the average it has spent $325 per relocation.

In many instances it helps the relocated person get training for the new job and it provides counseling to combat such social problems as homesickness. In its actions the Department not only is trying to promote employment but has in mind such broader goals as combating inflation by easing labor shortages in labor-tight areas. Economically this seems like a laudatory program, given the instabilities of employment opportunity that the federal government and major industries have permitted, such as I've been describing. A better long-range approach would be to work to minimize dislocations.

—Finally, the growth of big government itself has promoted a high mobility rate in the Washington, D.C., area. The facts of the reverberating turnovers created by congressional elections every two years and presidential elections every four years . . . the ebb and flow of Foreign Service, Central Intelligence Agency, and Pentagon personnel . . . the swarming of lobbyists and national association personnel all contribute to a turbulent living environment. Telephone records indicate that a third of all Washington residents change their addresses each year. The change in total telephone listings, including businesses, associations, etc., is even more imposing. There is about a 50 percent turnover in listings annually.

Each year a couple of hundred thousand people move into the Washington area looking for places to lodge. In the District itself they find that the major great divide is the meandering Rock Creek Park: west of the park is elite Washington with staggering rental costs, east of it are some excellent buys in terms of rooms per dollar and with many predominantly black neighborhoods. Most newcomers head for the suburbs in Maryland or Virginia. A few communities such as Alexandria have their own governments, but the major pattern is a mélange of development tracts run only by a county government, and there is little semblance of authentic communities. A doctor in one development, Waynewood, said he knew only one neighbor.

7.

Collegiate Breeding Grounds for Transients

It is no accident that the most mobile elements of the U.S. population—the professional, technical, and managerial types—have had at least some college education. Colleges are perhaps the greatest of all contemporary breeding grounds of super-mobiles. Going away to college offers millions of young people their first training in being uprooted—and in adjusting to it.

High school graduates who leave their home communities to go away to college tend in overwhelming numbers to settle, after college, somewhere other than their home towns. At the college they often develop acquaintances from several regions of the country. And they develop specialized skills which aim them toward job opportunities that either are not present in their home towns or seem more abundant—or rewarding—elsewhere.

One unsettling result is that hundreds of U.S. towns and

villages are stripped of about half of all their young people in the eighteen- to twenty-two-year age bracket. These tend to be the more talented half of the young people. And many never do come back, except to visit.

If the students are headed for business or professional jobs which require advanced degrees they usually must experience uprootings at a number of campuses before getting their union cards. And requirements for admission have been getting higher. A University of Rhode Island professor who was a native of the state told me that the biggest single obstacle he faced in getting his appointment there (after doing all his graduate work in other states) was that he might be viewed as a "local boy." He suspected the University had national pretensions and was therefore ranging broadly in its recruiting.

In 1940 about 13 percent of college-age young people actually went to college; by 1970 it was about 43 percent. In just five years between 1965 and 1970 there was a 60 percent increase in college enrollment. This has produced an explosive growth in the size of colleges, in the size of college staffs, and in the number of collegiate institutions dotting the landscape. There are at least 126 in small Massachusetts.

In many U.S. towns and small cities the local college or university has increasingly become the mainstay of the town's economy. For example the University of New Hampshire is in Durham, whose population is about 7,500. During the decade of the sixties student enrollment soared from 3,843 students to 7,729 students—2,000 of whom were from out of state.

An even more dramatic example of the change can be seen in Carbondale, in the coal-mining region of southern Illinois. The local teachers' college serving the area has swollen, as indicated, into the mammoth Southern Illinois University. Most of its approximately 26,000 students now are from outside the region. All of this has occurred in a town with a population of 22,000. A particularly intense town-gown hostility has developed.

Such antagonisms in many college towns have been aggravated in recent years by fears of what may happen locally if (or as) college students gain the right to vote on local issues. In many cases they have enough potential votes to run the towns.

In recent years, then, we have seen:

1. An enormous increase in the number of talented young people getting experience in mobility as students.

2. An increase in the recruiting and raiding of faculty members because of the growth in size of schools and the increase in newer schools urgently needing staff members. One result of this latter trend was a greatly increased proneness of academicians to become job-jumpers (at least until graduate schools began glutting some academic fields with qualified candidates for jobs).

The role of colleges in serving as a kind of conduit for changing talented local folk from low-mobility people to high-mobility people can be seen best at Morehead State University, Kentucky.

The town of Morehead (pop. 7,000) is nestled in the lumpy foothills of the Appalachian range in eastern Kentucky about fifty miles east of Lexington. Traditionally it has served as a trading center for the hill people who have their farming patches back up in the hollows of the region. In fifteen years the local college has grown from 800 students to 6,500—and has developed some spectacular, ingenious architecture to adjust to the knobby terrain.

It still seeks primarily to enroll the hill people of the region, most of whom, upon graduation, seek employment elsewhere. Sixty percent, in fact, say they plan to seek jobs outside the state, mainly in teaching. There are 200 teachers in Dade County, Florida, who came out of the hills of Kentucky via Morehead State University.

A number of Kentucky planners are seeking ways to keep its skilled young people within the state. In this they share the problem with many smaller cities and towns in the U.S. which complain that colleges are causing a "brain drain" from their area.

One reason West Virginia's Marshall University, in the hilly river city of Huntington, has had trouble getting financial support from state legislators is that so many of its graduates leave the state for other pastures. One such pasture, Ohio, begins several hundred yards from the campus, across the turgid Ohio River.

The surging of more than two million young people across state lines each year in order to "go away" to college is seen in data on out-of-state students. For example:

At the University of Colorado about 5,300 students, or 41 percent of all students in 1969, were from out of state. Thousands come from the East or West coasts. Cars loaded with students highball across the continent around the clock as passengers take turns driving and sleeping. The University of Colorado's ratio is exceptionally high, partly because of its spectacular locale nestled at the base of the Rockies near ski and trail-riding country. It has a reputation as a fun school. The University of Arizona, with its lush palm-lined campus surrounded by glorious jutting mountains and its nearness to ranches and the Great Outdoors, also has a fun-school image and attracts about 7,000 out-of-staters.

Similarly 5,000 collegians travel at least twenty-five hundred miles from their home each year to attend the University of Hawaii, a couple miles from the gentle rollers of Waikiki Beach.

Deep South state universities have traditionally had such low academic standards and been so state-oriented in their appeal that few outsiders have sought admission. All this is changing, especially at the University of Georgia, whose academic reputation is soaring. The school now attracts 3,300 out-of-state students a year, or around 17 percent of its enrollment.

Long-distance migrations of students to the better private colleges run at a higher rate than to most state-supported schools. At Oberlin College in Oberlin, Ohio, about 60 percent of the students in a recent school year came from outside the entire Midwest.

Then, too, there are the students who sample a variety of colleges, often in different areas. According to one estimate, 60 percent of the students at New York University are transfers from somewhere else.

*   *   *

Some U.S. states have far more college students for their population than others. This in part reflects differences in educational attainment within the states. But it also reflects differences both in the migratory patterns of students and in state support for higher education. Some states have become notorious exporters of young people seeking college educations; and others are conspicuous importers of students.

You see this in the contrast between New Jersey and Massachusetts, two nearby states that have comparable economic levels and public school systems up through high school. Massachusetts has one collegian per 22 population whereas New Jersey has one collegian per 47 population. Massachusetts has many fine colleges—mostly private— and attracts students from all over the world; New Jersey on the other hand has relatively few colleges and still fewer that would attract outsiders. I have repeatedly had the experience of asking college officials in Midwestern states where most of their out-of-state students come from and been told, "New Jersey."

Estimates prepared by the U.S. Office of Education on "Residence and Migration of College Students, Fall 1968," show that New Jersey imported only 18,000 students while it exported 117,000! The five states with the biggest *net* migration of students *out of* their state are:

1. New Jersey (− 98,710)
2. New York (− 55,716)
3. Illinois (− 32,454)
4. Connecticut (− 21,125)
5. Maryland (− 15,327)

And the states with the biggest net migration *into* their state are:

1. Massachusetts (+ 37,316)
2. Indiana (+ 26,495)
3. North Carolina (+ 23,556)
4. Tennessee (+ 20,037)
5. Michigan (+ 17,316)

Some state legislatures, especially in the Midwest, have started trying to discourage out-of-state students from coming to their state-supported colleges by calling for stiff tuition boosts for out-of-staters and for quotas of 18 or 20 percent on total enrollment for outsiders. Partly they have been trying to cut costs; but partly they have turned protectionist because they suspect the "outsiders" of instigating campus unrest.

The pursuit of excellence in scholarship is inherently a lonely business and traditionally college life compensated by providing intimacy-producing relaxation, clubs, and other activities. As universities and colleges have grown at an explosive rate, creating an uprooted environment in the process . . . as they have become more depersonalized with televised lectures, machine grading, and compulsory ID cards . . . as they have drawn more and more students from distant places . . . and as clubs have become less a part of the college scene, much of the old intimacy of college life has disappeared.

Contemporary Psychology carried an analysis in 1969 stating, "Evidence mounts that students are becoming more socially alienated, lonely and less able to establish close emotional ties with others. . . . It is sobering that 36 percent of the senior men at Berkeley said they did not have a close friend of the same sex."[2] At the University of Wisconsin a "rap center" has been established primarily for students who are lonely and yearn for a chance to talk.

In the campus upheavals of the past few years in which students occupied key campus buildings several student comments indicated that much of the gratification the students felt was not political but a sense of euphoria in suddenly achieving a feeling of community and comradery with other rioting or picketing students.

Lonely as student life can be, for many students the college experience still may be the last real community they will ever know.

And now a word about their cloistered and supposedly stationary professors.

As we noted, an aspiring professor today who has worked his way up through various schools to gain his credentials is already thoroughly oriented to mobility. O. Suthern Sims, Jr., a dean at the University of Georgia, has even called the new college faculty members "the nomads of the twentieth century." A sociologist at another Georgia college advised me that he and his family had moved five times in ten years.

The young faculty member is now usually expected to seek his first job at some campus other than the one at which he got his final degree. Some departments at the University of Wisconsin try to enforce five-year moratoriums on hiring their own graduates. Furthermore a faculty member possesses teaching and/or research skills that are usually readily transferable from one school to another.

David G. Brown, who has made the most extensive study of mobile professors, states that the idea of working one's way up in a single institution has become "foreign to faculties . . . each year every professor voluntarily considers new job possibilities." He added that "college professors now expect to switch schools several times, at least, during their careers."[3]

At Oberlin, located in Ohio, only a third of the faculty members did their undergraduate study *anywhere* in the Midwest. And only 15 percent did their undergraduate work in the state.

The wife of a college educator living temporarily in Connecticut said that she and her husband had moved fifteen times in the thirty-one years of their marriage, and ten of those years had been spent in one house.

A professor may start thinking about moving simply because he doesn't get along with his boss. But the main reasons instructors and professors *regularly* think about moving relate to the differing prestige of schools . . . to aspirations for higher rank . . . or to desire for more pay. One's own reputation, Brown found, is largely determined by the prestige of the school he works for. Academia is not a democratic world. It has its Siberias and its tight elite centers. Rarely does an academician move more than part way from one type to the other. Most emerging graduate students have to start off by taking a drop in prestige because the higher prestige schools have most of the graduate programs and couldn't possibly absorb all those they graduate. The schools that are in the top 10 percent in prestige, Brown found, rarely recruit members of their teaching staffs from any school outside their charmed circle.

The game of mobility in faculty ranks is most often a matter of trading off prestige for more pay or higher rank. If you want to move upward in prestige too you do it mainly by getting a reputation as a big publisher. This means getting ten or more journal articles or at least one book published. Faculty members at top schools, however, have a built-in advantage in getting published because their schools are more likely to have their own journals or monograph series.

Younger faculty members are more apt than older ones to be high-mobiles. A department head at the University of Northern Iowa told me that if he hires ten young instructors the best he can hope is that three will still be there after five years. Faculty members in the social sciences and humanities, who don't have to fight to get expensive laboratory equipment, are more apt to be high-mobiles than staff members in the physical sciences and engineering. Faculty members at schools with mediocre prestige move more often than faculty members of high-prestige schools.

Once a faculty member has been given tenure, by satisfactorily performing for a period up to seven years, he is assured a permanent post, short of scandal or outrageous performance. Thereupon he may become less mobile as to his home base, though in some cases he can transfer tenure to a new post. And he often roams as a visiting professor or takes a leave on a foundation or government grant. A substantial number of academic jet setters maintain a whirl of activities, consulting for a half dozen clients, giving visiting lectures, hitting the major institutional conferences, and occasionally getting back to home base to meet a few classes—and even, sometimes, grade a few papers.

To facilitate this movement of faculty personnel seeking to change jobs, informal "slave markets" have developed. A major activity at most academic conferences and conventions is the quiet sounding out that goes on between department heads and restless faculty members from other colleges. Some prospective employers post the job openings they have and sit in their rooms waiting for nibbling calls. Restless academicians also now have available as a way to make their restlessness known the hundreds of specialized employment agencies and agencies financed by professional associations.

In periods when there is a scarcity of qualified academicians to fill all the openings even the top schools find it hard to keep their stars, because lesser universities, desperate for prestige, will offer lush package deals. For example, they may specify that practically no teaching is expected. They may offer an eye-popping salary and "chair" that include a staff of research assistants in order to get a big-name superstar listed in their catalogues.

Just as with corporations, some colleges in the same city work out anti-raiding pacts to prevent jolting losses. And most colleges consider it dirty pool to find themselves raided by anyone after May 1, when they have to start putting together catalogues for the coming year. But such pacts affect only a small proportion of colleges.

All the movement about the landscape of students and faculty, while frequently salutary for the younger individuals involved, is denuding many communities of leadership talent. It is setting a pattern of generalized restlessness for the country. And it is creating millions of talented people who will be high-mobiles for most of their lives.

"GUY LOMBARDO WANTS YOU AS A NEIGH-
BOR."—*Billboard advertising Apollo
Beach, a development in the heart of
Florida's senior citizen area, south of
Tampa.*

8.

The Snowbirds
of
Centrifugal
Families

In the past decade a major new breed of migrant in the
United States, almost as predictable in his movement as
the migratory worker, has emerged. That is the retiree. At
least a million retirees and semi-retirees move south across
the continent in the fall and north in the spring. In Florida
they are known as "Snowbirds."

Partly they migrate to seek a more salubrious climate.
Partly they migrate in ever greater numbers because pen-
sions, Social Security, and savings make it possible. But
largely they migrate because of the crumbling of important
ties back "home" in the North caused by the engulfing and
destruction of once valid communities by urban sprawl,
the shifting ethnic groups, and the moving away of people
important to them. These changes have sent older people
groping for a new kind of life.

Many people find it disturbing—and a bit repugnant—
that older people should want to isolate themselves, seemingly, away from kinfolk, grandchildren, and the main-
stream of life, in places that are assumed to smell of
death. Yet the appeal of retirement communities is definite

87

and goes far beyond the search for a more salubrious climate. In a sense the people who migrate to retirement areas become rootless in order to escape a worse sense of rootlessness. For many the movement to retirement communities reflects profound yearnings.

They yearn to escape the prospect of facing old age in an uprooted, lonely, or unsafe environment where the familiar neighborhood has disappeared and is often devoid even of their offspring or other kinfolk. One study of 521 men who had retired to Arizona from the Midwest found that only one fourth of those with children had any children still living in their "home" communities.[1] For many, their grown children and kinfolk have largely centrifugated about the continent. And the sense of family splintering is aggravated by the fact that more than half of all marriages now end in divorce, annulment, separation, or desertion.

They yearn to escape from a feeling of being useless and unimportant, even though many retirees will remain vigorous and have a high potential for competency for many years. A former speech professor who after retirement moved with his wife into Lawrence Welk's Country Club Mobile Estates in Escondido, California, summed up a prevailing mood when he said: "Here you are not made to feel you are in the way, or that you are being laid on the shelf. You are a member in good standing in an active society."

They yearn for a life style not dominated by a youth-oriented culture, nor by the bewildering manifestations of disorder created by too rapid growth and social change. Many feel uncomfortable remaining in a culture that seems to offer little respect for the accumulated wisdom elders have to impart.

And most important, perhaps, they yearn for simple old-fashioned friendship, and seek it in a setting at least reminiscent of small-town intimacy. An official of the Sun City retirement communities who has made motivational studies of some of the 20 million Americans over age sixty-five compared many retirees with Dona Ana in Bernard Shaw's *Man and Superman*. Shaw wrote of her: "She wanders and wanders in her slow hopeless way . . . until she blunders against the thing she seeks: companionship."

Millions of older people feel too insecure financially to think of seeking another home base; and many are fortunate in still living in genuine communities, near kinfolk with whom they still have close ties.

But in greatly increasing numbers retirees are seeking alternatives. And meanwhile business entrepreneurs—including such favorites of senior citizens as Lawrence Welk and Guy Lombardo—are tapping this new restlessness by creating or helping create in many areas "villages" attractive to older citizens.

Most of these retirement villages or developments are found in the Southland: southern California, Arizona, south Texas and, in great numbers, Florida. Del Webb has started a chain of Sun Cities, in Arizona, Florida, and California. And a retirement development of many houses, aimed mainly at Americans, is beginning to take shape near a lake in the Mexican state of Guanajuato, seven hundred miles south of the border. But the concept is spreading to Oregon, the Midwest, to Northeastern states such as New Jersey and Connecticut, and to other areas where the north-south Snowbird pattern is not involved.

Yet many if not most who move a considerable distance want to migrate back "home" from the new "community" at least in the summer. Moving permanently to some out-of-the-way place is too hard on their sense of identity. A study funded by the U.S. Administration on Aging found that those who retired to Florida from the Midwest and established "regular" homes there were twice as likely to be disturbed by feelings of anomie as were retirees who stayed in their home communities in Wisconsin or who were "seasonal" visitors to Florida.[2]

Some of the retirement villages have grown naturally house by house. But most are run by entrepreneurs who sell the retiree a small tract house, or rent or sell space for a mobile home, or sell or rent space in an apartment complex. What such organized "villages" have in common is that the tracts are almost all age-segregated. Often you need to be over fifty to get in. Children and pets are usually taboo. Most tract operators promise security from such evils of the outside world as crime and rampaging teenagers. Many have walls or high fences. And many feature large tricycles, which offer a sensible form of local transportation for older people. Almost all stress a community center with an array of recreational and other activities that often are posted. This center-orientedness takes exaggerated form at Sun City, Arizona, where, from the air, the residences seem to be arranged in concentric circles around two bull's-eyes that are connected by a highway. Leisure World, south of Los Angeles, boasts more than a hundred clubs. The appeal of a return to villages, it should be stressed, is not confined to older people. Developers of apartment complexes in Madison, Wisconsin, where many young couples from the university live, have been advertising the "village" or "community" concept.

The interests of the people going to the retirement "villages" (some have 13,000 population) are perhaps well reflected in the advertisements published in a single issue of the *News-Sun* of Sun City, Arizona. There were ads for foot comfort shops, for organs, for "complete respiratory service," for a restaurant featuring "old-fashioned Sunday family dinner," for beauty palaces "for our beautiful senior citizens," for hearing aids, for cremation, for complete denture service, and for rocking chairs.

The nation's heaviest concentration of new retirement villages is on the western, or balmier, side of Florida. This "Sun Coast" has spread from the city of St. Petersburg, which has for several decades been a mecca for retirees. Today St. Pete still has about 60,000 retired people. It has repainted its famous drab green benches with gay colors. The newer retirement villages range north, past Clearwater and New Port Richey, which has grown 700 percent in five years, east to Zephyrhills and Winter Haven, and south past Bradenton and Sarasota. In the fall, the Zephyrhills *News* devotes a "welcome" page in each issue to new arrivals. They are listed by states with their home towns and local addresses included. In the issue I examined people from twenty states and Canada were listed but nearly a third of all the new arrivals were from Michigan. Such clustering of retirees by state of origin can be found throughout the Florida Sun Coast. Zephyrhills once was a typical Southern town but in 1972 it had 73 mobile home parks, almost all for retirees; and others were being built.

Not all older people who migrate to Florida's Sun Coast become Snowbirds. Some stay and sweat out the hot summer months, with the help of air conditioning and television. But tens of thousands do go north, usually to the area they consider "home," or to be near old acquaintances or their scattered kinfolk, or, if affluent, to summer vacation areas. They go by car, trailer, bus, train, and plane.

Most Snowbirds have left Southland by early May at the latest and most start returning after Labor Day. Many do not leave for either the North or South until after the third of a month because they don't want to risk having the Social Security check get lost in the mail.

Robert Cromwell, an official of the General Telephone Company, which blankets the Sun Coast area, advised me that most Snowbirds gear their flight to Easter. They plan to leave soon after Easter unless the TV weather reports indicate that spring is early up north. In that case they may leave a couple of weeks earlier. Sun Coast telephone subscribers—whether they live in a house, trailer, or apartment—have the privilege of paying a special reduced "vacation rate." The phone is not in use but is not disconnected. About 30,000 subscribers in the Sun Coast area go on the reduced rate. Many others have their phones disconnected, as do a great many residents who are not retirees. Altogether about 190,000 people in the six-county Sun Coast area have their residential phones disconnected. The two figures combined suggest that about 40 percent of all the people on the Sun Coast move temporarily or permanently each year.

Of all the towns in the Sun Coast area, Mr. Cromwell found that Bradenton's records showed the highest mobility. In 1969, 16 percent of the residents went on vacation rates and about 34 percent of the residential phones were disconnected—for a total annual moving rate of about 50 percent!

Bradenton is the main town in Manatee County. The town has many mobile home courts; and the part of the county surrounding Bradenton is literally packed with retirement villages, most of them made up of mobile homes. Altogether there are more than 110 mobile home parks in the county. A postal employee estimated that 50,000 people in the county go north every year.

One gets the impression that most of Manatee County is about five feet above sea level. At any rate, it is flat and semitropical. Beaches on the gulf are several miles west of downtown Bradenton. You reach the county immediately after coming off the long Sunshine Skyway from St. Petersburg, or on Route 41 if you come down the east side of Tampa Bay. The major highways leading south toward Sarasota are neon strips of gaudy billboard commercialism. For mile after mile one passes mobile home dealers with their wares on display, interspersed with motels, emergency oxygen supply shops, and shopping centers. The town of Bradenton—which calls itself "The Friendly City"—is a quite different environment shaped in an earlier America. There is an old-fashioned county courthouse, a riverside park, an art league, a planetarium, a municipal auditorium that alternately features "youth dances" and adult dances. There is now a handsome new library that has an adult entrance and a children's entrance.

Winter residents are made continually aware of how lucky they are to be away from winter's blasts up north. The radio and television stations of St. Petersburg and Tampa repeatedly list the Northern towns and cities where it is snowing. One owner of a 1957 trailer (quite unusual) in Bradenton muttered to me: "The older you get, the more you notice that damned cold." Since he hadn't been north in winter for several years the awfulness of cold must partly have been induced by Florida's news media.

With mandatory retirements being imposed in the United States at ever younger ages—while vigorous life spans are increasing—a distinction should be made be-

tween so-called senior citizens. There are the young retirees from fifty-five to seventy-five who enjoy sports,
partying, foreign travel, sociability. And there are the true
aged, starting at about seventy-six, who are more sed-
entary, lonelier, more prone to anxieties about health,
often for good reasons.

Manatee County is primarily young retiree country. Its
average age is four years younger than that of Pinellas
County, which St. Petersburg dominates. Still, the Grim
Reaper is always in the background, especially for males
with their shorter life expectancy. In Manatee County
deaths each year substantially outnumber births. Retirement village people living alone in trailers or small houses
usually have an understanding with neighbors that if the
lone person's window blind, for example, is not raised in
the morning the neighbors should investigate. At one
trailer village a man explained: "If we don't see a neighbor
by noon we knock on his door. It's become part of our
way of life."

Notices of deaths are usually posted on the community
bulletin board of a retirement center; and often there are
formal arrangements for dividing up the telephoning of
friends and acquaintances to make sure they know about
the funeral or visitation. O. M. Griffith, a leading Bradenton funeral director, estimates that about 40 percent of
deceased retirees are shipped to their home states for
burial, usually by air freight; 40 percent are buried in
local cemeteries; and 20 percent are cremated. Some
spouses arrange two funeral services: one in Manatee
County and one back "home" up north.

A Sun Coast informant, in commenting on the fact that
residents of relatively affluent Sun City just north of
Manatee County tended to an unusual extent to stay there
year round, added: "If they go out, they go in a coffin."
Along the winding driveways of Sun City, signs caution:
"Drive slowly. Grandparents playing." They are, practicing
pitch shots in golf or hurrying to bridge games.

Most of the retirement villages of Manatee County
forbid children, except for visiting a certain number of
days or living in restricted areas. Furthermore repeated

comments by retirees supported the restrictions. Retirees fondly showed me pictures of their own grandchildren up north. But children in the abstract seem to give today's oldsters in retirement communities the creeps. They fuss about the noise children can make and the way they can mess up one's flower bed. One retiree in a mobile home park said: "The older folks just don't want a bunch of kids getting into everything." A major Manatee County park developer, Robert E. Quinn, said: "The retiree parks just don't want children. And especially they don't want teen-agers if they can help it." Thus it would seem that the generation gulf is not created simply by the new scornful attitudes of youth toward elders, as often assumed.

A couple of technical reasons may contribute to the banishment of children from most mobile parks for retirees:

1. The mobile homes often are packed closely together and often aren't built to withstand noise as well as conventional houses.

2. Trailer park owners and dwellers throughout the United States are acutely sensitive to the local tax laws. The trailers are called "homes" (or "estates") but they usually escape taxes that ordinary homeowners have to pay since they technically are vehicles and require only the purchase of an auto tag. A third of all the "households" in Manatee County are mobile. Only the ground on which the mobile home is parked is usually taxed. If a substantial proportion of trailer owners in a park have school-age children, the parks are vulnerable to the outraged cries of taxpayers that they should pay their fair share of educational costs.

In Manatee County families with children live overwhelmingly in conventional homes—and an overwhelming proportion of the mobile home parks (97 percent) are occupied by retirees, almost all without children.

One retired woman vigorously dissented from this pattern. She lives in Bay Shore Gardens, a development which has over a thousand conventional homes, about half occupied by families with children, half by retirees. She said: "We like to be associated with young people. We like to hear children's voices. In retirement villages you only see blathering old idiots." But that, as indicated, is a minority viewpoint in Manatee County.

Life at the various mobile retirement villages in Manatee County is geared to promoting busyness, sociability, and fun for the over-sixties. Although the retiree population is overwhelmingly Protestant it is rapidly developing a pleasure-seeking, live-for-the-moment mode of life. One of the larger parks features "square dancing Tuesday night, round dancing Thursday night." Each of the better parks has a community center with a recreation hall that has a kitchen attached, where the wives associated with the various clubs vie in serving up their most mouth-watering dishes for pot-luck suppers. There are afternoons devoted to art crafts, pinochle, rummy, or bridge on the inside, or shuffleboard and sometimes swimming or fishing on the outside. (At Sun City in Arizona the newspaper each week prints a list of planned events for each day. The average is about twenty-five events, ranging from "Psychology Class" and "Lapidary Class" to "Scrabble" and "Beginners Round Dancing.")

One of the biggest and most posh mobile home villages for retirees in the nation is Trailer Estates, in Manatee County. It has winding paved roads and many canal inlets for its 1,400 trailer owners. Here you have to buy your parcel of land for your trailer, not rent it. Most of the trailer homes are at least partly double width (twenty-four feet). One resident even has an indoor swimming pool in his trailer home. There is not only a large community center but also a newspaper, volunteer fire department, and post office.

On the community bulletin board was an announcement from the Ohio Social Club stating: "Everyone from Ohio now living in Trailer Estates is invited to the Ohio Social Potluck January 3."

One retiree at Trailer Estates, Clifford Dentley from the Pontiac area of Michigan, told me that on Michigan Day 338 people showed up for the festivities. And when they held a Pontiac Day at the Trailer Estates Hall and invited anyone in all of Florida from Pontiac to come, more than 800 people arrived. Mr. Dentley used to work at Pontiac Engineering and said that several other fellows from the same plant also were at Trailer Estates. "I see more people here I know than I do all summer when I am back home." (He now runs a Christmas tree farm near Pontiac as an income-producing sideline.) He added: "I'm a volunteer on the fire department here in Trailer Estates." A lot of the calls are not for fires but for oxygen for residents with breathing difficulties.

A retired man who used to work for a golf club in northern New Jersey was tickled that he and his wife had a patio on a canal. It also tickled them both, status-wise, that some of their neighbors reportedly were former judges and business executives. When the two first looked in at Trailer Estates they liked the plot they now live on very much but didn't like the trailer on it. It was a year old. So they bought the plot for $5,500 and traded in the "old" trailer for a new 20 foot by 55 foot one with two bedrooms, one and a half baths, a pecan-type paneling in the living room, and three closets in their master bedroom. With trade-in, the mobile home cost $11,500 and they put about $3,000 more into masonry for the patio. Total cost to date was somewhat above $20,000. This was their first mobile home. They have nine grandchildren up north but had not yet had any down for a visit. The husband said: "Everyone is very, very friendly. And if you want to go to bed you don't wake up hearing babies crying or dogs barking." Other residents of Trailer Estates professed to be enthusiastic about their new way of life. All planned to go up north at least for a few months when summer came. On the basis of these discussions I began to suspect that some of their enthusiasm might be due in part to Trailer Estates' local reputation for eliteness, so I visited several smaller, untidier old-fashioned trailer camps near downtown Bradenton. These had smaller trailers of various ages—often with their wheels on or with cinder-block props exposed to the eye. The retirees there were more likely to have working-class backgrounds and paid less for renting their space (about thirty dollars a month) than is charged at the big new mobile home parks. I expected to hear grousing and disgruntlement but I heard none.

At Sunset Trailer Village I talked with a couple from a suburb near Detroit, who had been coming to Bradenton for eleven winters. They spend six months in Michigan, where their children still live, and six months in Bradenton. The husband said:

"I like Bradenton, it's like a little country town. The downtown looks like a little country town. Sunset Village is always full. There are an awful lot of Michigan people here. Sunset Village is dominated by Michigan." Sunset Village, it turned out, has a small community hall where the people have dances, play the piano, or play cribbage.

A neighbor who was sprinkling the flower bed around his trailer was from Akron. He said:

"Here you get acquainted. You are not alone. There are a lot of widows. They plant their men back up there in the North and then come back down here and we watch out for them."

At the Friendly City Mobile Court nearby, a man from Middleton, Massachusetts, whose own small trailer was on wheels, fussed about the untidiness of some of his neighbors, but quickly added: "I like it here. It's very friendly. The people are nice. It's not too big like some of those fancy new parks." A bachelor, he explained that he got a good deal of acclaim from the fact he is a former chef: "I cook them scalloped oysters and they go crazy." Friendly City Mobile Court also has a community center of sorts. He said one reason so many people kept returning to this park (which looked pretty untidy to me) was that "we are very fond of the owner. We gave him a $75 present for Christmas." The rent is a dollar a day. There was no phone but he explained: "You don't need one because there is a loudspeaker."

So I was forced by such comments, and by what I saw, to question some of my preconceptions about retirement villages and to modify somewhat my image of trailer homes. The retirement village may represent an unfortunate trend but it is at least a makeshift interim answer to our contemporary social fragmentation. I learned in

Florida that having a big solid house to retire into is not as important as being among people who respect you, who care about you, who share your concerns, and who have a chance to know you well enough to become an authentic friend. Later (in Chapter 16) readers will hear from an investigator at Harvard's Department of Psychiatry who contends that these are precisely the kinds of interpersonal relationships that *all* people need in today's world if they are to capture a sense of personal well-being.

"I'm a shell creature clinging stubbornly to a rock. The rock is being broken apart by the waves of change but it is the only home I ever had and I will not leave it."—A SEVENTY-ONE-YEAR-OLD WOMAN IN THE AUSTIN AREA OF CHICAGO, WHERE AN ETHNIC UPHEAVAL HAS BEEN TAKING PLACE.

9.

Ethnic Churning in People-Imploding Cities

The bloated cities of North America are proving to be quite a challenge to human adaptability. People have been imploding into the cities at an extraordinary rate. In this century more than 90 percent of all the nation's growth has been in urban areas.[1]

This bursting inward of people to metropolitan areas has greatly increased the proportion of the populace living in high-rise apartments, multi-unit complexes, or subdivision tracts. All tend to make people more isolated as individuals. A mass society is created in which people are less likely to achieve any sense of community. City planners are finding that people living in apartments feel more isolated than people who live in any other kind of dwelling.[2]

It is not just the increased anonymity which typically goes with big-city life, however, that is producing such a challenge to human adaptability. There is the further aggravation produced by the turbulence of people-movement within the cities which is wiping out thousands of familiar neighborhoods.

Prime causes of this turbulence in today's cities are the churning of ethnic groups as they collide with one another and the fragmenting of these groups as the bonds of many of them weaken over time. All this churning, displacement, and fragmentation disrupts the development and maintenance of stable communities within the cities. It has become a chronic source of instability and of temporariness in living patterns.

The ethnic groups have contributed greatly to the very rapid growth of many North American cities. At the start they often played the constructive role of providing a sense of community for severely uprooted people. It is their subsequent pressing upon each other and fragmenting that creates the turbulence which concerns us here.

The word "ethnic" means different things to different people. Some think of "ethnics" simply as being Americans of central, east, or south European origin. *A Dictionary of the Social Sciences* defines an ethnic group as one having a special status because of a complex of traits. In addition to national or geographic origin and religious and linguistic characteristics it included "the distinctive skin-pigmentation of its members." In short, Americans whose ancestors came on slave ships from West Africa are just as clearly an ethnic group as Americans whose ancestors came from Poland or from Mexico.

In this book I will use the broad dictionary meaning.

An ordinary American who moves from a rural area to a large city can live where he chooses but often finds the city cold, depersonalized, anonymous as compared with "back home." Immigrants, on the other hand, have always been likely to head directly for the neighborhood or ghetto where many people of their national origin live. Here they could ease uprootedness by quickly entering into intimate social relationships (despite a possible poor knowledge of the English language), and find organizations ready to receive and help them.[3] Approximately 90 percent of all immigrants from Europe have settled in major cities.[4]

*   *   *

A leading analyst of ethnic groups in North America, Stanley Lieberson of the University of Washington, advised me that the "most magnificent ethnic ghettos" in all of North America are not in the United States but in Canada's Toronto and Montreal. National policies toward immigration probably account for this. Immigration from Europe to the United States peaked soon after the turn of the twentieth century and virtually dried up after World War I because of restrictive legislation. In contrast Canada actively welcomed refugees and other immigrants after World War II. Thus its ethnic settlements are far newer and, perhaps consequently, still in a more stable stage than those of the United States. About 40 percent of Canada's postwar immigrants settled in Toronto.

Despite many visits to Toronto, I thought I had an image of the city as a rather formal British outpost. After consulting Lieberson, and then several Canadian sociologists, I took a closer look at this extraordinarily fast-growing city—growing fast partly because of immigrants. Toronto still has thousands of Smiths, Taylors, and Thompsons; but it also has more Ukrainian organizations (34) than polyglot Manhattan. The Ukrainians have settled mainly near Queen Street West, Dundas Street West, Bathurst Street, and Christie Street—all directly west of downtown Toronto. The city also has 10,000 Estonians and two Estonian newspapers; and it has large colonies of Yugoslavs, Portuguese, and Greeks. Its largest ethnic groups, aside from the British, are, in descending order: Italians, Germans, Poles, and Ukrainians. The Italian settlements blanket much of an area nearly two miles wide west of downtown.

Each of Toronto's ethnic groups has a host of organizations but four that are common to almost all are: community halls, ethnic newspapers, credit unions, and churches. These four ingredients seem to be most helpful in giving a newly formed ethnic group a sense of community.

My main interest, however, was in the shifting movement of ethnic blocs in modern cities and the upheaval and personal uprootedness this creates. For this, Lieberson recommended I ought to take a look at Chicago, U.S.A.

In my look at turbulent Chicago I had the good fortune to obtain on-the-spot advice from Pierre de Vise, De Paul University sociologist who has been conducting studies on the characteristics and movement of Chicago's population for the Hospital Planning Council for Metropolitan Chicago. He says flatly: "Chicago is the most ethnic and segregated large city in the country."

As recently as 1930 nearly a million Chicagoans were foreign-born. After legislative restrictions had forced a reduction in the flow from abroad, migrants continued to pour into Chicago, now from Puerto Rico, Appalachia, and the South.

The Near West Side of Chicago, for nearly a century, was the ground where one incoming immigrant group after another crowded out a predecessor. The earliest groups were the Irish, Germans, and Scandinavians. Next came the various and quite distinct Jewish groups. Later came the Italians, the Poles, the Lithuanians, the Greeks, and the Turks. Finally came the blacks from the rural South, Appalachia, etc.[5] Some groups reacted to newcomers with more instant aversion than others and moved out.

As Chicago grew the immigrant and migrant groups elbowed each other as they groped outward from the Near West Side for desirable living space. Trolley, bus, elevated lines, and finally subway lines and freeways gave shape to the major corridors of expansion.

De Vise cites these major expansion routes used by the European immigrant groups during the first part of this century:[6]

—The Poles moved northwest along Milwaukee Avenue out to Irving Park; and southwest from the stockyards.
—The Italians moved westward in a corridor between Roosevelt Road and Harrison to the Cicero Avenue area; and farther north they moved northwest along Grand Avenue.

—A great many German Jews moved southward along South Parkway and Drexel Boulevard and then swung eastward toward the lake into the existing, mixed communities of Hyde Park, Kenwood, and South Shore.

—The Russian Jews moved west from their ghetto on Maxwell Street out to Douglas Park and beyond. Under later pressure around 1950 they, and Polish Jews, migrated to North Shore communities in and out of Chicago.

—The Czechs moved down to Cermak Avenue and ultimately west to the suburbs of Cicero and Berwyn.

Author and Chicagoan Mike Royko described the dispersal of European ethnic groups more vividly, if broadly, in *Boss,* by explaining: "The neighborhood towns were part of larger ethnic states. To the north of the Loop was Germany. To the northwest Poland. To the west were Italy and Israel. To the southwest were Bohemia and Lithuania. And to the south was Ireland. It wasn't perfectly defined because the borders shifted as newcomers moved in on the old settlers, sending them fleeing in terror and disgust. . . . But you could always tell, even with your eyes closed, which state you were in by the odor of the food stores and the open kitchen windows, the sound of the foreign or familiar language, and by whether a stranger hit you on the head with a rock."

The change in character of neighborhoods, with all the ethnic shifting, has often been abrupt. Consider the case of much of the Hyde Park area near the University of Chicago. It has gone through four changes of character in the last thirty years.

Until World War II Hyde Park-Kenwood was primarily high-income WASP country with some Jews. After the war, news spread that a black corridor was pushing southward from near midtown along Drexel Boulevard in the general direction of Hyde Park. Panic selling began in much of Hyde Park-Kenwood that lies west of the Illinois Central Railroad tracks and north of 55th Street, and many of the buyers were poor whites from Appalachia and Orientals. By the early fifties much of the housing in this area was again being sold, now to blacks, mostly poor blacks. Then in the late fifties a large urban renewal project nearly a mile and a half long was launched, mostly in poor black territory. The bulldozers came in. Today the renewal part is occupied about 85 percent by whites and about 15 percent by middle-class blacks. The over-all area is one of two Chicago communities to show a decrease in black population from 1960 to 1970.

More than two thirds of all Chicagoans today are first- or second-generation Europeans or blacks. The major European stocks, in order, are Poles, Germans, Italians, Russians, Irish, Czechs. Most of the groups of European stock have been fragmenting, but there are still enclaves of particularly heavy concentration.

The various European ethnic groups give ground grudgingly to other European ethnic groups, with varying degrees of resistance. But the prime cause of ethnic scrambling in Chicago today is blacks making a breakthrough from their ghettos. Blacks are more tightly segregated in Chicago than in any major U.S. city. Three quarters of all of Chicago's one million blacks live in neighborhoods that are at least 90 percent black.

There are two principal black corridors, one going straight south from the midtown area and the other going straight west. The southern corridor is more massive and clearly defined, with occasional breaks for, and pockets of, white neighborhoods. It is about nine miles long and from one to three miles wide, and grew by several square miles between 1960 and 1970. The western corridor, smaller and considerably more irregular, mainly straddles the Eisenhower Expressway; and tips of it have reached close to the city limits.

The enclaves of people from Lithuania, Czechoslovakia, and Poland are the most clannish of all the European stock.[7] There are 4,000 Polish societies in Chicago and its suburbs. The fact that the westward corridor of the blacks by-passed Cicero is attributed in large part to the fierce resistance to change of Cicero's many Polish-

Americans and Czech-Americans. Interestingly Italian-Americans and Russian-Americans are less upset by black incursions.

De Vise pointed out that a sharp distinction must be made between Polish-stock Jews and Polish-stock Catholics. "They don't live together and they are worlds apart" in their resistance to moving. The Catholics are extremely resistant; the Jews are quick to move on if they feel pressured by some other ethnic group. This in fact seems to apply to Jewish groups whatever their national background. They are less attached to a specific territory and tend to yield.

Much the same seems to apply to WASPs and those of older immigrant groups who are more assimilated, such as people of German, Scandinavian, and Irish stock.

While the ethnics of central European background tend to resist fervently any entry of blacks into their enclaves they will usually accept and give way to Americans of Latin backgrounds. De Vise points out that this has created a fascinating ethnic picture along the western black belt. The Puerto Ricans and Mexican-Americans serve as buffers between the black Americans and the European ethnics. But since Mexican-Americans don't get along with Puerto Ricans one group serves as the northern buffer and the other as the southern buffer. On the north side, Puerto Ricans are strung out along the Division Street area—and thus largely separate black Americans from Americans of Polish, Ukrainian, and Italian stock. On the south side, the Mexican-Americans are spread out along the 18th Street area—and thus largely separate blacks from Czech-Americans and Polish-Americans, who, incidentally, mix pretty well.

Because the ethnic lines are so tightly drawn in Chicago, pressure points build up. When blacks seeking better housing appear they tend to create upheaval, consternation, panic selling, and a scrambling for new locations. By 1970 blacks were just a few blocks from the western suburb of Oak Park, which in that year had 62,500 residents, about 130 of them black. De Vise predicted that

Oak Park would admit blacks while nearby Cicero and Berwyn to the south, which are more ethnic-conscious with their heavy concentrations of Polish- and Czechoslovakian-Americans, would continue to resist integration. They have been called "rock resistant and lily white."

De Vise has concluded:

"If Negroes could move freely throughout the city they would tend to disperse rather than bring intense pressure to bear on just one community at a time. That pressure tends to eliminate the chances of that community's maintaining a real biracial population." And he might have added that the intense pressures would be still further reduced if blacks could move freely into Greater Chicago's hundreds of square miles of suburbs.

Contrary to common assumption, Negroes do not tend to expand into run-down, low-rent white areas near them. Most of their movement is into middle- or higher-income areas. One reason is that they are primarily looking for better housing. Another reason is that white people in higher-cost areas find it easier to move—and are more oriented to mobility—than are white people in low-income areas. Here are two other general propositions:

One: white families with school-age children will be more inclined to leave a neighborhood that has become, say, 20 percent Negro than will families with no children.

Two: people who are highly status-conscious (and they come at many economic levels) will also be more inclined to leave a neighborhood when black families start buying or renting than will people who are not particularly status-conscious. This may partly account for the frequent willingness of Jews to move on rather than fight black or non-Jewish European ethnics. In many areas United States Jews still have an anomalous status. That is, they receive less social acceptance than their incomes and educations would seem to warrant. This can cause them to be above average in their sensitivity to the status overtones of an address.

Early warnings that a neighborhood is likely to undergo a change in character are these:

—Doctors and dentists in large numbers start locating elsewhere. De Vise says, "Doctors and dentists are the real indicators of change."

—Owners of quality stores start making hasty exits.

—The better teachers in the local schools start getting themselves transferred out in abnormal numbers.

The blacks, in their probing for expansion points in their western corridor of Chicago, came up against a wall manned by belligerent residents, as indicated, when they reached the boundary of suburban Cicero. But directly above Cicero, and still inside Chicago's city limits, is the Austin community area. It has been a relatively cosmopolitan middle-income area with thousands of brick bungalows and duplexes on often tree-lined streets. Until recently it had few apartment buildings. It even boasts a town hall. In 1960 it was peopled by German-Americans, Italian-Americans, Jewish-Americans, WASPs, some Polish-Americans, and other white ethnics. Of its 125,000 residents a couple dozen were black.

For five years it has been in the throes of ethnic upheaval and in 1970 was about one third black. The blacks are concentrated overwhelmingly in the southern tier of Austin, which is rapidly becoming black. The northern part of Austin is still overwhelmingly white. The two parts still share many facilities, such as the Austin High School. School records in 1969 indicated that about twenty-nine blocks a year in Austin were changing from white to predominantly black. Realtors from all over Chicago swarmed in to encourage and profit from panic selling. Within five years the number of realtors in Austin grew from 40 to 210. One realty firm operated from seventeen miles away. The profits for the realtors show up in telephone records of residential telephone disconnects per year. In Austin, these records indicate about 37 percent of all Austin's residents changed their addresses in 1969 as against 19 percent in Cicero and 18 percent for Oak Park, just west of Austin and over the Chicago city line.

Those residents of Austin who have declined to move have been primarily struggling young couples without school-age children who found Austin one place they could afford to own a real home; or older citizens with long ties to Austin who are determined to stick it out. Also Austin has a number of public-spirited, well-educated, dedicated citizens who have chosen to live in Austin. Some are working for orderly integration; others are holding firm against further black incursions. Thus at this writing Austin's future character is far from clear, especially in the northern sector, which has traditionally been higher-income—and more Protestant—than the southern half of Austin.

The buffeted white people of Austin do not—in a sampling I conducted—seem for the most part to be bigoted, hard-hat types, which some accounts would suggest. But they are uneasy, bewildered, up-tight people. A young truck driver who had recently moved to the Austin area of Chicago "to get out of the city" explained, "The people here have never had to handle blacks before; they don't know how to react." Some approve integration as a concept but others add that they worry about "inundation" and economic loss.

An inclination to be fair-minded showed up in quite a few comments. A wife of a salesman who had lived in Austin twenty years said: "There's no way to stop people from moving in. As long as they keep things up, it's fine." An older woman who had attended black-white meetings offered the view that black families who were buying their own homes were "completely different" and more compatible as neighbors than those who were moving into large apartment buildings. And a resident of twenty years said that the real problem was that suddenly there were "too many strangers. If everyone could just get together and have a little more trust we could beat this problem."

But repeatedly informants indicated there was a new wariness of all strangers, a new isolation of people in once congenial neighborhods, a putting up of invisible barriers. There is less calling on new neighbors, white or black. A male teacher who had lived in Austin thirteen years said, "When we first moved here we knew everyone on the block. Now it's just the three close neighbors."

And residents of northern Austin are beginning to fight back against the hordes of panic-peddling realtors who have been flooding white homeowners in Austin with letters, flyers, or calls aimed at scaring them into selling. The residents found, belatedly, that they have a weapon in the state law which had set up a Commission on Human Relations. Under the law, if residents of an area notify the commission that they do not want to be solicited by realtors seeking to get them to put their homes up for sale, the residents can send the commission a form requesting that solicitation stop. The commission, although it has acted slowly, is supposed to send a list of all such petitioners to all of Chicago's realtors and brokers. If thereafter the homeowner is solicited the commission is supposed to notify the state's attorney general. It was largely the pressure generated by Austin's aroused residents that led the City Council of Chicago to ban the display of home "For Sale" signs in 1971.

Chicago has exceptionally few neighborhoods that have achieved anything approaching genuine black-white integration, except for certain upper-middle-income housing projects. When blacks begin buying in a neighborhood and the so-called "tipping point" (about 25 percent black) is reached, realtors as well as the Chicago Urban League begin referring to it as a black community. And realtors help see to it that it does become more fully black, at considerable profit to themselves. With tightly drawn ethnic lines, when a break is made into a new area, the pressure of other blacks behind the pioneers who also are seeking escape from their black slums assures that others will keep coming as long as housing remains available. The white flights might cease, De Vise suggests, if the whites could be assured that no more than 10 to 20 percent of their neighbors would be black.

Such a ratio would be especially easy to maintain—assuming a consensus was reached—if the blacks could disperse with reasonable freedom in suburbs as well as in the inner city. Although only 40 percent of the residents of the Greater Chicago metropolitan area now live inside the city limits, 89 percent of all blacks in the metropolitan area live inside the city limits.

On the famous North Shore beyond Chicago, for example, the city of Evanston has a substantial proportion of blacks—perhaps 16 percent in 1970. Many work in the city's fine hospitals. Beyond Evanston the North Shore suburbs are almost entirely white, except for a modest enclave of blacks in Glencoe. Of the ten most elite suburbs of Chicago as measured on a socio-economic scale in 1970, six were on the North Shore and were over-whelmingly WASP towns—Kenilworth, Winnetka, Glencoe, Lake Forest, Northfield, and Northbrook. Others of the top ten areas that were essentially WASP towns were Barrington Hills and Olympia Fields. And one of the top ten was predominantly Jewish—Lincolnwood, on the northern city limits. The top-ranking predominantly Catholic suburb, River Forest, on the west, was listed in fifteenth place.[8]

Throughout the United States in the past decade some blacks have moved out into suburbs, but still only one suburbanite in twenty is black. The blacks looking wistfully to the suburbs face economic as well as social barriers. They usually have to pay more for the same house than whites. And since most can't afford a car, and thus can't use the White Man's Expressways, travel costs to get to work will remain formidable until they can live near where they work.

"Parma residents just don't realize they now live in the ninth largest city in the state of Ohio."—SALLY SOEDER, FORMER OFFICIAL OF THE CHAMBER OF COMMERCE IN AN AREA THAT INCLUDES PARMA.

10.

And Three Novel Forms of Urban Sprawl

Many Americans still think of a suburb as a quietly affluent folksy town that is conveniently near the city where Father works, but is insulated from the city's turmoil by miles of nice pastures and woodlands. That image had some validity twenty years ago. Today the suburb of a major city is engulfed in a sea of urban sprawl. It can be a full-fledged industrial city, a bedroom town, a commercial area with gleaming twenty-five-story towers, a trailer park, or a spreading slum. It may or may not have its own government. It probably doesn't have a "downtown" and may not even have a center of focus.

This restless, swelling sea of suburbs creates quite different kinds of upheaval and rootlessness for its inhabitants than do the churning inner cities. Hanging over the sea is a sense of fragmentation, confusion, and diffusion. Breadwinners who travel some distance to work from these suburbs do not necessarily "commute" to the central city. They may go off in six different directions to earn their livelihood. In the thousands of square miles of municipalities and non-municipalities that make up Greater Los Angeles the traveling breadwinners are sometimes called "intercommunitalists."

More than four fifths of the nation's growth has recently been taking place in these suburbs. An example of the growth of quickie "communities" is Cypress, in Orange County, southern California. In 1950 it was not in existence. In 1960 it was a village of 1,700. In 1970 it was a city of 29,000.

Quite a few inhabitants of the sprawl called Greater Los Angeles that is seventy miles wide and thirty-five miles deep are often confused as to orientation, and certainly have little sense of place. I asked a number of people who had recently moved to Azusa, California, what their hardest problem of adjustment was after arriving. One woman responded: "Finding out where we are." She meant it literally. Most of the so-called towns, often centerless, and the housing tracts that are in limbo filling gaps between town lines in that area of California, all seem to run together. It is quite easy to be geographically disoriented until you see a familiar towering expressway.

In nearby Orange County a planning official has referred to Garden Grove (pop. 122,000 plus) as a phantom city: "You can't tell when you enter it, and you can't tell when you're leaving it."[1] A resident there was quoted as saying, "I live in Garden Grove, work in Irvine, shop in Santa Ana, and go to the dentist in Anaheim. My husband works in Long Beach. . . ."

The chaotic way that "suburban" growth has been permitted to occur in most metropolitan areas represents one of the major shames of mid-twentieth-century America.

Three of the newer types of suburb are of particular relevance to our exploration of the fragmentation of community living in the United States.

SPILLOVER CITIES

Parma, Ohio (pop. 100,216), is a new kind of city in search of a soul. Despite its rank as Ohio's ninth largest city, most Americans have never heard of it. And many Ohioans know of it primarily because a Cleveland TV comedian made it the butt of jokes. He called it the white sox town because a decade or so ago the elite of the town, many of Polish ancestry, reputedly wore white socks to social events.

Despite its relatively anonymous status Parma has several features that give it national significance as a prototype of things to come. For example:

Parma is probably the only U.S. city with more than 100,000 residents that doesn't have a daily newspaper. Its only paper is a weekly that is a part of a suburban chain.

Parma is one of those rare—but growing in number —U.S. cities of more than 100,000 population that doesn't have a downtown to serve as a community center. Its City Hall is thirty blocks away from its municipal court. Its commercial district is no district at all but rather stores strung out along streets that form a square about two miles on each side. Most of the residences are inside the square. Twenty years ago the "downtown" was thought of as being at the intersection of Pearl and Ridge and up to the north near the Cleveland city limits. Now the center of gravity has shifted more than a mile south toward the Parmatown Mall area.

Parma is probably the only 100,000-plus city that doesn't have a bus system of its own. The buses you see in Parma are part of the Cleveland transit system. They follow the main arteries into Cleveland. Thus Parma has virtually no crosstown buses. Almost any citizen without a car who wanted to get to City Hall would have a lot of walking to do.

Parma also is probably the only 100,000-plus U.S. city that does not have a decent-sized hotel (or sizable motor inn). It has a small motel that is called a "hotel."

The city furthermore has no TV station of its own though several of Cleveland's TV towers are located in Parma. And the city doesn't even have a map you can buy in the stores. When I asked at the bookshop for a map of Parma the clerk said: "I don't know of any map being sold just of Parma alone. We have maps of Cleveland that show Parma."

Until recently, Parma did not even have a telephone directory. Its phone subscribers are included in the Cleveland directory. Though a Parma directory has been issued, it is not widely used. One resident said, "Most people throw it away and keep on using the Cleveland directory."

A civic official in Parma explained: "Unfortunately most people here think they are residents of Greater Cleveland and not of Parma per se." He pointed out that there is still a store in Parma that advertises in neon lights: "Serving Clevelanders for 27 years." The lack of civic identity and cohesiveness helps account for the fact that it took four votes to get a school bond issue passed in 1969. Another problem was that a third of school-age children go to Catholic schools. Parma is 68 percent Catholic.

A great many people who live in Parma work outside Parma; and a great many people who own businesses in Parma live somewhere else. Some live in Parma Heights, which I guess we would have to call a sub-suburb since it is a suburb of a suburb. The mayor of Parma Heights in 1971 conducted his law practice from an office in Parma. Parma Heights is surrounded by Parma on three sides. Though it is called Parma Heights it is actually, on average, a few feet closer to sea level than Parma. At any rate Parma Heights fancies itself a cut above Parma in socio-economic eliteness, and probably is. It has more transients of the upward-mobile managerial types.

Despite its identity problems as a spillover city, Parma does have its assets. When land was plentiful to the south it had the good sense to reserve areas for a large park and a municipal golf course. It is a city of mostly modest single-family homes, white clapboard, that have about eighteen-foot lawns in front and are neatly kept up. There are a few somewhat elite areas where houses cost up to $50,000 or so. Within Parma there is a good deal of moving to upgrade by getting, for example, into Dogwood Estates.

Parma's people are trying to sink new roots. William S. Nigro, head of a leading realty firm in Parma, said many wives work and "there is more money in this little community of ours than one would suspect. They don't have to be sophisticated, but there are more mortgage-free homes in Parma than most. Forty percent of the houses are mortgage free."

The people are seeking to sink roots because most see Parma as an escape from where they came from: the lower west side of Cleveland, better known as the Flats, near the mills bordering the stench-laden Cuyahoga River. It was an area largely populated by people whose national origins were Slavic (Ukrainians, Poles, Czechoslovaks) or Hungarian or German or Austrian or Italian.

And those nationality groups are basically the groups that make up Parma's population today. Of Parma's total population these seven nationality groups in 1969 accounted for nearly 90 percent of the population:

Czechoslovakian	21 percent
Polish	18 percent
German	16 percent
Italian	11 percent
Hungarian	9 percent
Austrian	7 percent
Russian	6 percent

Parma's black population is less than .1 percent, although as one informant said: "We have some excellent black teachers in the schools."

In Parma—whose political outlook is conservative—the European ethnic groups intermingle more than they did back on the Flats of Cleveland but there are still heavy ethnic enclaves, especially among those who speak broken English and live in the lower-cost areas. Mr. Nigro pointed out that there is less of an ethnic-colony atmosphere in areas where property values are higher. To demonstrate he showed me in the crisscross street directory the names of people living on Westmoreland Road where houses are fairly high-priced ($25,000 to $50,000).

Names I noticed at random were King, Rusmanis, Drake, Street, Sosinski, Walzak, Jensen. In contrast on Liggett Drive where housing costs are somewhat lower the names were almost all Slavic, primarily Ukrainian: Markus, Chmura, Srnkia, Skorepa, Stankiewicz, Rymansky, Dobrovach, Labuski, Houska.

Parma is only one of a growing number of U.S. spillover or "outer" cities that hardly fit our conventional idea of a suburb. Los Angeles alone has several unorthodox suburbs of the spillover-city type. For example to the east there is El Monte (pop. 70,000), a dreary jumble of drab little houses and gaudy business places and a few factories. As a one-layer working-class city, it boasts that it is the first "all-American" community in Los Angeles County. As of 1971 it had no art gallery and no blacks. A third of the population is Mexican-American. El Monte is, for many, considered a way station. An El Monte businessman was quoted by *Time* magazine as saying: "We get them coming both ways. Those who are coming from other parts of the country and those who are leaving. Those who are coming up in life and those who are going down." Annual turnover of pupils in some El Monte schools approaches 100 percent.

Still another excellent prototype of the spillover city is Warren, Michigan (pop. 179,000). It has more of an industrial base (Chrysler, General Motors, U.S. Detroit Arsenal, etc.) but in some other ways it is more of a spillover-type city than Parma. In mid-afternoon as you drive due north in Detroit on Route 53 over urban flatlands that stretch to the horizon you see sections where most of the storefronts still have Polish names but the streets are bustling with black children just out of school. Then abruptly as you get near Seven Mile Road the children and people on the street are all white and stores have such names as Nowicki and Bulki. The Polish and other Slavic names continue to predominate for a mile. Then at Eight Mile Road you are across the city limits and into Warren, where the streets are named for automobiles (mostly of the past) such as Packard, Hup, Maxwell, Jewett.

In square miles the city of Warren is half the size of Washington, D.C. It is laid out on a grid, mile after mile, on flatland that once was swampy. The houses on the side streets from Route 53 are neat bungalows built mainly of brick. Route 53 is the main stem. There is a large factory every few hundred yards. The city's municipal building sits facing the Fisher Body Plant. A mile or so farther out on Route 53 at Twelve Mile Road you come to a sort of city center, part shopping mall with a couple of high-rise buildings.

Warren is primarily a Polish-American city. Its only daily newspaper, the *Macomb Daily,* is designed to cover all of Macomb County (pop. 500,000), not just Warren. Warren's population doubled in the past decade as people, mostly factory workers, moved out from Detroit's east side. Many were seeking more open space or escape; many say their old homes back in Detroit are now occupied by blacks.

Anyhow, Warren has recently achieved national notoriety because of its vehement feelings about blacks. About 100 of its 179,000 population are black at this writing, yet 30 percent of the jobs at the major Warren plants are held by blacks, who must commute to Warren from somewhere else—mainly Detroit. Since plenty of modest-priced housing is available in Warren it struck some federal officials that this was a clear case of minorities being kept out of a town for racial rather than economic reasons. So the U.S. Department of Housing and Urban Development decided to make Warren a test case for enforcing the fair housing law, using the threat of withdrawing about $13,000,000 allocated to Warren for urban renewal as leverage. A $3,000,000 project was already under construction.

Many of the citizens became somewhat hysterical at the prospect of fair housing really being enforced. Many began buying guns. When H.U.D. Secretary George Romney, a long-time Michigan public figure, came to Warren to explain the situation it took a police line to get him out of town safely. The city voted to scrap the urban renewal projects rather than bow to the fair housing law. And, at this writing, H.U.D., under a smoke screen of verbiage, has been backing away, not just in Warren but elsewhere, from actions that might be labeled "forced integration" of the suburbs, or any actions that might make these slices of sprawl into well-rounded communities.

PSEUDO TOWNS BASED ON SHOPPING MALLS

As America's urban areas continue to spread out over one-time farmlands—mainly in the form of development tracts—marketers are quick to follow. In the frequent absence of authentic existing downtowns to build upon the marketers have invented a new form of "downtown" much more efficient for mass merchandising. That is the shopping center; if it is large enough it may be called a shopping mall, or a covered shopping mall. In Madison, Wisconsin, the two largest plazas are called East Town and West Town and are located on the east and west sides of the city.

There are now about 13,000 of these centers of some sort in the U.S. A number of the great fortunes of the past twenty years have been made by entrepreneurs, such as Leo Corrigan of Dallas, who, with their staffs of specialists, planned and built these shopping centers all around the country (and some abroad).

These entrepreneurs, starting fresh, don't have to worry about their shopping center's stores being thinned out by unprofitable town halls, YMCAs, courthouses, police stations, and public squares. They have discovered the combinations and layouts of department stores, specialty shops, and discount houses that produce the highest volume of impulse buying by residents in various price-range housing tracts. They know precisely how many square feet of parking space are needed per hundred square feet of floor space. The shopping center's biggest contribution to mass merchandising is its acres of parking space, which makes it easier for an auto-loving society to haul home large quantities of goods.

The big mall operators have also learned what kinds of staged—or encouraged—events, such as charity bazaars, antique auto shows, and children's art shows, will be most effective in packing the stores day or night. Such events are known in the trade as "traffic builders."

Most of the people living in the vast new tracts of houses surrounding these shopping centers are relatively rootless; and they perforce see the shopping center as the only focal point in sight as a sort of "downtown."

One of the more awesome examples of sprawl-mall take-over is in Paramus, New Jersey, which two decades ago was a truck-gardening hamlet about ten miles west of the George Washington Bridge. Today it is a jungle of housing tracts and shopping centers that move a million dollars' worth of goods a day. And it has no downtown in any conventional sense. There are two whopping-big shopping centers: (1) The Garden State Plaza, which long boasted it was the world's largest. As a sample of monstrous civic planning it deserves a special prize since it is intersected by two major thruways, Route 4 and Route 17. Until afterthought precautions were taken, a number of shoppers were killed or injured trying, by racing across whizzing highway traffic, to get from one part of the center to another. (2) A mile away is the other giant, the Bergen Mall. The mall proper is on one side of Route 17 but a separate complex of big and little stores has sprung up across the highway.

The Town Hall of Paramus is on Route 17 between the Bergen Mall and a Holiday Inn.

East and south of Pittsburgh are another pair of enormous malls—the Monroeville Mall and the South Hills Village—both built by the same developer. Surrounding them are a sea of development housing tracts and apartment complexes that have engulfed and virtually obliterated the small villages that used to lie in these hills.

At many of the larger U.S. malls many types of business endeavor that normally would only be found "downtown" are starting to rent space. There are brokerage houses, psychiatrists' offices, movies houses, banks, night clubs, restaurants. And there are the beginnings of community-type facilities that normally make little or no profit: chapels, youth consulting services, playhouses, auditoriums. Some mall managers justify them by claiming it is good business to be a good neighbor . . . or that it builds traffic . . . or that they are trying to fill a vacuum, as when they permit late evening junior proms on the mall, or "marketplace ministries." At the Plymouth Meeting Mall near Norristown, Pennsylvania, for example, a Presbyterian minister has his office at the shopping center and his congregation holds weekly services in the covered mall. A music store loaned an organ and Sunday school classes are held in a barbershop and a restaurant.[2]

Still, almost all of these big shopping centers have a long way to go to fill the vacuum, really, and become true "downtowns" or community centers. A large proportion of store managers commute to the malls from their homes in nearby cities and have little to do with the surrounding tract residents to whom they sell their wares.[3]

The major obstacle to true downtown status, however, is that the malls—no matter how vast and filled with fountains, greenery, benches, and parking lots they may be—are private property. If we must think of them as towns at all, it is as company towns. They have no downtown squares, no street corners, no greens where political candidates and others can exercise their constitutional right to free speech. Some malls permit their parking lots to be used for political rallies, others do not. In 1968 Richard Nixon, running for the presidency, conducted seventeen major rallies at malls. But some malls turned him (and others) down. The Garden State Plaza at Paramus, for example, vetoed a Nixon rally, on the grounds that it might disrupt the flow of customers into the stores.

But the malls are becoming by default such frequent substitutes for "downtown" that their claims to private control of all activities is being challenged. Peaceful picketing of stores, for example, is constitutionally protected in ordinary downtowns. But are the stores which are located in a vast expanse of private mall property protected from such picketing? This has become a hot issue. Apparently the shopping center stores are not legally protected from picketing; although mall owners are still reluctant to acknowledge that they can't rely upon state trespass laws to chase pickets away. The Supreme Court in a 1968 decision involving a labor dispute at a mall near Altoona, Pennsylvania, ruled that as far as the constitutionally guaranteed right to peaceful picketing is concerned a shopping center passage is as much of a public place as an ordinary street or sidewalk.[4]

The private-property, company-town nature of these malls has become painfully conspicuous in their attitude toward young people looking for a place to hang out. Nearby housing developments don't have street corners; or at least not the kind that attract idle young people. There are no corner drugstores. So the youths from thousands of homes surrounding the bigger malls gravitate to the corridors, stores, and parking lots of the malls in order to meet friends and, sometimes, horse around and even smoke a little pot.

Most mall owners view them with distaste and hire security guards to eject them as trespassers if they can find an excuse, such as boisterous, obstreperous behavior. A few of the more sensitive mall towns have permitted youth counseling services to be established in the malls and have even allowed the young to use the "community room" one night a week as a coffeehouse. One such mall was the South Hills Mall south of Pittsburgh. Later the management changed its mind, explaining that too many of the young were creating confusion among customers in the corridors and using the community room as a place to loaf and, in the management's view, sometimes to be obscene.

A strong critic of the management's action was a young Presbyterian minister, Reverend Lyndon Whybrew, who was directing a counseling service there called Ministry in the Mall.[5]

The Reverend Mr. Whybrew was bitter and spoke

sharply to what I believe is the major point. He said of the youngsters involved:

"These are suburban kids, whose fathers have often been moved around the country by their companies. These youngsters don't know anything else but the shopping center as a gathering place. Even if you don't do anything for them here they will come anyway. *I don't think the developers have any moral right to turn away the kids when they are pushing so hard to get their parents in here to spend their money.*"

PSEUDO VILLAGES ON WHEELS

We glimpsed, in Chapter 8, a few mobile home parks in Florida inhabited by retirees. But mobile home parks are not confined to retirees and they are not confined to the Southland. (Some areas still call them trailer parks.) In the past decade their growth—by several hundred percent—has become an all-American phenomenon. About six million Americans are now said to be mobile home dwellers. About 80 percent of all new houses costing less than $20,000 that have recently been built are mobile.

Judging from the pages devoted in *Woodall's Mobile Home Park Directory* to listing mobile home parks presentable enough to get a Woodall rating (one to five stars), the eight leading states in espousing mobile homes are, in descending order, California, Florida, Texas, Michigan, Arizona, Illinois, Ohio, Washington. The Northeast is the only U.S. region that did not make the list. Compare the nation's two most populous states, the West's California and the Northeast's New York. California has about ten times as many mobile home parks worthy of listing in *Woodall's* as New York.

By my computation, if all the mobile homes in the state of Florida were hitched up to trucks and started a trek across the U.S. there would be a tightly packed line reaching all the way from Florida to California!

Tens of thousands of Americans have travel trailers in which they live much or all of the time. Retirees in particular are likely to cluster with other people owning same-make travel trailers and take off on junkets for months at a time. They become in effect truly mobile villages with elaborate committee structures, scouts, etc., to see that everything goes off all right. Some months ago more than 3,000 owners of shiny aluminum travel trailers staged a rally, with a vast circular layout, in upper Michigan.

However, the great majority of mobile homes stop being "mobile" after they are driven to their park site. One reason is that most have become so large that they cost a dollar a mile to move.

But still, there is an aura of mobility and impermanence in mobile home living. Mobile home owners know they can always pick up and move to another location or area in a pinch, which seems to appeal to restless Americans. Their mobile homes also offer such people a chance to make a minimum commitment to both home and community. While retiree parks feature community centers and offer a semblance of village life, this is much less true of parks in general. Of twenty-seven parks in Flint, Michigan, listed in a recent *Woodall's Directory* only seven had community halls.

The mood of impermanence is enhanced by the fact that mobile homes are merchandised like motor vehicles. Owners trade their homes in for new models every five or six years. The homes become obsolete in the eyes of both mortgage lenders and owners several times faster than conventional houses.

The parks often call themselves villages, communities, or even cities. We saw in Florida's retiree colonies that when there are community halls in the parks a community-like attitude is promoted, but there are some important differences. I have not seen a mobile home park that had a market place, where people historically have done most of their socializing. And in the few where I have seen children, the families with children were isolated in remote parts of the park. Most of the parks to which Woodall has awarded the coveted five stars are for adults only. And it says bluntly that a three-star park with higher aspirations possibly is being held back from a higher star level because of the presence of children and the disarray they can create.

No matter how you floss them up with peaked roofs, "expando" sections, and patios, most mobile homes are elongated metal boxes. But as one architect observed: "They're ugly as hell sitting out there in rows. But they allow people to buy a two-bedroom, air-conditioned home for $6,000. Where else can you do that?"

Their popularity springs partly from their movability, but a more important factor is the scandalous failure of the home-building contractors and the construction trade unions, with their high wages and stern rules against labor-saving innovations, to provide Americans of modest incomes such as young marrieds and retirees with decent housing. By mass-production techniques the mobile home builders can provide housing at nine dollars a square foot —or about half the cost of comparably sized conventional houses.

The walls around many parks seem, too, to suggest safety to people made fearful by reports of muggings and by the turbulence of contemporary society.

One of the new trends in mobile parks has been the introduction of the chain concept. If Holiday Inns, in expanding, can thrive by developing know-how and brand recognition, why not mobile parks? And the chain concept has an additional appeal to park owners. They can lure mobile home owners by assuring them that if for any reason they want to move on they will be given preference at any other park in the chain.

It was partly to inspect this chain idea—as embodied in Chateau Estates—that I was led after visiting Warren, Michigan, to proceed on out Route 53 to Utica.

Beyond Warren as you drive out the flatlands of Route 53 you come first to Sterling Heights, a brand-new stretch of urban sprawl running for several miles and consisting mainly of apartment complexes, housing tracts, and occasional shopping centers, amid still empty woods and farmland. Until shortly before my visit Sterling Heights did not exist as a "town." There was a Sterling Township.

AND THREE NOVEL FORMS OF URBAN SPRAWL

Woodall's guide described the largest Chateau Estates mobile home park (five stars) as being in Utica, Michigan. This intrigued me because Utica was listed as having a total population of 1,550 persons; and the Chateau Estates park had 760 mobile homes, which I assumed must house at least 1,550 people. Those 760 mobile homes made it one of the largest parks in northern United States. It turned out that the situation was not exactly as I assumed. Utica is a pleasant, traditional American small town. One of its major stores is called Chateau Estates Mobile Supplies. Chateau Estates had a Utica telephone number and for a while used the Utica Post Office. Its children went to the Utica Community School, which covers several school districts. But Chateau Estates itself is not in Utica. It begins exactly on the town line in what was the emptiness of Sterling Township but now is a part of the newly created fast-growing city of Sterling Heights, whose population has zoomed past 40,000.

As mobile home parks go, Chateau Estates in Sterling Heights is pleasant and relatively spacious, if pretentious. It has lawns, broad winding roads bearing such names as Normandy, Bordeaux, Versailles, and Notre Dame. About 25 percent of the residents have children and live in a special family section. If a wife living in the main, non-family part of Chateau Estates becomes pregnant she goes on the waiting list for a house in the children's section. At the heart is a community center building of French Normandy-style architecture with a lush lounge room in which, when I was there, several ladies surrounded by bedspreads were arguing about bedspread design. Outside the building was a swimming pool and an area for having barbecue parties.

The general manager of this particular Chateau Estates, Howard Todd, explained: "One appeal of the mobile home to people is that they have the *feeling* they can move any time they want to. It is their house. Some move their house when they leave." He added that the proportion that are actually mobile in the sense of moving their houses is only about 2 percent. But this may rise. Usually it is difficult to find a place to move to but with ten other

Chateau Estates being built in the Greater Detroit area the corporation will give preference to people moving to other Chateau Estates.

The sensitivity about children—and taxes in general—in mobile home parks was a hot issue when Chateau Estates first sprang up in Sterling Township. When I was there each mobile home owner had to pay a school tax of $36 a year. In addition the management was paying a property tax of approximately $88 a year on each mobile home site. Thus each dwelling was producing a total of about $124 a year in taxes. The cost of educating even one child for a year in Michigan costs many times that amount. So it is doubtful if Chateau Estates will ever permit the proportion of its residents who have children—especially school-age children—to rise much above 25 percent. It would just aggravate the pressures already existing in the state legislature, at this writing, to make mobile home owners pay a property tax on their vehicular homes.

Another new trend in mobile homes which is far more hopeful and portentous as a way of providing aesthetic lower-cost housing in urban areas is the modular unit home. It is sometimes called the plug-in home. The technology is well developed and buildings based on modular units are going up in Chicago, Vicksburg, Mississippi, and many other places. Modular unit builders in the mobile home industry are embracing the mobile home technology they have perfected but are stripping the dwelling of its gaudy metal sidings. Using the stripped-down dwelling units as a building block, they are making garden apartments and even high-rise apartments. Some smaller modules are sections of houses or apartments. Once a desired framework for an apartment house or multistory dwelling is erected the modules can be plugged into the framework by crane-type machines and connected to utilities.

And here again we get back to temporariness and mobility. If the owner of a module later becomes bored with his modular home or the apartment house it is a part of, or if he begins to consider his module obsolete, he can have it removed and trade it in for a new module which can be inserted in the space made vacant when he re-moves the old one. Or if he likes his module but wants it in a different part of town where there is a framework for modules—or in a different region—he can move it by truck to the desired site.

Thus—if the idea spirals—his home can be wherever he chooses to hang his hat for that year.

PART TWO

Problems
of
Adjusting
to
Fragmentation

"Remember that money goes down the drain every time a house changes hands —in improvements, closing costs, the 6 percent broker's commission, and other outlays."—ROBERT J. STAHL, CONSULTANT TO PEOPLE MOVING INTO THE NEW YORK CITY AREA.

11.

What It Means to Transplant Today's Family

The modern middle-class family that moves to some other town or state will take along at least seven times more tonnage in family possessions than the family in the covered wagon took. And this modern family on the move must make arrangements with at least ten times as many bureaucratic organizations as the family of a century ago did in making a move.

If the husband is an organization man, almost all the details of logistics and bureaucratic notifications are normally left to his wife. The husband is immersed in being briefed on his new job and in making office arrangements. North American Van Lines reports that 90 percent of its contacts in working out the details of moving are with the wife. An official of the Nike missile program—who had moved his wife and children sixteen times in fifteen years —said his wife typically handled the details of selling a house.

The millions of Archie Bunkers and other working people in the land who move suffer more losses in relation to income than do the organization men or women of cor-

porations and government. They don't have a protecting
organization to share some of their costs and headaches.
Usually they have to hire or borrow trucks or rent haul-
type trailers instead of using moving vans. They do their
own loading and unloading and they may have to take
several trips. Usually, too, the move is more upsetting because they are less used to moving and are likely to be
more uneasy in strange surroundings.

On the other hand the Archie Bunkers don't usually
move as far as the organization families, or as often. And
they are less likely than organization families to move
under pressure. Even the Bunkers of the world can be
under pressure to move, however, if they are military men
or if the breadwinners are cogs in a corporation that de-
cides to make a mass move, as Shell made from New York
to Houston. If so they may receive some cash help from
their particular bureaucracy, such as the payment of moving van costs.

One compelling reason why many corporations want to
check out a man's wife on her movability before they hire
the man for a managerial role is to guess how she will
react if he is asked to move. Will she sulk, rebel, or fuss if
the husband is tapped for a move? If that seems likely he
probably won't get the job.

Some companies also devise strategies to keep wives in
a moving mood. The wife of a Chevrolet sales manager in
the Chicago area showed me designs of charms on a silver
bracelet given to her—at a gala presentation—by a top
sales official of the company. From her bracelet dangle
charms signifying the numerous cities in which her husband has served. She is, nonetheless, not an enthusiastic
mover.

The hardship, turmoil, and family tensions are intensified when a man is asked to make a long-distance move
if his wife is one of the four out of ten wives now who has
her own career. If she is in the middle of an important
project will she stay behind until it is finished? Will she
have trouble finding as satisfying a job in the new town
where her husband is to be assigned? If the husband's new
job is less than a hundred miles away should they seek a

house somewhere midway so that she can continue, by commuting, to pursue her current career?

The well-organized wife who finds herself facing a long-distance move—whether she is a corporate manager's housewife or a Mrs. Bunker—begins making a list of the things that have to be done in order to get out of one house and into another in the coming weeks. If she is fairly thorough her list will look something like this:

GETTING OUT

NOTIFY

Contact gas, electric, telephone, and fuel oil companies about discontinuing services—and give them new address to which to send bills. Also make arrangements for same in the new town and specify date of arrival.

Arrange to stop milk, bakery, garbage, and newspaper deliveries.

Tell post office of planned change of address, and what is to be forwarded and what junk mail is to be thrown away.

Advise all magazines of address change.

Notify local creditors of move and try to get them to be patient.

Notify insurance companies (life, fire, theft, car, polio, furs, etc.) of change—and don't forget Blue Cross and Blue Shield!

Remember to close out charge accounts as bills arrive here or at new address, and be sure to tear up charge plates.

Notify the six credit card companies whose cards are held of change of address and ask for new cards. When arrive, tear up old.

Notify all friends, kinfolk, etc., of change of address.

DO

Try to sell the house. See about placing ads, contacting local brokers.

If a moving van is to be used interview moving van representatives and after making choice arrange to move toward middle of month to reduce chance of foul-ups.

Go with husband to see about buying or renting a new house. Be sure to check the school situation!!!

Have bank transfer money in checking and savings to the bank at new address, get traveler's checks, tear up present bank plates.

Pay up local pledge to church.

Have someone drain oil and gas from power mower. Arrange to have TV antennae removed.

Reserve hotel accommodations en route.

Have garage give car a thorough checkup for trip (especially brakes and windshield wipers).

Start defrosting fridge twenty-four hours before moving and freezer forty-eight hours before.

Arrange going-away party for children.

Ask Motor Vehicle Bureau what is to be done about auto registration and licenses.

Clean rugs and draperies a week before M day.

Start an inventory of all things to be moved, and decide what to throw away and what is not worth the shipping costs. Try arrange tag sale for things not going to take.

Arrange to have garbage man make special trip for things not being taken and can't dispose of.

Start packing, a room at a time. Save children's room and kitchen till last. Number each carton packed and keep a list of room it came from. Draw sketch of floor plan of new house (in duplicate), mark the numbers on cartons that should go in each room. If professional movers are being used give one copy of floor plan to movers. Keep the other for self.

GET

Get medical records from the dentist, family doctor, gynecologist, pediatrician, veterinarian.

Get children's school records, notify school when departing.

Get letter of transfer at church.
Get current prescriptions from druggist.

MOVING DAY

Tranquilize the dog.

Make sure water heater, furnace are turned off, utilities disconnected, windows and doors locked, and police notified of move.

If using a moving van company, be sure to have enough cash, money orders, certified checks, or traveler's checks to pay moving company when truck arrives at new place. (Otherwise they won't unload.) Don't leave town until load has been weighed and have been advised of exact cost of move. Also remain on premises until all boxes loaded and be sure to get bill of lading from van driver.

GETTING IN

Start unpacking by rooms as per floor plan. Unpack stuff for children's rooms first, then kitchen.

Arrange for stove, washer, TV, etc., to be hooked up.

Take children to new schools and make necessary arrangements.

Arrange milk and newspaper delivery and garbage pickups, and find out what day pickup is made.

See about dog license.

Find out if family wills have to be changed because of move to the new state.

Find out the local rules about keeping dogs fenced or chained.

Find out if children have to be inoculated for diphtheria, measles, tetanus, whooping cough, etc.

Start getting names of good doctors, dentists, and see if they are accepting new patients.

Check to see if must take driver's license test.

A wife in Stamford, Connecticut, who had moved six times in ten years, was quoted as saying: "I've taken so many driver's tests I could scream!" Given a society as mobile as America's, compassion as well as logic point to the need for establishing a federal driver's license and a federal title for motorcars.

After the first flurry of getting moved in, the husband, if he is a corporate transfer, goes off to his new berth with his corporate home. New colleagues, a few of whom he may know from an earlier assignment, are geared to induct him swiftly into his new milieu.

His wife and children, however, are likely to feel considerably more uprooted by the move.

An upstate New York wife who had moved twenty times in fifteen years of marriage had few complaints but added: "I am tired of remodeling homes over and over only to pass them on to other people." A Darien wife who had moved six times in fifteen years explained: "Moving is hard on the wife, children, furniture, and appliances. I don't mention the husband. He is usually enamored of a new job."

After the wife gets through the flurry of organizing the kitchen and retailoring drapes for the new house and locating the best cleaner and bakery nearby, she typically begins feeling what some psychiatrists call "psychological arrival." Some younger wives who have been well trained in mobility take the change of environment in stride, others complain of a general "lost" feeling for a while.

Whenever the newly arrived wife is out in the yard or on the street she is careful to look pert and presentable on the assumption that neighbors are watching her and trying to decide whether these newcomers are going to help or hurt the street's real estate value.

One incoming wife in North Stamford, Connecticut, became so disgruntled and irritable because she knew virtually no one that her husband paid her $15 a week to be cheerful. If he caught her grumbling in any week he didn't have to pay the $15.

Sociologist Robert Gutman of Rutgers University has found that while some women literally thrive on mobility there are four types—age aside—who seem to have the most difficulty:

1. Those who are, socially, downward mobile and resent the move as demonstrating they are moving into a less prestigious and favorable situation.

2. Working-class wives making a move from city to suburb.

3. Women who tend to be very expressive emotionally, especially from ethnic cultures such as the Italians and Poles. They have problems relating to a new settlement.

4. Women whose tastes and interests are so sparsely distributed in the total population that in a new location it takes quite a search to find people of similar tastes and interests, especially in a suburban development tract.

What it means in dollars to relocate a family depends on a lot of things, and can range from $200 to more than $10,000, depending on distances . . . whether a raise goes with the new job . . . how much the employer will help with costs . . . whether schools will be so bad in the new town that private schools will have to be considered . . . the length of commuting in the new town . . . and, most important, whether the family can sell its present house and get into the new one without too much loss due to price differences, lawyers' and brokers' fees, etc.

The answer to the last point depends partly on whether local real estate conditions are slumping or booming. A corporate manager living in Wilton, Connecticut, was reported still trying to sell not just one but two former homes in towns where he had been stationed. That can be pretty distracting. Consultant Robert Stahl, cited earlier, estimates that transferring a corporate manager is likely to cost about $5,000. The moving van cost is only a fraction of the total cost. In New York State, for example, the real estate closing costs for a house may run about $1,000. And then, as indicated, there are the costs of disposing of the old house. Many corporations located in the New York City area now feel impelled to give a cost-of-living differential to families they bring into the New York area.

In all parts of the country, in fact, companies that want a readily transferable supply of managers, professionals, and technical specialists have found it necessary or prudent to take over more and more of the moving costs. Policies on this vary fantastically from company to company. But an American Management Association study a few years ago of 329 reporting corporations found that 77 percent of all the companies had some kind of policy for providing benefits for transferees.[1]

Some companies also give an "inconvenience bonus" to families they move. For a junior executive this may be two weeks' pay but for a high-level manager it may mean nine weeks of extra pay.

In the course of my research I asked 74 newcomers to their areas a number of questions about their thoughts in settling in a strange community. Most of the respondents were wives. About half were from affluent Darien, Connecticut. The rest were from less affluent Azusa, California; stable Glens Falls, New York; and the Austin area of Chicago.

Here are some comments wives made about their major problems in settling in:

—DARIEN: "Finding a place to cash a check."
—DARIEN: "The children's loneliness—and never hearing the phone ring!"

One of the questions I addressed to the 74 newcomers who had been in their towns less than a year and a half was whether it had been easy or hard to come to feel they were a part of the new community. Of those giving a clear-cut answer, about half indicated it was hard and about half felt it was easy.

Perhaps the more fascinating responses to my probing of newcomers came from a couple in Darien. I had given the wife a form inviting her to comment at length on her "thoughts" about settling in a strange community. It included a number of questions to stimulate her thinking. The wife gave the form to her husband to fill out. Then, apparently later, she wrote me a long postcript giving her own thoughts. She explained that her husband's comments were those of an "organizational man."

This particular couple, since marriage, had been moving, on average, every two and a half years for nearly twenty years. Their last tour of duty, in the Midwest, had lasted less than a year. While he, in his comments, expressed some reservations about frequent moves, her comments were far more blunt. She was fed up and a bit angry.

The husband conceded that any move involves some hardship and that moving becomes more difficult as families grow older. He said the moves loom less as an adventure and as more of a challenge. But on my query regarding corporate policies about moving people every few years he said they were probably a necessary part of training and preparation for advancement. He said he accepted moving as a requirement for advancement.

The wife in her long postscript said: "It is hard for me to say what I feel without sounding like a bitter woman. I know a move is much harder on a woman. Continually decorating *another* house, having *another* new group of people for dinner, lining up *another* new church, finding *another* new doctor and dentist can be a challenge the first few times, but it can also be very hectic and tiresome.

"If you are ambitious, moving is a part of the package. Most of my friends seem to thrive as long as they are moving up."

She mentioned that their children had probably broadened their horizons by their many moves but added that their last move in particular had had a traumatic effect upon their teen-age daughter by taking her away from her friends. She said the daughter held her parents responsible and had become hostile to the point that a fine parent-daughter relationship had been destroyed. She continued:

"I think sooner or later every family has to decide what is more important—money and position or roots. For me, family and friends—*old* friends—mean a great deal. I am sorry my children will never know the same kind of family closeness that I did. Travel and new experiences are good for children. All the ladies' magazines keep telling us the good outweighs the inconvenience. I don't buy this any more. I think the security of having a real home with

family and friends around that I don't have to say good-
by to again means more to me than the security of a bigger
pay check." She concluded:

"I've said more than I meant to . . . but I wanted you
to know there is one soul out here who would like to
resign from the rat race!"

Another query I put to the 74 people who had recently
moved was whether they had developed any ideas or strategies for making relocations into strange areas easy and
pleasant for the family.

A number offered suggestions that seem worth passing
on. Several of these were in harmony with ideas I encountered elsewhere.

1. Get to know the new area well even before you
move. An upper New York State family that had moved
four times in four years said it always subscribes to the
newspaper in the new town several weeks before the
move.

2. Encourage companies transferring or hiring a person
to have a "buddy system" not only for the person hired
but for his or her family.

3. Have home furnishings geared to movability. A family in Azusa said: "We bought a sectional couch with
these thoughts in mind." A Connecticut wife admonished:
"Don't buy contour furniture if you are likely to move a
lot. It's better to have relatively simple furnishings, comfortable and of a size that will fit in any house, apartment,
or what not." Others own easily dismountable shelves and
bookcases. And a Darien wife said, "Don't worry about
whether the carpet and drapes match." The Whirlpool
Company, incidentally, has been offering a convertible
washer "for people on the move." You can park it in a
closet or install it permanently later if you choose.

4. Develop techniques for maintaining a sense of continuity wherever you live, to minimize the sense of upheaval. A family in Wheaton, Illinois, that has made
several moves has in its last two moves built houses identical on the inside. The wife explained to me that the family did this deliberately to provide a sense of stability

for the children. The cherished pictures and antiques, the furniture, the curtains, the refrigerator, and the children's rooms remain in the same spots in each new home.

Philip Slater, chairman of the sociology department at Brandeis University, wonders if we may have to learn to cope with mobility by dramatically de-emphasizing personal possessions.[2] He explains:

"Ultimately it seems inevitable that Americans must either abandon their nomadic habits (which seems unlikely) or moderate their tendency to invest their libido exclusively in material possessions. . . . The new culture is of course pushing hard to realize the second alternative, and if it is successful one might anticipate a trend toward more simply furnished dwellings in which all but the most portable and decorative items are permanent installations."

The four major problems most commonly mentioned by the 74 newcomers were:

1. *Obtaining needed household and personal services.* Here the wives most often mentioned problems of getting cleaning women and baby sitters. A Darien wife said: "If you want a cleaning woman here forget it." One woman complained her most aggravating problem was finding an adequate hairdresser.

2. *Overcoming mistrust of yourself as a stranger.*

A young wife in Azusa said it was hard there "to feel a part of things. There seems to be a lot of mistrust and that is hard to overcome unless you really work at it."

3. *Finding medical services.*

Pediatricians and obstetricians seem particularly busy, or choosy about taking on new customers. And there were complaints about the scarcity of family doctors. One wife said she always asked the advice of the local realtor selling them a house. And one studious wife said she checked out the background and training of potential doctors by consulting the American Medical Association listings in the local library.

A national report on the doctor shortage in 1969 indicated clearly that the worst shortages of doctors were in the new communities or rapidly growing areas.[3] The report stated: "Many families moving to new communities say they contact up to half a dozen doctors before they find one willing to accept them as patients. In waiting rooms the delays, seemingly, are interminable, and, the patients claim, illness often is treated perfunctorily, tardily, or not at all." It reported that in Willingboro, New Jersey, a Philadelphia suburb which had grown by 10,000 within a year, the town's three pediatricians hadn't accepted any new families as patients in the past half year.

4. *Making new friends.*

This was cited most often. And a Darien wife observed: "I have found it most difficult to make friends since moving to Darien. I am not speaking of bosom friends—just casual acquaintances."

I will take up this challenge of rebuilding a social circle in the next chapter.

12.

On Rebuilding
a
Social Circle

When I asked 74 newcomers to their areas what could be
done to ease the sense of strangeness occasioned by moving into a new neighborhood, about one fourth either
said, "Nothing much," or that they didn't know. One
woman said, "Nothing can ease the pain except time."

Studies indicate that neighborhoods vary tremendously
in the amount of time it takes before newcomers feel they
are accepted. For many people, this time factor greatly
influences the degree of satisfaction they will feel with
regard to their new neighborhood. Columbia University
sociologist Herbert Gans finds, too, that how the newcomers will feel they "fit," and whether they came by
choice or not, significantly shapes the feelings they will
have about the new neighborhood.

Much of the old gregariousness toward newcomers—so
characteristic on the lonely frontier—is disappearing from
American life. Newcomers I contacted complained bitterly
about the snobbishness and aloofness of people in older,
established neighborhoods. On the other hand the "per-
manents" in such established neighborhoods insisted they

were not snobbish but were just tired of having parties for newcomers—only to find them moving on within a year or two. A woman who is a long-time resident of a New England town near me put it this way: "I used to be critical of a lot of things here that looked like snobbery. Now I can see that when you've been here awhile you just don't want to be bothered by somebody who's new. You have your friends and the new people are probably only going to stay a couple of years—and I guess you forget what it's like to be the other one."

Several high-mobile newcomers told me they much preferred to look for homes in new areas rather than in established neighborhoods, when they haven't been cued in by their companies on areas appropriate to their status and that of their company. For those who rent, town-house complexes were mentioned as high-mobile places where the residents are outgoing about welcoming newcomers.

In new high-mobile areas, people tend to be more outgoing not only because they themselves are somewhat socially insecure but because of the special character of such areas. These still lack many normal amenities of a community such as churches, clubs, trees, day nurseries, and playgrounds. Incoming residents develop a shared concern over the need for such amenities.

Still, a new and more standoffish attitude toward one's neighbors has, as noted, developed in areas that are in flux or are fragmenting. Writers Arlene and Howard Eisenberg put it well when they said: "Today we seem more concerned with good neighborhoods than good neighbors."

Many people seem to feel that if you get caught up in neighboring you will find yourself in a whirl of making instant friendships—expected at daily kaffeeklatsches to gossip, constantly borrowing sugar, and taking turns having weekly barbecue-and-booze parties. Such things do happen, where frenetic neighboring gets out of hand. In a well-organized neighborhood a neighbor does not necessarily become one's friend, and that is mutually understood. You reserve your friendship for congenial people whom you enjoy being with and whom you learn to respect and trust. In a strange community it takes time to find these special people. But though an immediate neighbor's role may be less than that of a friend, he should be a person who welcomes you to a community, who sees that you have a chance to meet a variety of the neighbors who might interest you, and who has a special understanding with you that you will help each other in emergencies.

A young wife I know disclosed an interesting technique for assessing areas where she and her husband were considering buying a house. She said: "One of the things we did on this move that we hadn't done before was that I actually went around and knocked on doors and talked with neighbors to get a feeling of the neighborhood to be sure we would be reasonably compatible. We ruled out our favorite house because I didn't think we could have lived comfortably in that neighborhood."

Although the moving van companies frown on the jam-up in the summer, moving in the warm months, at least in the northern half of the United States, makes sense for quite another reason than that it is school vacation time. In the summer there are far more opportunities for a newcomer to have casual encounters outdoors with his new neighbors informally as they putter on their lawns, have playpens out in the yard, and sun themselves.

Children are also aids to settling into a new community. Less hindered by protocol in starting up acquaintanceships, their curious new acquaintances are soon tagging into their houses to look around.

The amount of the newcomer's education is also a factor in determining the speed of integration into a neighborhood. Working-class wives with no more than a high school education are usually more fearful of strange situations than college-educated wives, who not only are higher in socializing skills but often have moved enough times to be old hands at the techniques of integrating themselves into a strange neighborhood.

A good indicator of the changed attitude toward neighboring is the lack of consensus on who should call on whom first. Traditionally, simple good manners dictated that when a new neighbor moved in next to you it was up to you to extend some sort of hospitable greeting. This could range from dropping by to chat, to welcoming them the first day with a casserole, to forming a committee of wives or husbands to call on them, to inviting them over for a drink, to organizing a party for them or their children.

I first became aware times were changing about twenty years ago when a grande dame I knew in Connecticut confided how she was coping with the influx of new neighbors. She still felt compelled to observe the old etiquette but she did it by watching out the window till she was sure the newcomers were not at home. Then she would stride over to their house, knock and, receiving no answer, leave her calling card.

Today many people are simply confused about how they should treat new neighbors. In many cases, especially in cities, people resolve the puzzle simply by ignoring one another—or by nodding in the elevator. Of the newcomers I queried in four towns, about a third with definite opinions felt neighbors should do *more* to make newcomers welcome. A woman in Darien reported:

"No one on the lane of some twenty-two families phoned or called in person to welcome us to the community. We have been here a year and have only a nodding acquaintance with the neighbors—and not all of them."

On the other hand some enclaves within Darien—particularly the newer ones—apparently offer the more traditional warm welcome. For example, a young wife who had moved five times in six years of marriage said: "We were fortunate in our blind choice of a neighborhood. Our lane is very friendly. Our next-door neighbors greeted us on moving-in day with stew and biscuits."

The U.S. South and West have reputations for being more hospitable but a woman in Azusa, California, who had moved down from Oregon reported: "It could have been better. Nobody said 'Hi' for quite a while. It would be nice to have a welcoming committee." Another noted that "people are hard to get acquainted with here."

The result of all this wariness and confusion is a new assertiveness on the part of many newcomers, even at the risk of seeming too forward. United Van Lines, which provides clients with a consulting service on how to survive a family transplanting, suggests, "The days of neighbors welcoming new families are almost gone. You will have to make the first move in most cases." An official of Welcome Wagon echoed the same conviction when she said: "How do people get to know each other today? Newcomers are supposed to call on the existing neighbors. Don't expect the old to call on you."

And Helen Giammattei and Katherine Slaughter in their guidebook, *Help Your Family Make a Better Move,* suggested: "Go more than half way. Take it upon yourselves as a family to become active in areas of interest that involve other people."

Some realtors, in selling or renting a house, try to prod residents into welcoming the newcomers by sending reminders that they have a new neighbor. One realtor in my town sends a mimeographed letter that begins: "To introduce your new neighbors." It gives their names, where they are from, lists the names and school grades of their children, and identifies the house they have bought.

Informal techniques to develop acquaintances are evolving in many areas. The young wife of a new teacher in high-mobile Great Falls, Montana, said that though she still did not know anyone on her block, "We have developed a number of friends through the bowling alley where we play. I bowl one afternoon a week with a lot of real nice girls and we have met several couples at the alley. The alley develops leagues which any girl can join and you are periodically put on a different team with people you don't know."

Other newcomers to Great Falls indicated that Tupperware Home Parties were becoming a widely used way for wives to get to know one another. These parties are held in many parts of the United States. The wife who agrees to let her home be used for a display of Tupperware products gets extra points that she can use for getting products free or at discount; the number of points she gets depends on how many potential customers she can get into her house and how much they buy. She is supposed to serve coffee and dessert. In Great Falls people flock to the parties and may buy a product or two but what they are mainly seeking is sociability and a chance to meet neighbors. There are also Beeline home fashion parties and Fashion 220 cosmetic home demonstration parties that serve as ways to meet neighbors.

In more stable Glens Falls, New York, according to several informants, annual block parties are held for adults to which all newcomers are invited.

Since neighbors in many areas have become undependable at helping newcomers integrate into the new community, there is increasing dependence on affiliating with organizations that will quicken the newcomers' pace of involvement.

Churches play an important role here. Don't just *go* to church. The old friendliness of earlier decades when after the service everyone chatted with people in nearby pews has disappeared in many areas. The churchgoers are more likely to march out as from a funeral parlor and head for their cars. To become integrated you need to become an *active* churchgoer. Go to the Wednesday night discussion meetings that are followed by coffee and cake; volunteer for the choir or to teach a Sunday school class. Teachers in unsettled areas are usually badly needed.

Most ministers recognize that in our increasingly mobile society, service to newcomers is an important part of their mission. Many seek out newcomers by getting lists of new residents that are put out by many Chambers of Commerce. In high-mobile Wilton, Connecticut, the Zion Hill Methodist Church has "neighborhood cells" who are assigned to spot any incoming moving van in their area and report it to the minister.[1] This is supplemented by information the church gains through membership in a six-church joint welcoming committee that collects names of new arrivals from all possible sources. The churches take turns each month calling on newcomers, learning their denomination, and directing them to the proper church or one close to it in doctrine. About 50 percent of the membership of the Presbyterian church is transient, which perhaps reflects that church's strong appeal to corporate manager types.

A whole new literature is evolving to guide ministers in helping the frequent movers. One aspect of the literature that transients seem to respond to particularly, the Methodist minister in Wilton observed, is the emphasis on you-can-take-it-with-you values.[2]

The church is only one organization that offers instant involvement. Having observed life of high-mobiles in Birmingham, Michigan, and elsewhere, Helen Giammattei advised me that young families have become adept at using organizations—YMCA, Scouts, local politics, PTA, etc.—as a method of instant "plug-in" when they move to a new community.

The organizational role at which the newcomer is most welcome is that of fund raiser. Fund-raising organizations are chronically short of personnel, and the newcomer who volunteers to raise funds in his or her neighborhood is assured of being invited inside virtually every house when he or she solicits. Some residents who have let months go by without welcoming a new neighbor find it a bit embarrassing to have a first encounter when he turns up on the doorstep soliciting for the Red Cross. On the other hand one of my long-time neighbors expressed annoyance that the local chairman of a polio drive had called and asked if she would handle the soliciting in our area. She begged off, and blurted to me: "I don't see why they keep after me when there are so many new people on the road who want and need to meet people."

A wife near Birmingham, Michigan, complained that in the last town she had lived in she had had to start all over again as a block worker. To her this was obviously unreasonable. She felt that in a mobile society there should be criteria of experience in fund raising so that when you moved to a new town you could start off at the same level you had achieved by prior experience.

Another type of organization that is helpful for instant

plug-in is a national, good-anywhere-type group. These include, for women, the American Association of University Women, the Junior League (as noted earlier), the League of Women Voters; and, for men, their professional associations (such as educators have), the Rotarians, etc.

Then there are almost always the newcomer clubs. There are in fact at least 4,000 of these in the United States. Most have emerged in the last decade to meet a felt need of a high-mobile society. Many are launched by Welcome Wagon but others are sponsored by civic organizations. Their activities tend to be female-oriented, but they become couples clubs for gourmet dinners or dances. In New England, newcomer clubs are more *family*-oriented and put more emphasis on trips to zoos, boat excursions, and picnics.

The Newcomers Club in Darien, for example, is open to any newcomer in town and is extremely active. (Dues are $10.50.) In practice, the members are mainly couples and the male usually has a managerial or professional job. This may be due partly to the type of activities undertaken by the club and partly to the fact that most newcomers to Darien are of the managerial-professional sort. You can be a member for two years. In the yearbook of members I inspected a lot of names were crossed out. It was explained that they had already moved on. The gracious blond president in 1970, Mrs. William Haines, explained: "Boy, do they move fast. Eight months after I came into office I had lost two of my board members."

But while they are members Darien's newcomers have a dazzling array of events going and members can sign on for whatever activities appeal to them most. The arrangements of details for a single month's activities require a few thousand phone calls. Basically there are these types of events to choose from:

BRIDGE GROUPS
SPORTS GROUPS
EXCURSION GROUPS (*to early American villages, silversmiths, etc.*)

THEATER GROUPS (*busing members to New York matinees*)
GOURMET DINNERS

In addition there are two dinner dances a year and a lobster bake on the beach.

The intricacy of planning and the personal interaction that develops can perhaps best be seen in the regular gourmet dinners. Fourteen groups of six couples each are formed. On the scheduled night the fourteen groups meet in fourteen homes and eat the identical menu. Each couple is assigned a dish to prepare and given a recipe for it. On a recent German dinner night, the fourteen groups in fourteen homes feasted on:

Lachstuten mit Rahm
(*Smoked Salmon with Cream Filling*)
Kraftbruhe
(*Clear Mushroom Soup*)
Kassler Rippchen Glace
(*Smoked Loin of Pork with Sauerkraut and Grapes*)
Spinat, auf Salzburger Art
(*Creamed Spinach, Salzburg Style*)
Rumtopf and Meringues
(*Rum Pot and Bite-Size Meringues*)

Each of fourteen hostesses of the evening supplied her house, plus bread, coffee, and tea, and arranged for the group purchase of two suitable German wines.

For weeks afterward, newcomers meeting members from other dinner groups could compare notes on how the respective dinners went off.

When members of a newcomer club move on—as they typically do—they usually immediately check in with the newcomer club at the next stop. Thus newcomer clubbing becomes a way of life and a world of its own, usually quite apart from the world of the people who consider the town their home town. There is little likelihood that by building their social life around other newcomers they will become a part of the town they live in, in any real sense. But that, perhaps, is the way many have come to prefer it.

13.

New Institutions to Serve High-Mobiles

At hundreds of U.S. airports built for mobile Americans in the past twenty years the most conspicuous shop is usually one selling gift items. Some of these shops may also sell periodicals and they sell house-gift items for people you are going to visit. But it has been discovered that large profits can be made by selling tokens of love to guilt-ridden breadwinners who have been away from their spouses and children several days or weeks on business trips, and have to cope with that question, "Whatcha gonna bring me?"

At several points in this book I have indicated that the wholesale fragmentation of people has led to the creation of new kinds of institutions and services, from trailers and retirement villages to professional slave markets and telephone calling services for the lonely. I have also alluded briefly to new types of entrepreneurs serving people who move frequently. Here in this chapter I'll offer a closer look at several types of intriguing new institutions that have emerged to serve, or profit from, high-mobiles who are moving frequently or have to travel a lot.

EARLY SPOTTING OF PROSPECTIVE MOVERS

Entrepreneurs are discovering that getting advance tips on corporate personnel or other people who are about to move to another state or area can be big business indeed. U.S. corporations transferring personnel spend at least a billion dollars a year on the costs of house-hunting, plane fares, auto rental while house-hunting, household moving, house-selling, etc.; and the transferees themselves will be spending a few hundred million. The *Hotel Newsletter Weekly* estimates that corporate transferees now account for possibly 40 million "room nights" per year in U.S. hotels or motels. Transferees moving across state lines alone account for about three million real estate transactions a year.

But how do you spot and get to this family generating so many dollars before your competitors? Often the first clue comes when he approaches a local realtor about unloading his current house. Or it may come when he sounds out a local moving van company.

Out of this yearning of entrepreneurs to get first crack at helping the about-to-move family has emerged a remarkable cooperative. The prime mover in its formation has been a Towson, Maryland realtor named Donald E. Grempler, who set up something called the ASK International Real Estate Network. (ASK means Automatic Service Komputer.) This computerized network began sending out tips to affiliated realtors in the towns to which families were moving. At first the tips were provided mainly by a local realtor who had been approached about selling a house, usually that of a transferee. More recently ASK has been sending tips to—and receiving tips from—a number of highly interested affiliated companies outside the real estate field.

They have included: North American Van Lines, Hilton Hotels, Trans World Airlines, and Hertz Rent-a-Car. A hotel industry official called this tip-flashing combine "a brilliant sales package."

When the transferee, or any other mover, arrives in a new town, the news may be flashed to local businessmen by another type of organization that has emerged. In New York, for example, there is an organization called New Comers. It promises prospective clients: "Every month we provide the names and addresses of all new families moving into the area you specify at 25¢ per name. . . . New family names sold to you will not be sold to any competitor."

THE HOME FINDERS

People who move to a strange metropolitan area are often bewildered about where to start, looking for a place to live (as noted in Chapter 2). Greater Chicago, for example, has seventy-odd "community areas" inside the city—and even more suburbs. Greater New York covers twenty-two counties in three states. And the sprawl of Greater Los Angeles is endless. As one home consultant put it: "A buyer can waste days and days and days going to communities which might not be suitable for his family at all."

Back in the early 1950s a tall, taciturn neighbor of mine in Connecticut, a textbook editor named Donald McPherson, began wondering if this dilemma of the modern mover didn't spell opportunity. He opened up a tiny office in New Canaan, Connecticut, with the ambitious title Homerica. His slogan became: "Transplanting torn-up roots is our business." He would find an appropriate home for you anywhere in the whole of America. How? By getting all your specifications about what kind of neighborhood and house you wanted, matching them with a file he was building on America's communities—and then referring you to an affiliated realtor on the spot who would have your specifications and show you around. And you wouldn't have to pay Mr. McPherson a penny. He would be compensated by getting a split (then 40 percent) of the brokerage fee earned by any affiliated realtor who sold you a house.

Today it turns out that Homerica was too modest a name. The company has affiliated brokers also in such places as Canada, England, Belgium, Germany, Italy, and Switzerland. The organization now has more than 1,000 affiliated brokers, and it has regional offices in New York, Chicago, and Los Angeles. Since he began Homerica it has helped more than 65,000 families relocate.

Meanwhile in the late sixties a rival firm based in New York emerged. Executive Homesearch is a division of Previews, Inc., the international real estate marketing firm which serves as a clearing-house for posh homes all over the world. Its experience with mobile "upscale" families inspired Previews to move into the home search problems of executives both within the United States and Europe. Executive Homesearch works through more than 400 member brokers and the nine Previews branch offices located in major cities and Paris. Its staff of experts tries to help executives and their families prescreen communities.

An official says one of the trickiest problems his firm has in keeping up to date in its nationwide research is the quality of schools. With so many suburbs undergoing explosive growth, a fine school within a single year can become overcrowded. Taxes and school budgets will all of a sudden become a problem and a mass exodus of the school's best teachers often occurs over the summer.

Still another approach to instant home-finding for migrants, after undergoing experimentation by the National Association of Real Estate Boards, has become nationwide. About 2,500 real estate offices use a system called Realton, Inc.; and competitors with computers have sprung up. Under this system detailed information on all houses for sale in an area, such as northern Virginia, is fed into a computer. If you are planning to move to that area you fill out a form listing your specifications (or aspirations) for a home. When the proper buttons are punched, out comes a list of available houses—if there are any—that come close to fitting your specifications.

Guidebooks on communities and city areas are now being sold to house-hunting newcomers in airports of such large metropolitan areas as Cleveland, Detroit, and Pittsburgh.

A quite different and specialized approach to home finding is provided by Area Consultants, Inc. Originally it confined itself to serving as a guide to Greater New York but is now broadening out. Area Consultants is retained by corporations to help their transferees relocate —for a flat fee of $200 per relocated employee. Most commonly it is called in by corporations preparing to make a mass transfer of from several dozen to several hundred employees.

In a single month Area Consultants was helping Allied Chemical make a shift of operations from Manhattan to Morris Township, New Jersey, in which 1,600 positions were involved . . . helping Xerox move its headquarters personnel from Rochester, New York, to Stamford, Connecticut . . . helping Standard Oil of New Jersey move a subsidiary from Manhattan to New Jersey . . . helping Hoechst Pharmaceutical Company move from Cincinnati, Ohio, to New Jersey.

Mr. and Mrs. Robert Stahl got the idea for Area Consultants after their own tribulations in being transferred by an electronics company from California to New York City. A quiet, no-nonsense man, Mr. Stahl is now president.

The company's service to corporations in mass moves is psychologically oriented. It has a staff psychologist and draws upon the services of numerous behavioral scientists. The people at Area Consultants know the dread of the unknown that sweeps through a company when a mass move is impending. And they know that the wives are particularly apprehensive because, unlike their husbands, they identify with their homes, not with the company. So in addition to offering frank advice on the three best possible places to look for a house or apartment near where the breadwinner will work they conduct confidential surveys to find what is most worrying employees at the company about the move. And they hold dinner meetings, with wives urged to attend, at which they seek to ease

the fear of the unknown by a candid briefing, with color
slides, of the area to which the mass move is being made.

HOUSE DISPOSERS

Don McPherson's innovative thinking did not end when
he created Homerica to provide a nationwide home-
finding service.

As corporate transfers of personnel grew and grew it
soon became apparent to him that the bigger problem in
a move was frequently not in helping the transferee find
a new home but in helping him get rid of his current
one.

In areas where real estate was booming the transferee
could usually handle the sale himself and often at a profit.
But in overbuilt areas (a year or two ago these included
Midland, Texas; Oklahoma City, Oklahoma; and Cape
Kennedy, Florida), or in essentially one-company towns
where business had become sluggish, a transferee often
could not find a ready buyer at what he fancied his house
was worth. Morale sagged if he had to go to his new assignment and leave his wife and family behind until a
buyer could be found.

To prevent such collapses of morale many companies
set up real estate departments and offered help in various
ways: some even began to buy up slow-moving houses of
transferees. This practice got some corporations uncomfortably deep into local real estate and sometimes led to
tense situations. For example IBM had such a plan for
purchasing unsold houses and in one instance took over
the house of a man in the Philadelphia area who was
being transferred elsewhere. About a year later the man
was transferred back to Philadelphia. Since the company
had not yet managed to dispose of the house it had taken
over from him, it highly recommended that he move back
into the house and resume ownership. The man told
IBM officials that they were crazy if they thought he was
going to move back into that old shack again!

As Don McPherson began hearing about hundreds of

such touchy situations he created a new company called Homequity, Inc. At first it simply managed, for corporations, the disposal of houses of people being transferred. This didn't get the companies out of real estate and it didn't give Homequity the freedom it felt it needed. So in 1964 Homequity took the giant step of offering to purchase at appraised market value hard-to-move houses of transferees. It paid the taxes, insurance, maintenance, and cost of making the house more salable until the house was finally sold. Working for the corporate employer, Homequity's reward for its activities depends upon its effectiveness but typically averages out to more than 10 percent of the home's appraised value and is paid by the client corporation.

By the spring of 1972 more than 80 of the nation's larger corporations had turned over their housing headaches to Homequity. In 1972 Homequity was grossing about $24 million a year in billings and had moved into a splendid new headquarters building in Wilton, Connecticut. It expected to sell its twenty thousandth home before the end of the year. Further evidence that Homequity has become the tail that wags the dog is seen in the fact that still booming Homerica is now just a division of Homequity!

I should add that a number of other organizations eager to help corporations with their home-disposal problems have also been springing up across the country.

THE EMPLOYER'S OWN RELOCATORS

In the decade from 1959 to 1968 there was a sharp rise in the number of companies forecasting that they would be moving an increased number of employees in the future. This at least was the finding of a university study financed by United Van Lines, in which 649 companies responded by supplying information. The study found that over the same period there had been a decline from 92 to 76 percent in the proportion of employees who accepted transfers willingly.

Such factors have inspired the larger companies that commonly are involved in shifting divisions or headquarters to new locations or opening plants or offices in new areas to get more deeply involved in the human side of moving. IBM has a relocation department to handle large moves in its office products division. A spokesman for a major home search firm confessed that IBM's community profiles and information on housing in New Jersey were even more complete than its own files.

Companies with many plants and offices, such as General Electric, have a department that assesses communities; and a number of its experts are especially trained to size up the quality of life in each community, its amenities and any negative features that might cause talented personnel to balk at wanting to live there.

When Shell Oil decided to shift about 1,400 people from New York to Houston (see Chapter 3) its staff of relocation specialists thoroughly researched the school and housing situation in Greater Houston, conducted many orientation sessions for fifteen or twenty people at a time on what to expect in Houston, and tried to keep the employees' visits to Houston, which Shell financed, on an individual basis. A spokesman explained: "Some companies herd the new people being transferred around in buses. We think that is psychologically bad."

Apparently Shell overlooked, however, another "psychologically bad" factor, at least in the early stages. One Shell wife, upon discovering no provision was being made for her to accompany her husband on the inspection-house-hunting trek to Houston, rather fearfully wrote a letter to a top Shell official arguing that wives should be included. To her surprise the official replied that her proposal was commendable; and it was followed.

SCHOOLS FOR
GROOMING INTERNATIONAL MOVERS

Now that more than 3,300 American companies conduct business overseas, some with large international dealings have developed courses to help their movers avoid business and social blunders. In addition, several dozen companies have combined to set up the non-profit Business Council for International Understanding.[1] It offers a four-week course for any U.S. business manager headed for service abroad. His wife can take the full course too—or just a special one-week course on coping with servants, shopping, school, etc. It is conducted in Washington, D.C., at American University and is somewhat comparable to the U.S. State Department's Foreign Service Institute for government personnel.

Thousands of executives and their wives from hundreds of companies have taken this course designed to cushion some of the cultural shock of being transplanted into alien territory. One of the more fascinating cautions offered is how close to stand to a national when in his country. While Americans and Englishmen normally stand about thirty inches apart in talking face to face, Latins feel more comfortable discussing things while about eighteen inches apart.

THE MOVING FLEETS

U.S. taxpayers might note with interest that a half billion dollars of their taxes each year go to pay the moving bills of families in military service.

Civilians—mostly corporate transferees—who are moving now are paying close to a billion dollars a year to the rapidly growing fleets of moving vans. During eight recent years while the population of the United States was increasing by 7 percent, the use of moving vans increased 58 percent. And with the growing affluence of most Americans the stuff the families lug along on a move has been increasing nearly a hundred pounds a year and is now on average close to two and a half tons per family. The families take along everything from barbecue grills and several TV sets per household to the long-buried casket of a deceased spouse.

The migratory American also is moving increasingly

greater distances. United Van Lines reports that every year for nine recent consecutive years the average distance a client-family moves has been increasing. Its clients tend to be of above-average income or people being moved by private or governmental organizations. From 1960 to 1968 the increase in distance clients moved rose from an average of 403 miles to 529 miles.

Americans tend not to fall in love with their moving companies, partly because moving is often traumatic anyway, and partly because of the frequent late deliveries, the broken furniture, or the misunderstandings about bills. One fundamental cause of the complaints has been the fact that the industry has grown so fast in order to try to meet demand. But a larger cause is that about three quarters of all movers hire a van during the three summer months when school is out. And there are peaks within this peak period. The vast majority of all movers want to move in the week around the first of each month. What this means is that most of the moving van companies have to hire a lot of extra people—who are necessarily amateurs at moving your furniture.

The moving van industry is fighting back against this concentration of moves in the summer with a propaganda war on two fronts. It is questioning the conventional wisdom that it is a bad idea to take a child out of school during the school year. Allied Van Lines, for example, cosponsored a two-day symposium at Loyola University on "The Effect of Change of Environment on the Child" in the hope of getting expert support for the notion that it may be better to transplant a child to the new school while school is in progress (despite the break in continuity of classroom work). And its magazine for clients, *The Allied Shield,* carried an article entitled "Moving During School Term? Many Parents Say—YES!"

Its second-front campaign is to promote the idea that America should change to year-round school terms, with staggered vacations. The industry is urging all school systems to adopt something like the pattern Atlanta's high schools operate around the year on a four-quarter basis. A student can choose to stay out for any one of the four quarters or keep studying right through all four. Year-round school programs are springing up in more than a hundred school districts in many states. There is an economic appeal in the fact that they provide better utilization of buildings and teachers.

Another interesting development in the long-haul moving van industry, in which drivers may be on the road for many weeks, is that many husband-wife teams are starting to occupy the cabs. Companies such as Red Ball are encouraging the practice since it helps reduce poor morale caused by loneliness and seems to cut down on accidents to both truck and cargo. The wives often take turns at the power-steering wheels of 16-ton trucks and are proving there is no special trick women can't master in deftly coping with the 13-forward-speed gearshift pattern.

Meanwhile the cost of hiring a moving van service has inspired a great many mobile Americans—especially those not being aided by their bureaucracies and those who have moderate incomes—to do their own moving by hiring a truck. This is especially popular with those who can keep the load to under a ton or can readily make two trips.

With such a load an ordinary man can hire a truck he can manage. A hardy family willing to try this can cut the cost of moving by two thirds. Truck rental services that permit you to hire a truck in your home city and drop it off at the city you are moving to are thriving. In 1971 Hertz Corporation reported it had—within one year —increased the number of towns and cities where it rented one-way trucks from 300 to 1,300.

THE FURNITURE RENTERS

Some moving van officials have speculated that the growth curve in size of loads might come down. An official of United Van Lines commented: "Many Americans are adapting to their mobile way of life—younger families are tending to acquire less in the way of permanent possessions that would hinder their capacity to move long distances on short notice."

This mood—plus the growth of apartment living—is giving rise to a whole new business institution: furniture renting. In Ardsley, New York—which is surrounded by transplanted corporate headquarters—International Furniture Rentals advertises: *"Short or Long Term to Individuals, Companies, Apartment Owners and Managers— Complete Apartments Done in Excellent Taste, Economically. One Room to a Complete House."*

THE PEOPLE RENTERS

Because of the quick, temporary need for problem-solvers at plants or offices where the needed problem-solvers are scarce, a number of management consulting firms have entered the "body-renting" field. They supply chemists, physicists, and engineers, for example, to companies around the U.S. which have a short-term need for such special skills.

People-renting of a more exotic type is also flourishing because of the increasing transience of businessmen and others who attend conferences and conventions or take short-term assignments far from home. The entrepreneurs provide companions of the opposite sex on a contract basis. Some entrepreneurs are simply using their firms as fronts for providing call girls. But many others insist in their contract that the companion for the evening is to be treated just as that; and they have the endorsement of their local Chambers of Commerce. A number receive requests —which they are prepared to fill—for companionable females who are middle-aged. Clients often can pay the cost of the companion service by credit card. And at least one companion-renting service has developed a chain with offices in a number of cities in the Southwest.

THE PACKAGE RELOCATORS

A number of new enterprises offer to take over *all* or almost all of the headaches of getting you relocated.

One such firm, appropriately located in the transfer town of Darien, is called the Vanguard Executive Transfer Service. It is run by a robust, vigorous woman named Anne Wehmann, who began in the moving van business and spread out. She is, for example, a licensed real estate broker and does a good deal of co-broking. Four husky sons help her. She will, by adjusting the fee, do as much as you want, including:

—*Sell your current house*
—*Buy you a new one at the new location*
—*Pack your possessions*
—*Handle your personal transportation*
—*Have your rugs cleaned*
—*Get your animals transported*
—*Take charge of selling the possessions you wish to leave behind*

She does this last by having a tag sale—at which a dozen ladies help her. She has sold $4,000 worth of things people wished to leave behind in four hours. Those items that don't sell immediately, at the tag sale, go on sale in her consignment shop.

THE CHURCHES FOR A MOBILE SOCIETY

Churches are not only starting to appear in shopping malls; at least 65 drive-in churches have emerged on the U.S. landscape, from one outside Syracuse, New York, to a handsome glass-towered one in Garden Grove, California. Many improvise by taking over drive-in movie lots on a Sunday morning. Others build their own special drive-in structures. The sermons can be heard through window speakers.

Another manifestation of temporariness in churches is that one near Bethlehem, Pennsylvania, is rented on a twenty-year lease from a businessman who perceives there will always be a market for his structure in some denomination or organization.

These are not isolated situations; they represent a new concept that is taking hold in the minds of many leaders of at least Protestant Christianity. The journal, the *Christian Century,* a few years ago devoted a lead editorial to "A Time for Tents." It said that the "phenomenal mobility" created by the increasing speed of the redistribution of the American population was forcing churches to radically rethink their mission to the world. "The churches cannot minister effectively to a mobile population if they cling nostalgically to traditional forms of architecture," the editorial said. It called for "a mobile church for a mobile age. This is not the time for the churches to build permanent temples. . . . Rather this is a time in which churches should live in tents, prepared on short notice to move toward and with the people."

THE INNS FOR HIGH-MOBILES

A vivid measure of the increased movement of people is the explosive growth of motor inns located mainly on the edges of cities and towns. A very large proportion of their clients are people in transit to new homes or people traveling on job assignments. Almost all can sleep 150 to 400 people. There are the chains of Ramada Inns, the Howard Johnson Inns and, most conspicuously, the Holiday Inns. When my travels took me to the small, presumably sleepy Deep South city of Columbus, Mississippi, I worried about finding agreeable accommodations. What I found was a large Holiday Inn with three newly added annexes, and a car in front of almost every room. There are sizable Holiday Inns in Conway, Arkansas; Crossville, Tennessee; Santee, South Carolina; Seymour,

Indiana; Ephrata, Pennsylvania; Tewksbury, Massachusetts—and two in Dyersburg, Tennessee.

The first Holiday Inn was built just twenty years ago in Memphis, which became the world headquarters for a chain of 1,200 inns. The inns usually bed down more than 100,000 road-weary Americans per night. The company's affiliated International Inns operate in Europe and several countries outside Europe. Holiday Inn officials confidently expect that by 1980 they will have 3,000 inns going, in just about every corner of the globe.

THE ORGANIZED GREETERS

Memphis, oddly enough, gave birth to another now far-flung business enterprise geared to dealing with a mobile society. Welcome Wagon International, Inc., is managed and staffed mainly by women and the service it performs is to have its "basket ladies" call on newcomers in approximately 3,000 towns and cities in the United States, Canada, England, and Scotland.

These basket ladies, bringing a word of welcome, are often the first people to call on a newcomer in the strange new town, and for that reason alone are often welcomed in return. What they bring in addition to a word of welcome is in the basket: gift samples of merchandise from merchants, banks, etc., hoping for their patronage, and—so that they will not seem crassly motivated—a great deal of helpful printed material about the new community: its schools, churches, motor vehicle laws, town government, map of the town, etc. The revenue to Welcome Wagon International for this service comes from the local businessmen who pay a fixed fee for each call made. Usually the Welcome Wagon ladies find the newcomer being visited has specific questions—about doctors or Boy Scouts, for instance—which the basket ladies try to answer.

An additional function Welcome Wagon performs without charge—mainly to enhance its image of civic-mindedness—is the formation of social-civic clubs for newcomers

which each couple called upon is invited to join. Sometimes the club is called a Newcomer Club but more often
a Welcome Wagon Club or Welcome Wagon Newcomer
Club. As indicated, they provide a fast way for newcomers
to meet people—even if they are only other newcomers.

THE ORGANIZED
INVESTIGATORS OF NEWCOMERS

Reasons other than welcoming inspire local businessmen to take an interest in newcomers. The new arrivals
are potential customers and potential employees. With our
populace and work force more on the move than in earlier
decades—and with so many strangers in town—a major
national industry, with some multimillion-dollar corporations, has emerged to investigate potential customers and
employees.[2]

Businessmen are understandably eager to find out
whether newcomers or strangers interested in obtaining
their products, jobs, or services are deadbeats or slow
payers. Often they can get a line on the person from his
previous place of residence through the local credit bureau's information-swapping arrangement with thousands
of other credit bureaus. In some regions, particularly in the
Southwest, this information can be gotten instantaneously
by hitting computer buttons. But if up-to-date information
is hard to get the businessman may want some local
investigating done.

This need led a national credit association to set up a
subsidiary that had the word "welcome" in it. Its agents,
posing as greeters, made calls on newcomers to assess
their credit potentialities. Welcome Wagon International
went to great pains to establish that it was in no way
connected with any credit bureau and to deplore the
practices of its pseudo imitator.

PURVEYORS OF HUMAN CONTACT

The pervasive loneliness of our times has encouraged the growth of dial-a-shoulder telephone services in many parts of the United States and in England. In New York City a divorcee named Marion H. Parker, who had known loneliness, learned from the Census Bureau that New York City had 750,000 people who live alone. In short order she had a thriving telephone service, Care-Ring, that had a "telephone companion" call each subscriber twice a day at appointed hours, for a charge of less than a dollar a day. The companion and subscriber would chat for a couple of minutes during each call. From each subscriber Care-Ring obtained the names of his or her doctor, building superintendent, a neighbor, and a close friend. Thus when a subscriber failed to answer, and still didn't answer a half hour later, Care-Ring would go into action with the doctor, etc. One subscriber confessed that she was not particularly afraid of dying but dreaded the thought of her dog starving as a result.[3] Mrs. Parker is now in the process of franchising her services in other cities.

Loneliness also clearly accounts for much of the sharp upsurge in entrepreneurs offering people "group encounters." According to one estimate, six million Americans have flocked to at least one such session. The group encounter is an outgrowth—and in many cases a corruption—of the respected technique of "sensitivity training" pioneered by the eminent psychologist Kurt Lewin to promote openness in the expression of feelings. Most of the group encounter operators dabble with the "openness" of expression but their main selling point is the promise of close contact with others. With some groups it is the bodily contact of touching the hands or toes of another person. With many it involves feeling the nude bodies of males and females while in a pool or simply feeling and examining the genitals of others. The noted psychologist Carl Rogers, who studied group groping at a center in southern California, concluded that the people there were almost all transients in search of roots.

Parents without Partners is a rapidly growing organization to provide a meeting ground for some of the lonely people among the more than fifteen million families where, because of disruption or death, only one parent is present in the family setting.

In many cities radio stations—in search of new reasons for being—have moved massively into programs that provide the lonely or frustrated with one of the few remaining forums available where they can make themselves heard, pour out their problems, grievances, and prejudices or even their sexual puzzlements and fantasies. Philadelphia's stations WCAU and WPEN, for example, have gone increasingly into "talk radio" programs handled by "talk jockeys." A Chicago psychiatrist suggests that as loneliness has become endemic these jockeys have become surrogate friends for a great many lonely people.

At first the format was that the jockey would interview a celebrity, then open the show up to questions and comments by listeners. Now increasingly the listeners are permitted to talk or argue directly with each other, with the jockeys mainly moderating.[4] While I was driving in a rented car in Livonia, Michigan, I happened to hear one of these person-to-person exchanges of total strangers via my car radio. A lady in Grosse Pointe asked the universe of the program's listeners for help because she always had trouble getting her chopping block clean. In a matter of seconds a lady in Detroit was on the phone telling her, via radio, to use peroxide, from her hair-care closet.

Since television is more costly to produce, this medium invites the listening public to call in mainly on shows when celebrities have guaranteed listener pulling power. However television is very much involved in catering to isolates and other stay-at-homes. An example is the fact that every Sunday morning tens of thousands of Americans kneel in prayer before their TV sets at the direction of a TV evangelist such as Rex Humbard.

All in all, as these new institutions I've cited (perhaps religious aside) indicate, the mobile American has generated billions of dollars in business for firms that have the patience to cope with him.

PART THREE

Impact
on
the
Way
People
Behave

"It is reasonable today to view the whole continent as one's community for play and place of opportunity for success."—A HIGHLY MOBILE MARKETING EXECUTIVE CURRENTLY LIVING IN WILTON, CONNECTICUT.

14.

The Arguments for a High-Mobile Society

In a society that has traditionally been restless and now, in addition, has become hedonistic, geographic mobility is widely seen as a positive characteristic. It is often equated with progress.

Since the tens of millions of moves individuals make each year account for much of the uprootedness and social fragmentation occurring in America, I will here set forth the main arguments made for a nomadic society.

I will cite in this chapter what are seen as the positive aspects of high mobility and the arguments that the disadvantages have been overstated. Then, in succeeding chapters, I will present what seems to me persuasive evidence that high mobility and other causes of uprootedness today indeed have disturbing implications for the individual, the family, the community, and society at large.

POSSIBLE ADVANTAGES TO
THE INDIVIDUAL

There is, first, the broadening effect on people who move frequently.

I asked the 74 newcomers in four communities for thoughts they had on the advantages or disadvantages of moving every few years. Of those offering opinions about advantages, 44 percent mentioned this broadening effect in one way or another. They felt there were advantages in getting to know more about the different parts of their country, and that the exposure to the country and different communities made their children more adaptable to life.

Second, there is the fact that you have a chance to make new friends.

This was mentioned by 20 percent of those who mentioned advantages. A man who had moved sixteen times in twenty-two years of marriage contended he had at least acquired "a few close, lasting friends at every stop."

Then there is the fact that you may, by moving on, escape present frustrations or assumed stagnating situations.

John Steinbeck, in describing people he encountered on his camper jaunt around America with his dog Charley, observed: "They spoke quietly of how they wanted to go someday, to move about free and unanchored, not toward something but always away from something. I saw this look and heard this yearning in every state I visited."

A Darien wife who had moved five times in eight years of marriage said: "One cannot stagnate. You have to adapt, learn to change. There are always new, interesting people, fascinating places." Another Darien wife commented at a luncheon meeting where we were discussing mobility: "I lived in one place sixteen years. Charleston, South Carolina. And now we have moved three times in three years. Having experienced both, I find it very refreshing to move because I think you can get very stagnant in one place."

An editor who had lived an early life of high transience in New York and California apartments married a lovely girl he happened to encounter in a small city in South Carolina. Commenting on the marriage, he told me, "One of the things that attracted us to each other was that I needed more stability and she needed more mobility. It worked out well. When I see what happens to locals in her town who marry within the old families there is something rather frightening."

Fourth, there is the fact that moves can add to the zest of life.

A young wife in upper New York, who had moved three times in three years of marriage, said: "I am looking forward to moving again in a few years."

The remarkable wife of a plant manager in predominantly stable Glens Falls, New York, who had moved twenty times in fifteen years of marriage seems a prototype of the ebullient wife so cherished by corporations. She explained: "I move to a new area with the feeling I will meet new people and will have many happy experiences—and I usually do. I join groups right away and get involved. . . . I try to portray each move as an exciting new experience—the same way one would look at a vacation trip!"

Fifth, there's the fact that moving can often broaden an individual's economic opportunities.

A man who has moved at least twenty times since he was a young man and who became very successful as a corporate marketing executive likes to scoff: "Roots are ruts." He feels that people who become "stuck" in a town like Jamestown, New York, "never know what wonderful opportunities there are in the rest of the country." I might inject a possibly contrary comment made to me by a faculty member of Findlay College in the relatively backwater small city of Findlay, Ohio, which is in some ways comparable to Jamestown. He said: "There are more millionaires per capita here than in any city in Ohio. But you wouldn't know it from looking at their houses."

Sixth, there's the strong probability that a big journey

or move while one is young creates a challenge that promotes personal growth.

Such an event before the age of twenty-one can be found in the background of a great many people who by their achievements have become well known. The big journey or move can provide rigorous training in helping one relate to new people and new situations and it can, of course, broaden one's horizons.

Whether repeated transplantings through life continue to promote the same marked effect of stimulating achievement and creating breadth of viewpoint is, I believe, arguable. Some of my informants contended that they did. A wife in Darien who had moved seven times in nine years of marriage cited as a major advantage of moving that it forces you "to extend yourself as a person in order to meet people in a new location."

Seventh, there's the fact noted earlier that mobility is often helpful in preparation for a professional career.

During the decade when talented young people are between eighteen and twenty-eight their quest for the best education for their special interests may require, as the present system works, several moves and take them substantial distances from their homes.

Eighth, there's the contention that mobility promotes closer family ties and more equalitarian marriages.

It is unquestionably true that the members of an isolated, nuclear family which is frequently on the move tend to depend more on one another for companionship and for simple talk than a family immersed in a network of community friendship ties. The isolated family thus may become "closer."

As for mobility producing more equalitarian marriages, it seems reasonable to assume that the mobile wife is more apt to become lonely while spending the day at home alone being a housewife specialist in a relatively strange neighborhood, and may seek a job partly to ease the loneliness. The job-holding wife who also is a housewife tends to develop more clout in the family power structure and thus has a more equalitarian marriage.

Finally, there are the arguments that high-mobiles

theoretically have a wider range of choices in picking a spouse, an occupation, or places to live.

POSSIBLE ADVANTAGES TO THE ECONOMY

From a purely mechanistic viewpoint, there is little question that corporations with many offices or plants can be more efficient if their personnel can be treated as interchangeable cogs. And it is equally true that an over-all economy can come closer to operating at what is called "full capacity" if manpower can be depended on to flow automatically to areas where developments have opened up manpower shortages. It also eases unemployment if people will move into areas of shortage instead of being stick-in-the-muds in areas of surplus like much of Appalachia.

In erratic industries such as aerospace a highly fluid work force would seem, from the purely mechanistic viewpoint, especially desirable. Multibillion-dollar plane or missile contracts go to a contractor in the East and then may be canceled or phased out, sometimes in favor of a contractor in Texas, California, or the state of Washington. Scientists, engineers, technicians, and skilled craftsmen promote efficiency by scrambling cross-country to fill any available openings.

Further, such movement can prevent the development of acute shortages, which give unions the power to run up wage rates—and perhaps trigger local inflation.

An array of economists in industry, government, and universities have lauded a mobile work force. For example:

—Harvey Hamel of the U.S. Bureau of Labor Statistics contends that in a dynamic economy "a substantial degree of job mobility is needed to achieve full utilization of the labor force and enable the economy to operate at full capacity."

—Noted economist Peter Drucker: "Men and capital, the two mobile resources of any economy, must

be able to move into the most productive allocation
and out of employment in yesterday's work."

—Economist John B. Lansing, Survey Research Center, University of Michigan: "The geographic
mobility of labor is one of the basic processes of
adjustment in the economy of the United States.
. . . Failure of human resources to adjust to . . .
changes lead to inefficiency, poverty and dependency."

—The business journal, *Dun's Review:* "How can we
increase labor mobility? The right answer will go
a long way toward the elimination of 'pocket' unemployment. It also could mean a stronger, health-
ier and more profitable economy."

Still another economic argument for high mobility is
that people who move a lot buy more at the stores than
more stable types of people. At any rate the high-mobiles
are the darlings of the marketing world. There seem to be
four reasons why the high-mobile is a bigger spender,
whatever his income:

1. People who move a lot usually undergo a strong
"upgrading urge." They feel they should reward themselves
by seeking a bigger home with more extras.

2. At least one merchandising study indicated that
high-mobiles are faster to accept new kinds of products.

3. Frequent movers have to replace things they have
left behind, buy new rugs because their old ones won't
fit, etc.

4. High-mobiles—especially those who are emotionally
insecure—often are anxious to demonstrate to new neighbors that they are persons of substance by putting on
display evidences of their affluence, as by the kinds of cars
or boats they buy.

POSSIBLE ADVANTAGES TO SOCIETY

Many areas of the United States would not have become developed if it were not for the assured inflow of a mobile population.

The rapid interregional circulation of populations has helped areas that have been behind the country as a whole on such measures as education, development of the arts, spending for mental health, and social concern reduce such differences. The recent profound changes in the South, as noted in Chapter 1, are cases in point.

THE ARGUMENTS THAT NEGATIVE FACTORS HAVE BEEN OVERSTATED

Some contend that the concept that a lack of roots is unhealthy and a negative factor is outdated. With jet flights and expressways, it is argued, a person's "community" can be more diffuse geographically.

Actor and jet-setter Richard Burton in talking about life with his wife, the actress Elizabeth Taylor, said: "But travel has become to us, as to most itinerant professionals, a part of our lives. We have been forced by habit to become doomed nomads, incapable any more of being sweet stay-at-homes. . . . We find nowadays that staying in any one place for more than . . . three months is intolerable."

Saul Bellow, the novelist, who guesses he has "lived" in a couple hundred places, has a character in his book *Mr. Sammler's Planet* say, when asked if he had no desire to inherit his uncle's home so that he could have a sense of roots: "No, of course not. Roots? Roots are not modern. That's a peasant concept: soil and roots. Peasantry is going to disappear."

Several sociologists also have contended that the ill effects of mobility have been overstated.

Until about a decade ago sociologists were in pretty solid agreement that high membership turnover at least tends to break up small primary groups, whether kin, neighbors, or close friends. Then a few sociologists, led by Eugene Litwak of the University of Michigan, argued that this was not now necessarily so. Modern conditions, they held, provided new mechanisms for maintaining group cohesion.[1] This position is viewed skeptically by some, but what follows is the essence of the thinking of Litwak and those who have collaborated with him:

Group cohesion can be maintained where turnover in neighborhoods is rapid. You can do this by speeding up the process by which newcomers are inducted to the neighborhood. Group norms would state that newcomers are to be welcomed on sight; special "subunits" of the neighborhood would seek out newcomers and introduce them.

Contact with kinfolk can be maintained despite separation by distance. Modern means of communication—the telephone and the airplane—make it "increasingly easy" for families and individuals to communicate with each other even though not living within "immediate geographic proximity" of each other.

Contact with close friends can be maintained despite separation by distance. In this contention they advance most of the same reasons used regarding kinfolk.

Perhaps still another argument for contending that the negative implications of high mobility have been overstated is that it is unwarranted to assume people want to be friendly with their neighbors. This might be assumed from some of the comments already cited in this book. Perhaps we are witnessing a withdrawal syndrome. When I asked a husband and wife who were newcomers to high-mobile Azusa if they felt too many people were strangers there they said no, things "were as they should be." Implicit in their response was the view that people bother you when they are too friendly. Another Azusa man said: "It's the kind of a town that leaves you alone."

Judith Chayes Neiman, an official of the company that is pioneering new concepts in neighborliness at Columbia, Maryland, explained:

"Some people don't want to make the investment of

close acquaintance. Being someone's friend is a very involving process—but gratifying. You have to give something of yourself, and many are afraid of getting hurt."

Perhaps, too, today we have less functional need for congenial, dependable neighbors. We don't call upon neighbors to help us raise the barn roof as people did five decades ago. We don't even need neighbors to borrow ice from because we have our own ice makers.

And then there is the fact that television sets—which typically stay on several hours a day—provide instant neighbors such as David Frost and Lucille Ball who can be invited in at the flick of a switch, and sent away with another flick. A number of research scholars have started alluding to the "companionship substitution function" of television.

Many people isolated in cities, especially retired people, literally build their daily lives around TV programing. I know a retired couple from Missouri now living in a twelve-story Brooklyn apartment who have a nodding acquaintance with a few people in their building but know no one else in New York City except a relative. Each morning they shop and putter until their TV day begins. That is at 11 A.M. when they have a wide choice of serials and game shows to choose from. They watch fairly continuously until 4 P.M. when the kid shows start dominating the airways. At this point they stop and prepare dinner. After dinner they kill time for an hour by strolling, reading the paper, or hooking rugs. Then at 6 P.M. their TV day resumes and continues until 11:15 P.M. when they finish with the late news. After ten and a quarter hours communing with television they go to bed. It doesn't seem to bother them much any more that they know few people in their neighborhood even on a nodding basis.

More fundamental, perhaps, millions of Americans are now seeing their fellow men in general not as allies but as nuisance makers. We are so closely packed together—and walls often are so thin—that other people interrupt our solitude, clog the highways, and keep us from getting to work on time. They beat us to a parking place at the mall, they roar past our lakeside cottage with their 100-

horsepower boats going full blast. In short, people *in general* are seen as problems to be coped with.

There is also the argument that it is unwarranted to assume that temporary relationships are inevitably superficial ones.

Many people can recall having developed a deep sense of camaraderie and trust with another person on the basis of only a few months' acquaintance. When the other person moves on the experience becomes an important part of our memories. Reunions may even occasionally be arranged. But the relationship remains a pleasant—if past—episode in one's life.

Finally, one could argue that many people in the modern world are moving from a traditional *place-bound* society to a society in which they are involved in groups whose members may be widely scattered geographically. The most important colleagues of heart specialists, geologists, or atomic physicists, for example, may be scattered in many states yet in a sense the colleagues are their primary group, to use the sociological concept.

Whether such new kinds of affiliations are cutting people free from traditional patterns or whether almost all people still need some kind of sense of place remains to be settled. Possibly some clues will emerge in the chapters that follow.

"Once they arrive [in California] hardly anyone 'settles'—no familial or community traditions bind them. 'That's why we have so many nuts out here,' says Los Angeles pollster Don Muchmore. 'People come and do things here they wouldn't normally do back home because such behavior is unacceptable.'"—FROM A REPORT IN TIME MAGAZINE, NOVEMBER 7, 1969.

15.

Curious
Life Styles
of
Loosely Rooted
People

Not all Americans—or Californians—who find themselves uprooted or isolated are "nuts" or even convention-breakers. Many aren't fleeing conventions but just moving to or being transferred to a new area. And many of the uprooted, as we have seen, are not even mobile: the communities around them are undergoing upheaval or depersonalization.

But, for whatever reason, when a person finds himself caught up in an element of a society that is fragmenting with unusual rapidity the experience has, with uncommon frequency, a predictable impact on his or her life style. Six predictable kinds of impact seem particularly noteworthy:

First there is a tendency, as just indicated, for people to do things "they wouldn't normally do back home because such behavior is unacceptable." Or they shrug and tolerate such behavior in others. To put it another way, there is, in general, less concern for the social consequences of one's behavior and less sense that anyone cares how one acts.

Some newcomers are anxious to make a first strong impression on new neighbors to reduce their own sense of strangeness; but in an area where the populace is churning, concern for the good opinion of neighbors tends to diminish rapidly.

Unofficial social controls as traditionally enforced by disapproval of or ostracism from the community hold little terror for uprooted people. And official social controls as enacted by the local government—beyond such universally accepted controls as stopping for red lights—are often dimly understood and are viewed as the dictates of strangers.

For some, this lessening concern for the consequences of one's actions can seem liberating. For others it can seem disquieting. Those who find it disquieting feel themselves slipping into a normless environment that threatens interpersonal chaos.

A thirty-year-old salesman in high-mobile Sunnyvale was one Californian who seemed more uneasy than liberated. But he didn't feel his neighbors shared his concern. He recalled that in Canada as a boy he knew everyone in his neighborhood but that in Sunnyvale he knew none of his neighbors. And he added as a general comment, "There's no morality here and I guess it is because nobody knows anybody so that you can get away with stuff you couldn't in the old days when everybody knew everybody and what they were doing."

Consider some apparent symptoms of this new lessening of concern in many parts of America for the consequences of one's behavior.

For one thing personal bankruptcies, in which others get hurt, tripled during a recent ten-year period. What is most noteworthy is the increasing casualness with which people take this move that once represented an ultimate in humiliation. Two possible contributing explanations are that high-mobile people may be more prone to take chances on thin ice; and instant credit cards issued through anonymous, computerized credit card companies tend to depersonalize one's mounting indebtedness to individual creditors.

Patterns of crime also seem to be involved. There are many causes for the soaring U.S. crime rates involving dishonesty and stealing; but certainly a major cause is the depersonalization of metropolitan life. I will examine this in more detail in Chapter 17. People are far more willing to steal from strangers and institutions than from personal acquaintances: witness the contrast between life in small towns where doors frequently are left unlocked and life in big cities where residents often have three or four locks on a door.

Even the confused state of the U.S. economy in the early 1970s seemed to reflect lessened concern for the social consequences of one's behavior. Edwin L. Dale, Jr., a leading economic analyst for *The New York Times,* was trying to explain, in late 1971, the puzzling fact that inflation was persisting despite high unemployment. This was contrary to conventional economic wisdom. He speculated that perhaps a dramatic change in attitudes of Americans in recent years toward being greedier and more out for oneself has disrupted the normal market mechanism. Dale suggested: "A bitchy society will be a more inflationary society, no matter what the supply-and-demand curves of the economists may seek to prove." He noted that the nation had been seeing a new abuse of union power. And he added that such abuse "is far more likely in a condition of general psychological abrasiveness, in which the rank and file push the leaders into positions that are unreasonable." I would suggest that this apparent new greediness, abrasiveness, and unreasonableness are at least in part related to the rapid social fragmentation, created by both mobility and depersonalized living environments, which has been developing in much of the country. There is a lessened concern for social consequences of personal actions all along the line. And this attitude is not confined to the U.S.A. Perhaps it is reflected in the popular British quip: "I'm all right, Jack! Bugger you."

Perhaps too it is significant that the decline of the family doctor whom everybody knows has in the past few years been accompanied by an epidemic of negligence suits against doctors. In many cities medical service has become so depersonalized—and so many rootless residents never come to have a personal relationship with a doctor —that citizens in our bitchy society are suing the system. It is surely not a coincidence that the state that leads the nation in malpractice suits, California, is also the heartland of U.S. rootlessness.[1] While for the nation in general about 15 percent of all doctors have faced malpractice claims, in California the figure is close to 70 percent!

Finally there is the startling rise in premarital sexual relationships during the last two decades, along with an apparent increase in extramarital intercourse, premarital pregnancies, and the clear general rise in casualness about sexual intimacy. All are unquestionably related to some extent to the lessened concern for the social consequences of misbehaving, or what has historically been considered as misbehaving. There is less worry about and less awareness of society's disapproval in a nation of strangers. The mobility of families, the upheaval of neighborhoods, the travels of husbands (leaving lonely wives behind), the anonymity of big-city living and of multiversity living for young people far from their home communities all have undermined normal modes of social control. One of the grimmer sides of the new sexual permissiveness is that gonorrhea, despite wonder drugs, is rampaging throughout the country and involves all social classes. More than a million and half new cases are being reported each year, with some cities reporting 200 percent increases within one year. Public health officials in thirty major cities who were surveyed by *The New York Times* attributed the epidemic to a number of factors including "relaxed sexual morality," "increased promiscuity," and "greater mobility of the population."

The lessened concern about social consequences and the lessened awareness of social disapproval are also reflected in the decline in the permanence of marriage, which has produced a great increase in the millions of children who are products of broken homes.

While mobility intensifies the emotional dependence of husband and wife on each other for human companionship, the loosely rooted life style often creates immense strains that sour a love relationship. One obvious strain is disagreement about moving again if the husband wants to and the wife (perhaps having her own career) does not. And if there are quarrels there may not be anyone within a hundred miles who gives a damn whether or not they stay married, except perhaps small children caught in the middle of the quarreling. These stresses have led sociologists Warren Bennis and Philip Slater to conclude: "The future of marriage in a society of temporary systems remains uncertain."

It is undoubtedly more than a coincidence that the incidence of divorce by regions in America shows some rather striking similarities to the American Telephone & Telegraph Company's records revealing the incidence of mobility. And the similarity extends to Europe. AT&T finds that mobility in Western states is double that in the Northeast. Regarding divorce, the U.S. Office of Vital Statistics finds that the divorce rate in the West is more than four times as high as that in the Northeast. Mobility in the United States is far higher than that of European countries where comparisons can be made and much the same applies to divorce. No Western European nation has a divorce rate that approaches that of the U.S.A.

The contrast between divorce rates in Western states and those in the Northeast is in part due to the fact that several of those states now have passed laws making it simple to get a divorce; but perhaps the laws are symptoms of the regional mood arising from higher rootlessness. As with many other signs of rootlessness, California is the U.S. heartland of divorced individuals and their offspring. State records show approximately six divorces for every ten marriages. In Orange County southwest of Los Angeles, where the population recently grew 600 percent in thirteen years, eight divorces were recorded for

every ten marriages; and approximately the same ratio
applies to Los Angeles County. With adversary divorce
proceedings jamming the courts of California, the state
recently acted to remove the requirement that one partner
must prove in court that the other partner has been somehow at "fault" for the faltering marriage as part of a
general easing of grounds for gaining a divorce. Regarding the proneness of married Californians to shed partners and perhaps turn them in for new models, sociologist
Clinton E. Phillips of the American Institute of Family
Planning made this assessment:

"In California we have a highly mobile, anonymous,
transient, striving, thrill-seeking, experience-seeking population . . . people here have no roots, no family ties."[2]

The increased mobility of corporate managers, it might
be added, has been accompanied by a dramatic increase
in divorce among those who get near the top of their companies. In the 1950s, according to a study by Eugene
Jennings, only about 5 percent of the officers and presidents of corporations were divorced or legally separated;
now the proportion is approaching 33 percent.

A second way that a loosely rooted pattern of life affects
people's behavior with uncommon frequency is in their
approach to socializing. They either resign themselves to
relative aloneness and privatism or they tend to become
adept at instant gregariousness.

A man can become a pal for two hours with a stranger
he meets on the golf course with full knowledge that he
probably will never see the person again. The trick is the
knack for affability. The new gregarions can be fairly
indiscriminate in their selection of new friends, who become as interchangeable as cars. At least one investigation
of high-mobiles in new real estate developments has shown
that their "friends" are mostly within a hundred yards
and—allowing for friendships made with new company
colleagues—the friends thin out predictably with every
additional hundred yards from the house.

And if the recently arrived male commutes to a job his

socializing at home will be with husbands of women his wife has met while he is off at work.

I asked the wife of a plant manager who had moved twenty times in fifteen years of marriage and who had been in upstate New York only four months how many "close friends" she had within five miles. (Her closest relatives was 351 miles away.) She replied, "Six." But later when I asked her if she wished she had more good friends she could see every week she replied "yes."

Neil Morgan, San Diego columnist who is perhaps the most perceptive diagnostician of California's life style, had this to say about the Californian's socializing pattern in his book, *The California Syndrome:* "He drifts between communities of amiable strangers. He may be immensely affable with his neighbors, but he chooses to avoid personal entanglement: his closest friend may be 20 miles distance by freeway. He finds a sense of community with his neighbors only on the occasion of accidents, dog fights, wife beatings, fires, flash floods, or earthquakes."

The wariness about "personal entanglements" of the loosely rooted is not confined to Californians.

All this instant palship—while being careful to keep it at a superficial level—is producing a new widespread blandness in human relations. Keeping friendships bland and readily disconnectable seems harder on women than on men. They make more effort to keep in touch with friends in former locations. An oil company executive's wife in Connecticut confessed that in her family's first few moves she made really close friends. "It was painful when I had to leave. Now I have a tendency not to get so close. I don't like that but it's a protection—not to get hurt so much."[3]

Along with this, a new coolness is for many people coming over traditionally warm, supportive relationships. There is a wariness of involvement. People in emotional distress are often shunned because their acquaintances are losing the urge, or knack, of being compassionate. When an acquaintance dies and it is announced that friends are invited to call at the funeral home, many wonder if they really knew the deceased *that* well to get involved. Really close friends may be widely dispersed.

A couple of years ago an up-to-date mortician in Atlanta offered a modern solution to the "viewing" problem; he built a drive-in mortuary where the tilted body of the deceased could be viewed through a window. People could drive by, perhaps leave a card, and keep on going. They didn't have to get dressed up. And they didn't have to get involved in the uncomfortable business of personally sharing grief and offering compassion. It seems a logical innovation for a cool land of fragmenting people. Another logical innovation—since so many people are dying far from their immediate families, who upon hearing the news rush to arrange the funeral—is that many funeral parlors now routinely offer to provide pallbearers.

A third distinctive pattern in the life style of loosely rooted people is their peculiar approach to establishing and furnishing a house and buying possessions.

James Mills, president of Home Facts, Inc., and a consultant to builders, was telling me about the nesting habits of corporate transferees. He explained: "The transferee doesn't want to get zapped. He looks at a house, and its location, strictly as an investment. He's thinking about getting out even before he buys."

A long-time resident of Darien (where, incidentally, the national headquarters of Home Facts, Inc., are located) amplified Mills's comment by explaining the kind of house the transferee in Darien wants: "He always has to do the surer thing than your or I, who stay longer. He just doesn't want to make a shaky move. So he wants nothing unusual about the house. It's either a ranch or a colonial—and it is typical. Nothing different. The transferee doesn't want any surprises. We don't have many contemporary houses here. The contemporary house is a big risk if you are going to move on because it is a house with individuality. The transferee knows that a distinctive house with individuality is harder to move in a quick sale than a house without individuality."

The loosely rooted person is willing to pay high interest

rates (which encourage inflation) because he is not ex-
pecting to be stuck with the mortgage very long. He's
going to move on.

The transferee's wife in decorating the family's new
house also tends to be careful. For example, a wife near
Schenectady who had moved during almost every year of
her fifteen years of marriage told me:

"In decorating a new home I stay clear of vivid or
unusual colors that would only fit in a certain room. In
other words I settle for something that will move well,
rather than what I really like."

Transferees are wary of putting money into original
paintings because they might not fit in the wall space or
color scheme of the next house they occupy. They are also
wary of built-in bookcases because the prospective buyer
may not have any books and would find the empty bookcases an embarrassment.

During the spring of 1971 Fairfield County, Connecticut, with its tens of thousands of transferees, had a crisis
of sorts. Predictions were that thousands of trees would
be defoliated by insects. The towns were split into violent,
almost hysterical factions on how to cope with the bugs.
Many wanted to call in airplanes and spray entire towns
with chemicals of vaguely understood side effects. Others
wanted to keep the spraying on the ground and preferably
be selective and just spray important trees near their
houses. It was noted in several instances that it was people in the high-mobile areas who wanted to call in the
planes and spray everything in the county that had leaves.
They were worried about getting caught with a denuded
property when orders might come from their company to
move on. Old-time residents on the other hand tended to
take the view that over three hundred years bugs have
come and gone in Connecticut and the sensible approach
was selective ground spraying. Usually the view of established residents prevailed.

Among people who are loosely rooted because of neighborhood upheaval even though they may not be high-
mobile themselves there is a clear tendency not to take
pride in keeping up their part of the street. Who cares?

Competition for approval diminishes among strangers. This is a major cause of the continued spread of gray areas and desecration in large urban sections.

As for the attitude toward possessions of frequent movers, temporariness affects many decisions. It is not accidental that more people lease cars in California than in any other part of the country. Many people don't want to get tied down even to a car. As for landscaping one's home, William Roos, the mystery writer and playwright who with his wife lives in several different houses each year, summed up one obvious solution by quipping: "We don't plant bulbs. We plant annuals."

A fourth distinctive pattern characteristic of a loosely rooted people is a relative indifference to local happenings in the towns they inhabit and to the social life in the area. We noted in Chapter 10 that the new spillover city of Parma, Ohic, with more than 100,000 population did not have a daily newspaper. In Chapter 16 I will describe my search for a prototype high-mobile small city that could be compared on the sociability dimension with a conspicuously stable small city of the same size. One of the accidental findings I began noticing in my search was that only one out of nine of the high-mobile towns I examined most carefully had a daily newspaper of known circulation; whereas every single one of the eleven stable towns had one. In high-mobile areas even the weeklies often have "controlled circulation," meaning that they are "free" and are sometimes referred to as advertising "throw-aways."

In high-mobile areas that do have newspapers the announcements of marriages and engagements are skimmed at most whereas in stable communities they are still read with considerable interest.

At the same time people in high-mobile areas such as southern California are more egalitarian in their socializing patterns and less preoccupied with status overtones than are people in more settled areas of the United States such as New England.

As U.S. society has become more fluid, "coming out" parties have gone into a sharp decline. My college class-

mate, Count Lanfranco Rasponi, who has spent a number
of years engineering and publicizing the events of America's high society, is discouraged. He complains that all
the mobility and travel is destroying society. People are
moving about so much that it has become frustrating to
try to put together a big glittering social event.[4]

A fifth possible characteristic commonly found in loose-
rooted people is an uncertain sense of self. That at least
is the contention of historian Arthur Schlesinger, Jr., based
on his study of recent Presidents of the United States. And
as a case in point he cited Richard Nixon, soon after he
became President.[5] Since Professor Schlesinger is not only
a historian but a Democrat his view may be somewhat
partisan. At any rate he stated:

"Nearly every other American President has had deep
and sturdy roots geographically and socially. . . . In contrast, Mr. Nixon, born in California, trained in the law in
North Carolina, elected to the Presidency from New York,
seems sectionless and classless," and carries a particular
appeal to others who are rootless, sectionless, classless,
mobile. Schlesinger believes this rootlessness accounts for
the fact that Mr. Nixon seems to many an "elusive" figure
and has a wavering sense of self that he works hard to
control, especially in his public appearances. Rootless
people, he added, are often quick to feel angry or threatened.

I suspect that if Mr. Nixon is indeed "rootless" that
condition springs also from the nature of the locales where
he has spent much of his life: he is a product of southern
California with its large proportion of loosely rooted people, and he has spent much of his time in Florida, which
also has a high proportion of relatively rootless people. It
is also possible that the responsibilities, deference, and
trappings of power that go with the U.S. presidency can
help the occupant of the office grow in his sense of self.

A sixth predictable impact on the life style of loosely
rooted people concerns their values.

Nomadic individuals, as we have seen, are far more

uprooted than nomadic bands moving together, and tend to develop a distinctive set of views of life that might be called nomadic values. Perhaps most conspicuous is a greater tendency to live for the moment. This perhaps accounts for what Bennis calls "the new immediacy."

The wife of a high-mobile manager in the Northeast said most transients feel that one learns to live each day as fully as one can and not to worry too much about the future. Much the same sense of immediacy swept over the restless, high-mobile alienated young of the late 1960s and early 1970s. They gloried in their impulsiveness, and sometimes called themselves the Now Generation. They were wary of getting themselves committed to any long-term activities for the future.

A facet of this living for the moment is a hedonistic tendency to live it up, to be disinclined to postpone immediate gratification in order to work for long-term goals. Have fun while you can.

In the West, mobility now is generated not only by job transfers and job moves but by a generalized yen to be on the move. Some of the extreme movement there is in search of physical pleasures; some of it is a quick inclination to escape frustrations. As historian George Pierson has noted: "Flight can be an escape from the future as well as from the past." This philosophy was neatly summed up in a comment by actor Jack Nicholson in the award-winning movie *Five Easy Pieces*. He was a West Coast floater. Much of the time he seemed to be enjoying himself but at the end as he embarked on a new, seemingly irrational move he explained:

"I keep moving not because I hope things will get better but because I know they will get bad if I stay."

*"They all come from somewhere else
and are looking for friends."*—A HOUSE-
WIFE WHO HAS LIVED IN AZUSA, CALIFOR-
NIA, FOR FOURTEEN YEARS. HER HUSBAND
IS A PLANT MOTOR OPERATOR.

16.

Two Towns:
A Comparison
in
Personal
Relations

In today's world is it really essential to one's sense of
well-being to have meaningful relationships with other people? If so, what kinds of relationships are of particular
importance? And how does high mobility affect the possible development and maintenance of such relationships?

These are important questions to consider in trying to
assess the various ways that uprootedness and social fragmentation may affect the way people behave.

The first two questions have been answered, I think
quite impressively, by Robert S. Weiss in a report on
research conducted by himself and associates at the
Department of Psychiatry of the Harvard Medical School
while working in its Laboratory of Community Psychiatry.[1] The research was supported in part by federal
grants. They studied the lives of people who had been
uprooted by broken marriages, by retirement, and by
moving substantial distances.

In the last case, for example, they studied in depth the
lives of six middle-class couples who had moved across at
least two state lines in order for the husband to work in

195

the Boston area. The husbands had their new on-the-job colleagues to talk with about common interests and were not particularly upset by their moves. But soon after the moves four of the six wives were seriously unhappy and complained of isolation. One of the wives took to drinking heavily; another pleaded with her husband to give up the promotion that had brought them to Boston and to return to her home town. Of the two wives who were not seriously unhappy, one, childless, broke out of her isolation by getting a job; and the second had, with her husband, intentionally moved into a new development where their neighbors were also newcomers to the region. They deliberately spent much of the first week getting acquainted.

From their studies Weiss and his associates concluded that people do indeed have needs that can *only* be met within relationships with other people. Furthermore individuals require a number of different kinds of relationships in order to have a sense of well-being. These different relationships that were on their "required" list served five different functions. And Weiss concluded: "It seems as though the absence of any relational function will create some form of dissatisfaction accompanied by restlessness and occasional spells of acute distress."

So what were the five kinds of relationship that provided the functions necessary to a sense of well-being? I will mention one of them only in passing since it is confined to a relationship within the family. That is the opportunity of parents to nurture children. Let us focus here on the four other categories of relationships that serve a required function and so help provide us with a sense of well-being:

1. *Knowing people who share our concerns.*
We develop these shared concerns with others we know as we work to cope with common problems or achieve similar objectives. The important function served by this type of relationship, Weiss found, is *"social integration."* The absence of this type of relationship in our lives leaves us with a sense of social isolation, which is often accompanied by feelings of boredom.

2. *Knowing people we can depend upon in a pinch.*

Traditionally this need has been provided primarily by our kin relationships. But today with kin usually scattered we are as likely to get such reassurance from friends and neighbors. This relationship provides us with the needed function of *assistance,* to use the Weiss term. The absence of such reassuring relationships in our lives leaves us with a sense of anxiety and vulnerability.

3. *Having one or more really close friends.*

Our relations with such people must be so trusting and close that we can express our feelings to them freely and without self-consciousness. And they must be people to whom we have "ready access." If we are in Indiana, they can't be down in Texas. In Weiss's words, such relationships serve the vital function of providing us with our need for *"intimacy,* for want of a better term." Without such intimate relationships we experience a sense of "emotional isolation" better known to us as loneliness.

4. *Knowing people who respect our competence.*

Such respect cannot develop at a cocktail party. It takes knowing. If we have jobs we gradually win the respect of colleagues by the quality of our work, if we deserve it. Or we may win admiration by achieving a successful family life or having homemaking skills. The important function this kind of relationship with people provides is *reassurance of worth*. The absence of this evidence, from others, of our worth results in decreased self-esteem.

The above findings by Weiss and his associates offer reasonably convincing answers to the first two questions I raised at the outset of this chapter. That is, we do need certain specific types of relationships with other people in order to achieve a personal sense of well-being. But what about the third question: How does high mobility affect the possible development and maintenance of such relationships, if it does?

I decided to try to test this out. My objective was to examine the interpersonal relationships of people in two towns chosen as prototypes of high-mobile and low-mobile areas. The towns I was looking for would be very much alike in size and income level.

The heart of the questionnaire I developed—four of the sections—was designed to probe the four types of relationship that Robert Weiss found were "required" for a sense of well-being.

Choosing the two towns turned out to be a major search project in itself, consuming several months' time and a few thousand miles of travel. For assistance I had scouts—most of them doctoral candidates in the behavioral sciences—who provided information I requested on certain of the towns I couldn't get to personally. And I examined a yard-high pile of reports sent in response to specific questions I put to a few dozen Chambers of Commerce.

Just finding a way to measure the mobility of people in specific towns was at first perplexing. The Census Bureau had no such records. Gas and electric company records often did not follow town lines. Post office officials varied in their cooperativeness in providing change-of-address information. Finally I concluded that the local telephone companies, with their disconnect records for main residential telephones, were the most dependable source; and happily they were uniformly cooperative.

In searching for my prototype of a stable town I considered only long-established, self-sufficient "towns" (actually small cities) outside the fringes of any "greater" metropolitan area. And I tried to find towns that were not dominated by one industrial plant controlled by a large national corporation, or by a university or a military establishment. Such institutions are known to generate mobility.

The U.S. towns I explored most carefully in my search for a prototype of a stable town were:

Bloomington, Illinois
Paris, Texas
Kingsport, Tennessee

Glens Falls, New York
Findlay, Ohio
Williamsport, Pennsylvania
Taunton, Massachusetts
Sheboygan, Wisconsin
Greenfield, Massachusetts
Hannibal, Missouri
Watertown, New York

As for the search for a prototype of a high-mobile town, I arbitrarily decided to focus on the dozens of satellite towns ringing Los Angeles. One reason was that I could assume from mobility data then available that most would be high-mobile by national standards. Also I was interested in getting a closer look at the alleged gay, carefree, restless, uninhibited life style of southern Californians.

Finding a good prototype of a high-mobile town there was more complicated than I had assumed. Many possibilities—especially in Orange County—had to be ruled out because they were growing so fast that outward mobility rates based on telephone disconnect records could be misleading.

At an early stage I received much helpful comparative information from a report called *Social Profiles: Los Angeles County* put out by the county's Welfare Planning Council. Only later did I discover that many of the "communities" it described were not communities at all in the sense of being incorporated towns or cities. They were clusters of Census tracts. For example in San Fernando Valley several of the "communities" that even many southern Californians think of as independent towns are not towns at all but part of the city of Los Angeles. Three promising "towns" there—Northridge, Granada Hills, and Chatsworth—were eliminated for that reason. And east of Los Angeles a very promising "community" listed in *Social Profiles,* Covina Highlands, near Covina, turned out on inspection to be in limbo. Most of it was neither incorporated nor a part of the city of Los Angeles and had no definite boundary but was just a lot of houses and stores that came under the general jurisdiction of Los Angeles County.

Thus the final list of towns I used in my search for a prototype of a high-mobile town was:

Arcadia
Baldwin Park
Altadena
Covina
Azusa
Monrovia
San Gabriel
Temple City
Monterey Park

The final choice for the high-mobile town was Azusa, in the foothills of the San Gabriel Mountains in the East San Gabriel Valley, twenty-five miles east of downtown Los Angeles. And the final choice for the stable town to match it with was Glens Falls, New York, isolated in the foothills of the Adirondacks.

Both had populations of approximately 30,000 when Glens Falls' thin ring of suburban growth was included. Both were very close in average family income at the time of the research. *Sales Management's* 1970 "Survey of Buying Power" listed the average "effective buying income" per household in Azusa at $9,620. And its figure for Glens Falls was $9,495, or a difference of only $125.[2]

Furthermore both were close to the average of the family buying power reported for the fifty U.S. states. The average for the fifty states was $9,664.

Earlier in 1969, when I was still trying to reach a choice of two towns to match, the income figures were even closer:

Azusa	$9,164
Glens Falls	9,152
Fifty states	9,137

In short, all three were identical to within $27!

While the two towns were very much alike in size and income, they differed conspicuously on mobility.

Telephone disconnect records of the New York Telephone Company indicated that roughly 19 percent of the people of Glens Falls had changed their home addresses during the previous year. This was well below the national average of telephone subscribers. And the comparable records of the General Telephone & Electronics Corporation indicated that about 38 percent of the people of Azusa had changed their address in the same year, more than double the Glens Falls rate. Azusa was high in movement even by southern California standards.

A brief word about the two towns:

Some Glens Falls residents like to call their small city "Hometown, U.S.A.," and they have some justification. The Swedish Broadcasting Corporation a few years ago chose Glens Falls for a documentary on life in a small American city. And in 1944 *Look* magazine designated Glens Falls "Hometown, U.S.A.," and devoted six articles to life in that area.

Originally a lumbering and logging town on the Hudson River, it now has sixty-five large and small industries and an insurance company. There are two General Electric plants in nearby towns but they draw less than a third of their employees from Glens Falls. Almost all the jobs held by Glens Falls residents are within a few miles of their homes.

Glens Falls has poverty areas and it has $250,000 homes, with a smattering of just about everything in between, including quite a few mobile homes. It has downtown squares and some tree-lined streets.

The town has a good many WASPs in its population but also a good many people of Italian, French-Canadian, and Irish descent, Jews of several different nationalities, and a few hundred Negroes.

When you ask people there what they like about the town they are most likely to mention the friendliness of the merchants and people on the streets . . . the nearness of recreational facilities . . . and their feeling that it is a "safe" place to live and bring up children. And things they may mention that they don't like are its class-consciousness . . . gossipiness . . . and the reserved attitude of people—especially natives—until they really get to know you.

As for high-mobile Azusa, it first reached national attention in the 1930s when comedian Jack Benny repeatedly—in a play on funny-sounding words—alluded to Azusa, Anaheim, and Cucamonga as purportedly remote, rustic outposts of southern California. Now all three have been swallowed up by the sprawl of Greater Los Angeles.

From the sleepy citrus-growing village of Mr. Benny's early joking days, Azusa has grown several hundred percent into a sizable industrial center. The peak of its growth rate was in the early 1960s. Now it is substantially filled up. The city is split by two major freeways and two major railroads.

The slogan of the local Chamber of Commerce is that Azusa has "everything from A to Z in the U.S.A." And the opening page of the Chamber's promotional brochure showed a picture of a confident young man labeled "Profile of a Man on the Move." The implication was that he was upward mobile both vocationally and geographically. The picture was in a housing developer's ad.

A truck driver in Azusa put this "man on the move" in less enthusiastic terms to me when he stated: "Neighbors are constantly moving. You hardly get to know them before they move away."

When you ask Azusans what they particularly like about their location they stress most often the conveniences for shopping, the schools, the nearness to southern California's recreational spots, and the weather, except for the inflowing smog, which many fuss about.

Far less than in Glens Falls do they mention friendliness of the people. Instead they often make a virtue of being left alone. A male telephone worker said, "You can stick to yourself." The wife of a laundryman said, "People leave you alone." And a divorcée in Azusa four months, thirteen hundred miles from "home" in the Midwest, said:

"The way of life is more individualized. People seem to enjoy life here in California."

Probably no one town could be singled out as "typical" of southern California. Although Azusa is typical of many aspects of the southern California life style we have been noting, it differs in several respects:

Azusa has a longer history as a distinct town than most.

Azusa, more than most towns in the L.A. area, has a downtown of sorts with a city hall complex surrounded by stores, mostly small. The center of commerce, however, has shifted toward the southern and eastern rim of the town where several shopping centers swarm with shoppers.

Azusa, far more than most towns in the area, is a major job center, including aerospace plants.

Azusa, being more industrialized, has an income level that, while typical of that of the U.S.A., is somewhat lower than the income level of most surrounding towns. Although it has pockets of higher-priced homes in the foothills the average home—usually a tract house—is modest, costing in the $20,000 to $30,000 range. It is basically a skilled working-class and lower-white-collar-class town with its jobholders primarily skilled blue-collar workers, technicians, and salespeople. There is no conspicuous ethnic caste to the town aside from the fact that one in six residents had a Spanish surname and blacks were a rarity.

Azusans, possibly untypical too, are not strong for night life. They seem more earnest than the southern California stereotype, and less restless. They move more for practical reasons than because of a generalized itch to keep going.

Perhaps most important from the viewpoint of my inquiry, Azusa is untypical in that most of its dwellers live in single-family dwellings which they own and the people are relatively young. Apartment living—though it exists—is far less conspicuous than in most towns in the Los Angeles area. This raises a puzzle. Why are Azusans so mobile? Usually very high mobility rates are associated with apartment living. One explanation is that people working in Azusa's industries are involved in a good deal of job-hopping within the Greater Los Angeles area. And another explanation, apparently, is that Azusa is seen by many of its residents as a stopover town for young families. An astonishing 47.5 percent of its population, according to *Social Profiles,* was under the age of twenty. Azusa teems with children. Local informants suggested that a great many young married families settle there because they can get a three-bedroom house for $25,000 and when the family grows or the husband gets a better job they move on.

With this introduction to my choice of two towns for comparison—one high-mobile, one low-mobile—let us turn to the results of the two samplings.

In each town I sought to obtain responses from more than 100 residents to an identical four-page questionnaire, which provided space for them to make amplifying observations. Responses were voluntary and, if they wished, anonymous. The respondents were virtually all chosen on a door-to-door sampling basis in a predetermined six-block area in each town which I had been assured was representative of the town.[3]

First a few facts about the people responding:

The people in Glens Falls had lived at their present addresses more than twice as long as the people of Azusa (six years vs. two and a half years) and had lived in Glens Falls more than four times as long as Azusans had lived in Azusa.

The Azusa respondents were on average clearly younger than Glens Falls respondents. And in the Azusa families more of the wives had their own outside jobs.

Since marriage, the Azusans had changed their home addresses, on average, every three years whereas the Glens Falls couples had changed theirs every four and a half years.

Although the questionnaire was designed primarily to test the two samples (mobile and stable) on the four types of personal relationships Weiss found essential to well-being, I also included several questions designed to assess the degree of rootedness and sense of belonging of these people from the two towns.

Was it possible that high-mobiles today are accelerating the process of integrating into their communities? And have they learned ways to maintain solid ties with old friends? Here are the questions, with the responses listed by the name of the town. Some readers, incidentally, might be interested in rating themselves on all the questions from the questionnaire that follow in this chapter.

—How many local shopkeepers, clerks, etc., know you well enough to chat with you by name?

Azusa	3 (median number)
Glens Falls	6 (median number)

—Do you know the mayor or other elected city officials personally?

	MAYOR	OTHER OFFICIALS
Azusa	6 percent	11 percent
Glens Falls	28 percent	48 percent

—Have you voted in a municipal election, here or elsewhere, in the past four years?

	YES
Azusa	55 percent
Glens Falls	80 percent

—Think of your closest friends in high school. Have you seen or talked with any of them in the past year?

	YES
Azusa	46 percent
Glens Falls	61 percent

—Approximately how many of the people living within a hundred yards of your home do you know well enough to chat with in neighborly fashion?

Azusa	4½ (median number)
Glens Falls	10 (median number)

—In the past year have you occasionally wished your way of life was less lonely?

	YES
Azusa	33 percent
Glens Falls	25 percent

One Azusa wife who said yes had lived in the same house fourteen years. She explained: "The way the neighborhood has changed, I don't have very many friends as neighbors now." She had no "close friends" within five miles. Another woman who had lived in Azusa two years said: "Back east people are more friendly. Close friends are closer there."

—Do you feel that too many people in this area are strangers?

	YES
Azusa	38 percent
Glens Falls	27 percent

A truck driver in Azusa said, "Life here is okay, but people don't mix in much like they used to in our fathers' day." And a male teacher there explained: "It's to be expected. People move in and move out. They move for opportunity. These people are not interested in other people." In Glens Falls one respondent complained there was an "in group" in town; and another said: "Especially in the suburbs there are too many strangers who do not get involved."

—In your neighborhood is there any common practice for welcoming new neighbors?

	NO
Azusa	90 percent
Glens Falls	64 percent

These responses would in every case indicate that the people of Azusa had a lower degree of rootedness or sense of belonging than did the people of Glens Falls. In fact most Azusans didn't seem to think of themselves as Azusans: they were oriented to their tract development or to southern California in general. They emerge, on the basis of these questions, as more indifferent citizens in the usual sense, lonelier, more weakly integrated into their community and neighborhood.

There was one noteworthy surprise and exception, however, in the Azusa responses dealing with the degree of rootedness. At first I found it baffling. And I still find it a fascinating anomaly. Two of the questions dealt with kinfolk relationships. Here their roots were at least as strong as those of people in Glens Falls.

In one question I asked:

—*How near is your closest relative (brother, sister, parent, uncle, aunt, first cousin)?*

On a simple average-distance basis, Azusan relatives would seem to be farther away. The average distances were:

Azusa	121 miles
Glens Falls	87 miles

But when the responses were analyzed to find how many had a close relative within five miles there was a surprising turnabout:

Azusa	53 percent
Glens Falls	43 percent

And the other question asked:

—*Have you attended a family reunion-type festivity in the past four years?*

	YES
Azusa	62 percent
Glens Falls	61 percent

We can only speculate why in a high-mobile town such as Azusa kinfolk ties seem at least as strong as, if not stronger than, in relatively stable Glens Falls. And why were there substantially more kinfolk nearby in Azusa than in Glens Falls? A possible explanation is Azusa's relatively flat social spectrum with a high proportion of craftsmen and white-collar workers of the limited-success variety in the population. "Working people" in general have a much stronger tendency to cling to kinfolk ties than do professionals, creative people, and managerial types. Many moves that "working people" make, as I reported in Chapter 1, are to get near relatives from whom they have become separated. The amount of family reunion-type festivities Azusans engage in suggests that, though they have fewer ties with neighbors and townsfolk than Glens Falls residents, they compensate by seeking sociability in family reunions and get-togethers.

Now we come to the heart of the survey results. Earlier we noticed four kinds of relationships that Robert Weiss of Harvard found to be essential to a sense of personal well-being. We wondered how these might be affected by mobility and decided to attempt tests in towns nearly identical in size and average income but in sharp contrast on the mobility dimension. Respondents in the two towns were asked nineteen questions that might provide clues on how much they experienced these four kinds of relationships. I give the responses here and group them under the four kinds of relationships cited by Weiss that I was seeking to test.

1. KNOWING PEOPLE WHO SHARE OUR CONCERNS

—*Are there any community projects currently that you are promoting, encouraging, or actively supporting?*

	YES
Azusa	24 percent
Glens Falls	36 percent

One Azusan said, "They haven't had any around worth getting into." From the reports received, Azusa seemed to have relatively few community affairs or projects and not many people knew about the few that existed. Some Azusans asked plaintively for information on any projects or activities they could get involved in. This did not happen in Glens Falls.

—Are you a member of any local clubs?

	YES
Azusa	30 percent
Glens Falls	53 percent

—Are you active, or fairly active, in the affairs of a church beyond possible attendance at weekly services?

	YES
Azusa	20 percent
Glens Falls	53 percent

—In the past two years have you attended any local gatherings of citizens about some local or national issue?

	YES
Azusa	31 percent
Glens Falls	36 percent

The kinds of meetings mentioned by the Glens Falls people seemed on the whole to reflect substantially more social concern than those mentioned by Azusans. Glens Falls respondents mentioned such gatherings as "urban renewal," "retarded children," "clean air," "zoning," "mayoral election," "black problem," seminars on "drugs" and Vietnam. Azusans mentioned such gatherings as "sidewalks," "John Birch Society," "traffic signals," "schools," "American Legion poppies," "servicemen's organizations," and "drug problems."

—In the past two years have you spoken up at any neighborhood or town-wide meetings?

	YES
Azusa	12 percent
Glens Falls	19 percent

SUMMARY: On each of the five questions above designed to explore the concerns that respondents shared with other people, the respondents in Glens Falls indicated more shared concerns in every instance, usually by emphatic margins.

2. KNOWING PEOPLE
WE CAN CALL UPON IN A PINCH

—*Do you know a local doctor who would feel personally concerned if you became seriously ill?*

	YES
Azusa	51 percent
Glens Falls	77 percent

A male technician who had lived in Azusa several years said: "I know a couple of doctors in town, but *personally concerned,* no." And a design worker in aerospace in Azusa complained: "You can't find a doctor anywhere who cares about anything but the dollar." In Glens Falls a wife who replied yes to the question added: "That's absolutely one of the good things about small towns."

—*If you had an emergency need for a lift some night around ten o'clock and no cab was available, how many people in this town would, if you called them, be glad to give you such a lift?*

Azusa	5 (median number)
Glens Falls	6 (median number)

—*How many people (would you guess) would try to come to visit you at the local hospital, if you were there recovering from a broken leg?*

Azusa	9⅓ (median number)
Glens Falls	9⅔ (median number)

—*If you had to go away for a week is there anyone in the block who would be glad to water your plants while you were gone?*

	YES
Azusa	89 percent
Glens Falls	96 percent

—If you had an emergency need for money temporarily how many people within fifty miles would you be willing to ask for a loan of say $100 for a few days as a favor? (Banks not included.)

Azusa   2 (median number)
Glens Falls   3 (median number)

Within fifty miles, an Azusan, of course, would have about fifteen times more people to draw upon than a Glens Falls resident would.

A woman living in Glens Falls thirteen years made the general comment that "neighbors are dependable in trouble but do not impose on you socially."

SUMMARY: On all of the five questions above that were designed to probe how much confidence respondents had that there would always be people ready to assist them, the Glens Falls sample produced higher rates of positive responses than the Azusa sample; but on four the margin of difference was small. Only on the question about knowing a doctor who would be "personally concerned" if they became seriously ill were the positive responses of the Glens Falls sample emphatically higher. This perhaps is significant because it was the one kind of support tested that could not be supplied by a relative. Azusans, although statistically more mobile, could confidently expect help in such matters as emergency lifts, loans, and hospital visits because they had substantially more kinfolk available nearby, as noted earlier. Kinfolk are usually expected to be helpful in such matters.

3. HAVING ONE OR MORE REALLY CLOSE FRIENDS

(AND HAVING READY ACCESS TO THEM)

Measuring the intensity of friendships on a questionnaire is, of course, difficult. The following five questions however should, in total, offer us a clue.

—*How many of the people that you regard as close friends (as distinguished from casual acquaintances and friends) live within five miles of your home?*

Azusa	3 (median number)
Glens Falls	6 (median number)

One Azusan wife answered "0."

—*How many friends within ten miles could you confide in if, for example, you had a child who was in a disciplinary jam at school or if you had a husband who was having a serious quarrel with his superiors?*

Azusa	2 (median number)
Glens Falls	2½ (median number)

—*Do you sometimes wish you had more good friends that you could see every week or so?*

	YES
Azusa	47 percent
Glens Falls	43 percent

One wife in Azusa commented: "I wish my two good friends who moved away were here."

—*Have you socialized in the evening with any friends or acquaintances in this town in the past two weeks?*

	YES
Azusa	56 percent
Glens Falls	61 percent

—*Do you think of this as a relatively friendly town or a relatively cold town in which to live?*

	FRIENDLY
Azusa	64 percent
Glens Falls	74 percent

Here are a couple of the negative comments:

AZUSA—Wife of a computer programmer: "I've been here a year and two adults have spoken to me from this neighborhood."

GLENS FALLS—A female resident of nineteen years: "You have to live here a long time to start feeling like a 'towns' person."

SUMMARY: On each of the five questions designed to probe how much sense of intimacy the respondents were enjoying from people in their area, the Glens Falls respondents offered the more positive responses. However, the margins of difference were impressive in only two of the five, those related to the number of "close friends" they had within five miles and whether their town was friendly or cold. On the other three questions where only the words "friends" or "good friends" were used it is possible that some Azusans included kinfolk among the "friends" whom they could count upon to help meet their need for intimacy.

4. KNOWING PEOPLE WHO RESPECT OUR COMPETENCE

—*Have you been an officer of any local club in the past three years?*

	YES
Azusa	13 percent
Glens Falls	22 percent

—*Have you been elected or appointed to any position of responsibility in community or neighborhood affairs in the past three years?*

	YES
Azusa	20 percent
Glens Falls	20 percent

—*Do you have any children between four and ten? If yes, have they been to the place where their father works?*

In both Azusa and Glens Falls approximately 40 percent of the respondents said yes, they did have such chil-

dren. Of them, the proportion whose children had been
to their fathers' place of work was:

	YES
Azusa	68 percent
Glens Falls	86 percent

*—Are there people locally who presumably respect you
for the way you are living—either because of the way
you run your home, or the kind of work you are doing,
or what you are doing in the community? Yes: No:
Wouldn't know:*

	YES	WOULDN'T KNOW
Azusa	52 percent	42 percent
Glens Falls	79 percent	12 percent

SUMMARY: On three of the four questions designed to
discover whether the respondents had reason to believe
they were respected in some way for their competence,
the Glens Falls respondents offered the more positive
responses, all by emphatic margins. But on the fourth
question, about being elected or appointed to any position
of responsibility in community or neighborhood within
the past three years, one respondent out of five in both
towns answered yes. The proportion in both towns is not
particularly impressive, but it is surprising that they were
the same. Perhaps we have a puzzle. Or perhaps the word-
ing of the question was so broad and so directly confronted the egos of respondents that they strained to come
up with "yes" answers. Perhaps those who belonged to
unions, for example, included elected or appointed posts
in on-the-job union organizations. Some Azusans did
list "union."

CONCLUSION: We set out to try to determine what kind
of environment would most encourage—and discourage
—four kinds of relationships which Robert Weiss found
were essential to a personal sense of well-being. The testing was confined to the dimension of mobility-stability,
with the Azusa sample drawn from a high-mobile environ-

ment and the Glens Falls sample drawn from a stable environment.

The responses to the first part of the questionnaire on degree of rootedness confirmed that the people of Glens Falls by a definite margin had a greater sense of rootedness and of belonging than did the people of Azusa.

As far as the four kinds of relationship being tested were concerned, the picture that emerged, while far from overwhelming, suggests that a stable environment does indeed provide more of the satisfactions of human relationships that Weiss found to be essential to personal well-being.

On eighteen of the nineteen questions the more positive responses were made by the people from Glens Falls. And in eleven cases the margin of more positive responses by Glens Falls respondents ranged from clear-cut to emphatic. By contrast, in not a single instance did the Azusa respondents show any clear-cut margin of more positive responses. The differences in response on some questions were not substantial, so that we are not looking at a black and white picture. Puzzles remain if we hypothesize that Glens Falls respondents should have shown an emphatic and consistent pattern of more positive responses on all four of the types of relationships being tested. Perhaps this absence of a thoroughly contrasting pattern can be attributed in part to certain characteristics of the Azusa respondents already noted. They proved to be somewhat younger. A majority were under thirty-five and few were over fifty. Perhaps as a result they tended to be more adaptable than Glens Falls respondents to the uprootedness ordinarily created by mobility. And as it turned out—perhaps because the town is much closer to being a one-layered community of well-paid "working people"—Azusans had more kinfolk nearby than did the respondents in relatively stable Glens Falls. To me, this superiority of Azusans in reporting they had kinfolk nearby was the most tantalizing surprise in the sampling results. We must also surmise from the nature both of the people and of the town locations that Azusans who move are less likely to make long-distance moves than are the movers of isolated, broad-spectrum Glens Falls.

The question of the impact of the mobility of an environment on various interpersonal relationships deserves extensive testing. But the results here do suggest that in general a stable environment is more conducive to the development of shared concerns, helpfulness in emergencies, close friendships, and respect for individual competence than is a turbulent one.

17.

Proneness to
Malaise
of
Loosely Rooted
People

What happens emotionally to people who are uprooted, or who lead highly transient lives, or who live in relative anonymity for these or other reasons?

Obviously such people are likely to find themselves with a shortage of solid connections with people or places. But is that likely to bother them seriously? Some people can lead relatively unconnected lives more blithely than others. But by and large, is there evidence that the unconnected people are more prone to a sense of malaise— or even actual emotional or physical disturbance? Webster defines malaise as "an indefinite feeling of uneasiness, or of being ill; also, generally a feeling of discomfort."

We have just seen in one specific examination comparing high-mobile with low-mobile people indications that the low-mobiles revealed a greater breadth of interpersonal relationships in at least three categories which a Harvard-based study found were essential to personal well-being.

Let us, here, broaden our exploration to see if there is any clear evidence in situations involving relatively unconnected people of any proneness to emotional uneasiness

217

—or actual emotional or physical upset—which may be triggered by malaise.

A good place to start perhaps is to examine the impact, if any, resulting from mass family relocations generated by urban renewal or superhighway construction. These types of upheavals have involved hundreds of thousands of American families in the past fifteen years.

What happened after urban renewal hit the West End of Boston more than a decade ago deserves special notice because it has been so thoroughly researched by psychiatrists, psychologists, sociologists, and city planners.[1]

The forty-eight-acre West End area that was involved lies down behind Beacon Hill. Officially it was classified as a slum, but sociologists found it was more accurately a working-class community of low-cost, walk-up apartments reasonably well maintained on the inside, if dingy on the outside. West Enders liked to boast that their area had people of twenty-three nationalities living in harmony. Italian-Americans predominated. The fact that West Enders were strongly attached to their neighborhood is seen in its very high stability: nearly three quarters of the people had lived in the area at least nine years.

These residents intensely enjoyed group life and—unlike middle-class people—they thought of their "homes" as being not just their own apartments but also the hallways, stoops, the street in front, and the street corners. Most residents were surrounded by relatives and friends and they attached more value to sociability than to success in life.

Under urban renewal, approximately 2,700 families were ordered to move elsewhere so that the forty-eight-acre area could be razed to make way for a luxury apartment house complex. The city's planners apparently felt that the renewal would add to Boston's tax base and brighten up the mid-city area.

Some of the relocated residents were able to find homes within a mile of their old ones but the majority were widely scattered, settling from one to seven miles away. Many settled in middle-class rather than working-class areas.

One of the major follow-up studies of these relocated people during the two years following the move was made by the Center for Community Studies, created by the Harvard Medical School and the Massachusetts General Hospital. It found that a third of them were happy with their readjustment. But, for the majority, leaving their West End neighborhood had generated feelings of long-term grief. Nearly half of the women—and more than one third of the men—gave evidence of fairly severe grief reactions.

Psychologist Marc Fried, a director of the study, who more recently has been at Boston College, reported: "There are wide variations in the success of post-relocation adjustment. . . . But for the majority it seems quite precise to speak of their reactions as expressions of *grief*. These are manifest in the feelings of painful loss, the continued longing, the general depressive tone, frequent symptoms of psychological or social or somatic distress. . . ." He found indications of an upswing in rates of psychiatric hospital admissions after relocation.

The people who had been best able to handle the transition successfully were those who were relatively well educated or were relatively high in occupational status or income, and those who, in terms of national background, had achieved a relatively high degree of assimilation into the U.S. and were fairly familiar with the world outside the West End. Such people, some experts contend, can actually grow in emotional maturity as they cope with the stress of relocation. Also, those who had moved *in groups* to new areas seemed to fare better.

But by and large, for the *working-class* people involved, Fried concluded that "these feelings of being at home and of belonging are . . . integrally tied to a *specific* place." And he felt the findings of his group imply the necessity for providing such people with *a sense of continuity*. This involves trying as far as possible to keep the people whose area is being renewed somewhere within that area. And when that is not feasible it involves trying to get them to new areas which are conducive to familiar life styles. Much more supportive effort and guidance would seem to be indicated.

Urban renewal has been a laudable concept and certainly should not be abandoned. But far more thought should be given to the impact on the people living in areas to be renewed. And as far as possible residential areas should not be "renewed" to meet such objectives as trying to save downtown shopping areas, or building parking lots, or ousting minority groups. The West End experience indicates that for unsophisticated working-class people, at least, loss of a sense of place is likely to have long-term adverse effects on their mental health.

Another question that arises concerning possible malaise is whether people *in general* who migrate are any more prone to mental upset than those who don't. This question also has been extensively explored and analyzed in the U.S. and other countries.[2]

Almost all of the studies have been confined to mental ailments severe enough to require admission to a hospital, which for research purposes can be easily checked.

On an over-all population basis, the evidence points emphatically to a greater proneness to mental ailments among migrants who move across state or national lines. Sociologist Everett S. Lee, a leading researcher in this field, has concluded: "It is now evident that rates of admission to mental hospitals are much higher for migrants than non-migrants." And two officials at the Illinois Department of Mental Health have stated that geographic mobility "produces a unique high-risk group for mental disorder."

Oddly, studies of hospital records in New York, Ohio, and California all point to the fact that people who were born in other states show up as even more prone to mental illness than people born in other countries.

When the analysts try to account for the reasons why more migrants than non-migrants show up in mental wards there is less consensus and more head-scratching. Are people who migrate more prone to mental instability in the first place? Or is the mental upset created by the stresses of relocating in a strange and possibly hostile environment the major cause? An early Norwegian study indicated that people who had schizoid personalities were somewhat more likely to leave Norway for America. They were predisposed to move.

A more recent study of black migrants in Philadelphia by anthropologist Seymour Parker and associates would seemingly tend to support this predisposition concept. Mental attitudes seemed to predispose some more than others to mental illness.

On the other hand, a McGill University doctor, in a reappraisal of all the research, tentatively summed up prevailing opinion a few years ago by saying: "Today there is a tendency to regard the stresses of migrational experience as the most likely explanation, with selection playing a secondary role." And more recently Christopher Bagley of London's Institute of Psychiatry supplied supporting bits of evidence for believing that the stress of relocation was a major—if not the major—cause of hospitalization. He cited evidence from Canada indicating that British immigrants to French-speaking Quebec had higher rates of mental illness than British immigrants to English-speaking Ontario, where the environment presumably would seem less foreign and possibly more receptive. He also pointed to a 1967 finding by Benjamin Malzberg, a leading mental health researcher, that mental illness rates decrease the longer a migrant has been settled in a new area.

As far as I know, none of the migrant studies has taken into account whether the migrating family moved on its own volition or was transferred. As we have noted, an element of coercion is often involved in the latter. This deserves investigation since increasingly long-distance migrations in business and government are semi-mandatory assignments to tours of duty in faraway places.

We noted in the West End relocation that those of higher educational and vocational status were less likely than those of lower status to suffer prolonged grief. This, however, does not seem to be the case in the studies of hospitalization of long-distance migrants. Lee could find little evidence of differences based on educational or vocational level. On the other hand it has been pointed out that refugees in America from Nazi Germany—who tended to be high in education and skills—managed the transition on the whole with little apparent impairment. Perhaps the explanation lay in the fact that relocation was a breeze when compared with the traumatic experience of living under Hitler. Also the refugees to America tended to be received warmly as heroic survivors. Certainly the supportive warmth migrants receive on arrival and the speed with which that supportive warmth is extended can be critical factors.

There is substantial impressionistic data that highly educated people who migrate frequently are likely to suffer, at the least, a good deal of malaise, if not mental upset. The engineers, scientists, and technicians at American aerospace centers and firms offer a case in point. They are said to be standing on the horizon of tomorrow not only because they are space-oriented and developing the technology that increasingly is influencing our lives but because they tend to be a highly rootless group. The rapid growth and shifts of focus of their industry and the ebb and flow of government contracts have made it common for them to move five times in eight years. Even before the major cutback in jobs in the early 1970s psychiatrists and family specialists were already referring to the "aerospace syndrome" as a conspicuous deep-seated malaise among many in the industry.[3]

At aerospace centers from Cape Kennedy, Florida, Houston, Texas, and Huntsville, Alabama, to southern California have come reports of a peculiar life style among these people, including frequently these elements:

—Very little community involvement. Most do not think of themselves as actually "living" at the place where they are employed.
—Few close friends. Thus, husbands and wives depend on each other to a marked degree for emotional satisfaction, which, as one psychologist put it, often breeds hostility.

—A conspicuous number of alcoholics. A Florida consultant on alcoholism estimated the alcoholics at Cape Kennedy at a third higher than the national norm.

—A considerable amount of infidelity, often by mutual agreement. A psychiatrist at the Huntsville, Alabama, space center said that in twenty years of practice he had never encountered so much infidelity.

What seems so significant in the peculiar life style reported among many of these people is that ordinarily engineers and scientists are among the steadiest, least flamboyant, and most earnest citizens on the national landscape. The alcoholism, the infidelity, the indifference to community of so many of those in aerospace must certainly be attributed in large part to their new migratory life style.

We have seen, then, evidences of the impact of uprooting on the mental health and life styles of three types of people: relocated city dwellers, migrants, and high-mobile aerospace employees. Perhaps for the remainder of this chapter the evidence of possible impact of being loosely rooted can be most succinctly stated if I take some specific symptoms of emotional upset and anti-social attitudes and note the evidence that they seem to be prevalent to an unusual degree among people whose connections to other people or to places are few or tenuous. These symptoms include not only peculiarities of behavior but certain actual physical ailments.

AGGRESSION AND ANONYMITY

A sense of anonymity may result from various kinds of rootlessness but is especially likely to become a pervasive feeling among people in the larger metropolitan areas. It is in such areas that aggression in the form of crimes against people is, to a spectacular degree, most common. Kenneth Watt of the University of California at Davis has assembled documentary evidence of this.[4] He found that as the population of a U.S. city increases the number of crimes per 100,000 citizens consistently increases. Consider the crime of assault:

Annual Assault Rate (per 100,000 population)

In cities with less than 10,000 population	29
In cities of 100,000 to 250,000 population	83
In cities over 250,000 population	154

If you live in a town of over 250,000 you are four and a half times as likely to be assaulted as you are if you live in a town of 15,000 . . . you are seven and a half times as likely to be robbed . . . and nearly three times as likely to be murdered. And women are four times as likely to be raped. All this happens despite the fact that as the size of cities grows the amount you, as an individual resident, must pay in taxes for police protection consistently increases, at least in cities above 90,000 in population. In a big metropolitan area you are likely to pay nearly twice as much in taxes for police protection as you do in a city of under 100,000.

A Stamford University research psychologist, Philip G. Zimbardo, has made an extensive study of the association between anonymity and aggression.[5] In a test of vandalism he and a colleague left a car, seemingly ailing, on a street of a small city, Palo Alto, California, and another on the street of a big city, the Bronx area of New York City, where he had found there was "a pervasive feeling of social anonymity." In each case he had raised the hood and removed the license plates as possible "release" stimuli. In each case the car was in a white, middle-class neighborhood and across the street from a large college campus.

In Palo Alto the car was left untouched for more than a week, except that when it rained a passer-by lowered the hood so the motor would not get wet! In the Bronx within a matter of hours and in broad daylight clean-cut adults and young men began stripping the car of its usable or salable parts often within eyesight of others. There was no observable evidence that anyone cared or disapproved. There seemed to be a diffusion of individual responsibility for social acts.

Then the next stage of reaction began; this fascinated Zimbardo more. At first, younger children began to smash the front and rear windows. Then over the next days well-dressed, "responsible-looking" white adults broke, bent, or ripped all easily detachable parts. Next they smashed the remainder of the car with rocks, pipes, and hammers. In less than three days "what remained was a battered useless hunk of metal, the result of 23 incidents of destructive contact." On a more recent visit to New York he learned that cars are now apt to be stripped if left for a day or two, even without any visible "release" clues that suggest the car has been abandoned, stolen, or is seriously ailing, such as cars in distress left on the Long Island Expressway and other highways.

In another test of anonymity and aggression he arranged for a series of laboratory experiments in which coeds were permitted to apply a painful electric shock to two girls. They could see the victims but the victims could not see them. One "victim" was depicted as sweet and altruistic, the other as an obnoxious transfer student. The victims were presented one at a time to the group.

The coeds manning the shock machines were, on signal, to apply shocks to the victims as they tried to perform a learning task—purportedly just to see how the victims would react—and purportedly to study to what degree the "shockers" identified with the situations of the victims. The girls who were to apply the shocks were divided into two groups. Zimbardo made a great effort to give one group a sense of anonymity and to deindividual-ize members. They had hoods over their heads and operated in the dark. No names were ever used. For the other group the individuality and identifiability of the girls in the group was stressed and they could see one another's faces when they were assembled.

During the experiment the anonymous girls, on average, continued to press the shock button twice as long as the individualized girls did. Furthermore, as time passed, the anonymous girls gradually showed less and less discrimination. They applied pain to the obnoxious girl and the nice girl almost equally. Some pressed the pain button as long as they were allowed to do so.

Zimbardo observed that, where social conditions of life destroy individual identity by making people feel anonymous, what will follow is what he saw in the laboratory. This led him to conclude that assaultive aggression, senseless acts of destruction, motiveless murders, and great expenditures of energy directed toward shattering traditional forms and institutions (such as we have recently seen to an unusual degree) are likely to be associated with a feeling of anonymity on the part of the aggressors.

Anonymity and deindividualization in his view cause us to change our perception of ourselves and others. The result is a "lowered threshold of normally restrained behavior." He suspects this may be a factor in the upsurge of social disorder of recent years.

"What we are observing all about us," he said, "is a sudden change in the restraints which normally control the expression of our drives, impulses and emotions."

The growing anonymity of American life, he suggests, comes not only from the growth of vast cities but from the feeling of powerlessness in the face of big institutions, the renting of apartments (instead of owning homes), and the immense mobility of Americans. He suggests the one best hope for change from all this is somehow to recapture our dwindling sense of identity within a meaningful social community.

Zimbardo's thoughts about mindless acts of aggression reminded me that the most publicized assassinations of our time—those of John and Robert Kennedy and Martin Luther King—all involved assassins who were high-mobile loners who had been constantly changing jobs or residences. An analysis financed by the Army of 137 men who had threatened to kill U.S. Presidents over a recent twenty-year period found that the most conspicuous characteristic they seemed to have in common was that they were "socially isolated persons." In 1972 the man charged with attempting to assassinate presidential candidate George Wallace was widely described as a "loner" who had from childhood avoided social contacts with people. His mother (an orphan from birth) was described as a person who kept to herself and seldom said hello to anyone.

The assassins of the Kennedys and Dr. King and the alleged would-be assassin of George Wallace also had in common severely unstable home lives while they were small boys. All had fathers who were absent or derelict. And all had an impaired social capacity, a subject I'll return to shortly. They were loners without friends. One report said that the young man who attempted to assassinate Wallace would respond to anyone who greeted him with a "vacant stare."

MARITAL DISTRESS AND ROOTLESSNESS

A woman who has handled a great many long-distance transfers of professional and managerial personnel for a nationwide home-finding service volunteered this observation:

"I have recently had quite a few divorces after transfers. Maybe the problem already existed and the act of turning over a new leaf triggered the breakup. But if the wife is in California and he's in Washington, it's a long way away. . . . Often when a house is not sold for several months and they can't buy another until the old one is sold, they get into financial strain. And being separated intensifies the strain. In one case it was simply that the young wife was in California, loved being there and didn't want to leave, and so a divorce resulted. A very sad situation. In another case a Main Line wife in Philly couldn't accept the idea of going to California."

The wife of a high-level executive in a high-mobile Connecticut town mentioned to me that two recent suicides in that fairly small town involved wives distressed over job transfers of their husbands.

As I have already indicated, California has an extremely high divorce rate. In Los Angeles County it is about three times the national rate. In that county more than 50,000 dependent children are involved in marital break-ups each year. The widely known marriage counselor Paul Popenoe, of Los Angeles, has concluded that the area's high incidence of divorce can be traced to its qualities of "social vagrancy."[6] Two of the traits he includes under this form of vagrancy are very high mobility and lack of family ties in many areas.

In Darien, the transfer-bedroom-traveling-man town we examined in Chapter 2, officials of the local Family and Children Services say that a large proportion of the problems they get are primarily marital, although often concealed behind problems involving children. One factor is that the husband invests so much of himself in his out-of-town job that he alienates his wife.

Darien is no exception: case workers in Family Service agencies throughout the country have reported that the uprooting of families accounts for many ailing marriages.[7]

The families of construction workers have usually had a good deal of experience and expertise in moving to new job locations, and those who are cohesive and resilient take it quite well. Even so, when the Atomic Energy Commission began a plant construction program in southern Ohio, back in the fifties, involving 25,000 workers, many with families, the Family Service Association of America helped set up an experimental counseling service there. Among the mobile families that sought counsel, it was estimated that 62 percent of the problems were somehow related—in a real or imaginary way—to their mobility.[8]

ROOTLESSNESS AND PRONENESS TO FANTASY

The scant evidence I've encountered here is confined to comments by California psychiatrists who have tried to explain the unusually large proportion of people in that state who have visions of disaster or are firm believers in occult phenomena. A number of psychiatrists have tended to explain away the prevalence of fantasy there by contending that it is linked in part to the high degree of rootlessness of the people and the high proportion of residents who are newcomers. Anxieties for many tend to take an apocalyptic turn. And the widespread obsessive concern that part of the state will soon tumble into the sea as a result of an earthquake represents—in the view of a University of Southern California psychiatrist—a localization of "free-floating anxiety."[9]

Although rootlessness can help cause various forms of psychological upset and distress, it should also be noted that the opposite can be true: distress can produce rootless behavior. It has even been given a name—"flight syndrome." Rod McKuen put it to words in his poem "Lonesome Cities" when he wrote that maybe, when he had seen all there was to see,

> *I'll find out I still cannot
> run away from me.*

The noted Philadelphia psychiatrist Martin Goldberg, of the Institute of the Pennsylvania Hospital, supervised an extensive study of runaway Americans. This study of 1,000 clients, many of them of the runaway type, of the Travelers Aid Society of Philadelphia was funded by the National Institute of Mental Health.

Goldberg found it was common to encounter a client who had arrived in Philadelphia "by way of a totally unplanned geographic movement from another community and was obviously less concerned with *going to* some place than with getting away from where he had been." Such a person, he said, often had a history that revealed frequent impulsive moves with little or no planning involved.[10]

Goldberg and his colleagues found that people in flight revealed to an unusual degree five characteristics:

—They had great difficulty in sustaining any close relationships with others.
—They had a very low tolerance for frustration.

—They were markedly impulsive.
—They presented patterns of chronic dependency.
—They had a marked tendency to misrepresent themselves.

Goldberg suggests that a sensible approach to flight people would have to be based on an effort to provide them with the acceptance, self-respect, and *sense of community* that has been lacking in their lives. He says, "The sense of community seems particularly important since only this could furnish them with motivation to restrain impulses, delay gratifications and enter into more open human relationships."[11]

To this end his group has recommended that "halfway house" facilities be gradually developed in major urban areas of the United States. Such centers should help the runaway find an almost family-like—or commune-like—setting conducive to the development of group identity and a sense of community.

UNCONNECTEDNESS
AND A LONELY COLDNESS

The emotional distress of loneliness does not necessarily mean the person involved is reaching out for human warmth: it may mean that he has trouble making contact in today's world. Many who were the lonely children of lonely parents grow up with cold personalities. Or they may be unable to make human connections for other reasons related to the way they were reared. An official of the Columbia College Counseling Service noted that many students who are wary of interaction with others wear dark glasses.[12] They feel endangered by human contact and personal involvement. They were raised by lonely parents and their own lives have been so profoundly lonely that loneliness significantly affects their personalities. My own observation is that dark glasses are also worn to an unusual degree by intensely alienated young blacks, whether at college or not.

The fragmenting of social groups that has been occurring in the United States for more than a generation is leaving a legacy of coldness. George Homans, Harvard sociologist, warned of such consequences back in the fifties.[13] He said that all the evidence of psychiatry showed that membership in a group sustains a man against the ordinary shocks of life and helps him bring up children who are happy and resilient. When that group is shattered something pretty terrible can happen not only to himself but to his children, who may grow up socially impaired. If the adult whose group has been shattered finds no new group he can comfortably relate to he will develop disorders of thought, feeling, and behavior. He will become compulsive, and he will be lonely while serving as a parent. And if the process by which the child learns to relate easily to others is a social process, then Homans thought it obvious that the lonely adult will "bring up children who have a lowered social capacity." He explained:

"The cycle is vicious; loss of group membership in one generation may make men less capable of group membership in the next. The civilization that, by its very process of growth, shatters small group life will leave men and women lonely and unhappy."

One way a young person may react to having a "lowered social capacity" is to withdraw or develop a cold personality. He may become aloof in his human contacts as the easiest, least embarrassing way of coping with them.

More recently Yale psychologist Kenneth Kenniston in his study of the alienation of modern youth said that, whatever the gains of our technological age, many Americans are left with an inarticulate sense of loss, unrelatedness, and lack of connection.

Many of these people who lose a sense of relatedness begin to find life meaningless and become indifferent to the troubles of, and the assaults against, their fellow men. They can become callous.

Writer Nat Hentoff cites an encounter with a district attorney in Queens, New York, who was bemoaning evidences of public apathy in his vast metropolitan area. The official explained:

"They talk about an Affluent Society, a Great Society, a Free Society. You know what we really are, chum? We're a Cold Society."

UPROOTEDNESS AND ALCOHOLISM

Selden Bacon, director of the Rutgers Center of Alcohol Studies, advised me that people who later become alcoholics show a marked tendency to break connections with human groups they are in, whether it is a job or membership in a high school class. Also, as one moves toward alcoholism he goes through a series of stages that end up with his being an "unperson," out of control. In reversing the process and bringing the person back into control of himself, Bacon has been impressed by the approach used by Alcoholics Anonymous. The crucial element is that the person once again becomes a full, participating member of a group. He is helped by others in the group and, when he becomes capable, he begins to take responsibility for others. There is a deeply shared concern. Bacon believes this entire approach is directly relevant to "uprootedness."

It is also possibly relevant that cirrhosis of the liver, commonly caused by heavy alcohol intake, ranks about twice as high as a killer among people in California, where rootlessness is widespread, as it does among Americans in general. Also, alcoholism correlates fairly directly with population density (which tends to promote anonymity). For example, the extent of alcoholism in New York State is three times that of North Dakota.

LONELINESS AND MENTAL UPSET

In the lead article in *Psychiatry,* February 1959, Frieda Fromm Reichmann pointed to the probability that loneliness plays an important part in the genesis of mental disorder. Two other investigators of mental disorder,

Robert Faris and H. W. Dunham, found that certain types of schizophrenia have their highest incidence in the central districts of cities, and especially among rooming-house and hotel lodgers—who tend, to an unusual degree, to be lonely people. Much lower incidences were found among homeowners and their families.

To move a step further, C. Tietze and associates found, in an early study, some support for the view that the duration of residence in a particular house is related to personality disorders, which were higher among people who had short periods of residence than among those who had lived in the same house at least ten years.[14]

The chances that a woman who has given birth to a baby will suffer a postpartum depression are directly proportional to the distance she is from any female relative or friend, anthropologist Margaret Mead has stated.

In recent years psychiatrists have started giving far more attention to the instabilities of society in their treatment of neurotic patients. In Sigmund Freud's day the tendency was to assume society was stable—in fact so much so that its stern demands generated a conflict with the true nature of the individual. Today society is no longer assumed to be stable. In fact it is now widely believed that society's instability and lack of supportiveness are factors in creating many personality disorders.[15]

UPROOTEDNESS, LONELINESS, AND PHYSICAL AILMENTS

There is now an impressive body of evidence that people whose lives are in a state of flux are more prone to serious illness than those who lead stable lives. Repeated changes put a strain on the body's adaptive capacity. Medical officers of the U.S. Navy at San Diego found they could anticipate illness patterns among 3,000 sailors who would be at sea six months. Before the voyage each sailor was asked to check from a varied list any changes that had occurred in his life in the preceding year. The list included job changes, residence changes, heavy job traveling, change in circle of friends, etc. It turned out that those who were in the top 10 percent in reporting the most changes were nearly twice as likely to become ill—and seriously so—as those in the bottom 10 percent.[16]

—Cancer proneness. Claus Bahnson of the Eastern Pennsylvania Psychiatric Institute has made an extensive study of people most likely to develop cancer. In 1971 he reported to the American Cancer Society Seminar that the cancer patient shows a tendency to be lonely, emotionally isolated, and to have difficulty forming deep relationships with other people. He has a cool personality.[17] A study at the Institute of Applied Biology in New York City has come up with much the same findings.

—Coronary disease seems to show some relation to stresses created by uprootedness. Leonard Syme, a research sociologist working with the National Heart Institute, analyzed the backgrounds of a number of coronary patients and of a control group. He noted two types of people in particular whose background made them high risks for coronary disease. One was the white-collar man of rural background who had experienced a number of job changes. The other was the American male who had been geographically mobile.[18] Syme theorized that coronary proneness occurs when a person is subject to a good deal of change in his life situation and when his experience had not prepared him for such change.

Some of the evidence cited in this chapter is only suggestive. Still, taken as a body, it strongly points to a quite definite relationship between disrupted or anonymous life patterns and emotional stress. The stress can in mild cases produce simply a generalized feeling of malaise, or it can in more stressful situations produce serious mental, physical, or personality disorders.

The kinds of disruption that seem especially stressful are those that shatter—or deprive us of—bonds to friends, kinfolk, and community. These are bonds that help us feel comfortable with ourselves and give us a sense of place among our fellow humans.

18.

Impact
on
the Children

What does a youngster whose family has moved into five different towns during the eight years of his lifetime say when asked where he is from? What happens to his sense of place? What training is he getting in uprootedness as a way of life?

Eugene Jennings of Michigan State University, who has conferred with many business managers in their homes, overheard the son of one mobile manager ask his dad when they were going to move again. The son had noticed they had lived in the community for almost two years and he was starting to wonder when they would be packing.

Mobility as a major cause of social fragmentation in America obviously has to have some sort of impact on the tens of millions of youngsters who find themselves being moved each year. For an urban child under ten a move of ten blocks throws him into a stranger environment than a move of twenty miles would for his parents.

Yet the impact on children is not readily predictable. It varies with the family. Many children are resilient and seemingly learn to cope readily. They are less inhibited than their parents about making acquaintances in new neighborhoods. A year can seem like a long time to a four-year-old. And, as I have noted, moves often do contribute to broadening their horizons and training young people to respond to challenges.

One easy place to check the impact of moves would seem to be in school performance. That is readily measurable and it is a special wrench to take children in and out of school systems. A great many children reach the age of ten without ever finishing a single grade in the same school where they began it. In Montvale, New Jersey, I found that out of 110 high school seniors questioned only two were now living in the house where they were born. Nearly half had spent some of their high school years elsewhere. A school official in Wheaton, Illinois, exclaimed: "Most students here have moved and moved and moved!" An official of Florida Tech University told of one student who had attended seventeen different schools. And a wife of a manager in Darien, Connecticut, who had moved sixteen times in her twenty-two years of marriage told me: "Our youngest son, now fifteen, has been subjected to three different school systems in the past twelve months. This is our price paid for progress."

But what is that price, for youngsters in general?

In the several studies I've encountered that compared the school grades or I.Q. test scores of mobile and non-mobile students only minor or subtle differences seem apparent, and even these are not entirely consistent from study to study.[2] Mobile parents worried about the commonly held belief that they handicap their children academically by moving apparently can ease up on their worrying, at least if they are not supermobile, if they don't keep moving during school years, and if their children are reasonably good students.

R. Keith Thomas, principal of the Loy School for children of military personnel at Great Falls, Montana, mentioned to me one interesting thing he had noticed. He said the children of above-average ability tend to adjust to a new school situation rather well whereas adjustment is often a hardship on the student who is average or below average in ability. Schools vary in what they teach at different grade levels and for the struggling student the frustration of academic problems created by moving can lead to emotional problems.

The age of the children at the time of a major move unquestionably is a major determinant of how well they will adjust to the move socially and emotionally. The three- and four-year-olds and those from thirteen to eighteen appear to be most vulnerable to difficulties. Louise Bates Ames, a top official of the famed Gesell Institute of Child Development in New Haven, Connecticut, advised me:

"At the very earliest ages (infancy) probably children don't mind too much. Then you come to the rigid pre-school years (twenty-one months to four years for some) when everything has to be *just the same* (even within a house or room). Moving may be quite traumatic in that it disturbs this rigidity. Five- to ten-year-olds might, hopefully, accept moving without too much trauma, but then come the teens when their lives are *shattered* by leaving their home towns and their home-town friends."

The problem of teen-agers is not only leaving their old friends but finding friends in the new town. Loneliness may become a problem because in the teens it takes longer to make friends than in the grammar school years. By junior and senior high school, cliques have become a big thing. A school official in Darien explained the incoming teen-agers' problem there bluntly:

"With the new students we often see the problem of not being accepted, being isolated, and looking miserable. Progressively it becomes more difficult to adjust if you are a newcomer from the seventh to the ninth grade. The ninth grade is where it is most difficult. But if you are from an affluent family you will fit in. It is at this period, from the seventh to the ninth grade, that the mothers are so concerned that their children get in the right set that they push them into dating. They want them to be popular with the right people."

A mother, who called the ninth- and tenth-grade years the ones that are "murderous" for newcomers, said it was such youngsters from high-mobile families who tended, under the pressure for popularity, to get on "the fast track" and to get "too far out in their behavior."

At a forum I was conducting with members of the Darien Newcomers Club one mother raised an extremely interesting point. She asked: "How do parents who are new in a town help their children evaluate their friends? How can parents counsel wisely since they don't know what kind of parents these friends of their children have? Do the parents thus feel they are losing touch with their children—and are thus losing their relevance?"

This woman, I felt, was unwittingly putting her finger on one substantial cause of the so-called generation gap. The network of parental and community guidance that traditionally has helped orient teen-agers as they hit the testing phase for adulthood is coming apart. Too many of the people who would normally be involved in the process are strangers. They have no frame of reference on what constitutes appropriate behavior. Thus the teen-agers are forced to make their own decisions. For guidance they turn to their peer group, which at the early teen level instinctively tends to take an adversary position regarding adults and adult values.

And as the parents continue moving, the teen-agers must continually become acceptable to new peer groups. If the moving continues while the teen-ager is away at college or boarding school he comes "home" on vacations and in the summer to a totally friendless environment. After a few days his inclination is to take off in search of his scattered friends.

One mother I know who moved several times in the U.S. and abroad while her children were of college age made this further observation: "The worst thing about moving as the children get older and into college is that you find you have dropped them all over the landscape—from California to Rome."

After college it usually never occurs to the graduate to seek employment in the "home town" where his or her parents are currently living. He looks elsewhere. Thus social fragmentation is reaching into the family not only because of divorce but because of generalized mobility.

A young man who had been raised in the military establishment confessed to me that since boyhood he had had difficulty developing close friendships. He was certain it was because his close friends while he was growing up were inevitably from military families and they were usually rotated out every two years. The pain of losing friends repeatedly caused him unwittingly, he suspected, to start shunning close friendships.

A different kind of possible loss centers on the family homestead. This obviously is intangible. But imagine the incalculable loss to millions of children today who can no longer spend hours in a homestead attic playing with uniforms or relics belonging to their grandparents, or leafing through a family album covering the span of a century.

If, as projected, the mobility of Americans accelerates, it seems inevitable that the so-called generation gap will become even wider and social fragmentation will increase.

The possible negative impact of frequent moving on the mental health of children remains to be tested and pinpointed by anything resembling an impressive body of studies. One systematic study in the 1940s found evidence that childhood disorders increase with frequent change of residence. But most of the evidence that there is some negative impact comes from convictions developed by academic experts and by cases in point.

Sociologist Philip Slater has pondered extensively the impact of the fact that the whole socio-economic structure of the United States is moving toward producing a society of "temporary systems." These would take the form of task forces organized around problems to be solved by groups of relative strangers. The concept would apply primarily to handling work problems. But even marriage, he suggests, conceivably may become a temporary system tied to a particular locality and task. He is convinced that a child moving from place to place suffers social impairment. He advised me: "I still find it difficult to imagine how the raising of children can be reconciled with temporary systems. I think, in fact, that it cannot be. Of course children grow up one way or another and I do not in any way mean to imply that under such an arrangement everyone would end up in mental hospitals. The kinds of personality development we could expect under such a system are simply incompatible with our society as it now exists. Something altogether new might emerge from this. I really cannot imagine what it would be."

Another academician who, a few years ago, expressed concern for mobile children was social philosopher Helen Merrell Lynd at Sarah Lawrence College. She noted:

"It is hard to overrate the importance of continuity for children. Some children I know began to stutter after their families had made several moves that for the families had been 'a good vacation' or 'a step up in the world.' In one family it took a child psychiatrist to find how much more was involved for the child . . . a tearing up of roots which severely threatened his security." She said the moves had been traumatic experiences in the negative sense.

In my queries to Darien newcomers on the advantages and disadvantages of moving every few years, the disadvantage most often cited was the unsettling effect on the children. One mother said that her family's move had been "a most traumatic event" for her daughter, a senior in high school. The daughter had had no previous experience in winning acceptance in a teen-age society. "It was very rough for her," the mother said. "She went to the refrigerator and gained forty pounds."

While I was visiting the home of a man who had moved into a Maryland community from Roslyn, Long Island, the man described to me in glowing terms the fine features of their new community. His family had been there more than a year. While he was talking his nine-year-old daughter came into the room. I asked her how she liked their new home town. She frowned and said, "It's okay, I guess. But I miss my friends back in Roslyn very much."

The family doesn't have to move to produce uneasiness in its children: the father can be a commuter-traveler. One study of commuters to New York concluded that they felt their commuting had hurt their relationships with their families. How might it hurt? Consider these three comments by three people in Darien, our prototype commuter town.

—A junior high school official: "If the father works nearby, say in the Stamford-Greenwich area, the youngsters can understand, and if the commuting hours are moderate the father commands a good deal more authority with his children. Many problems at school stem from the fact that parents are not home. The male image is lacking and ought to be there. Often both parents are working. I frequently have to contact parents about disciplinary problems and I can't get either of them because both are working or else the wife is running around all day to teas and bridge parties."

—A businessman who has been in affluent Darien more than fifteen years: "Because the commuter is in New York or traveling most of the time or works late and stays in the city overnight a gap develops between him and his children. This is bound to have an effect on them. It frequently takes the form of vandalism, drugs, and thievery." In the early seventies Darien ranked among the highest of all the towns in Fairfield County in drug arrests of young people.

—Mrs. Helen Miller, a mother, volunteer school worker, and long-term resident of Darien: "I've watched one whole generation grow up here. The doctors and lawyers and the ones who stay here all day, they have yet to turn up a serious problem that I have seen. Almost all of the serious problems come out of the families where the family is split or the father commutes or travels a lot. It's unbelievable how shocking the difference is. In Darien there is no grandfather to fill in while the father is away. The difference is that the mother can be a drunk or run around a lot, yet this doesn't show up so sharply in the kids as the difference that develops when the father isn't there. It's unbelievable."

Mrs. Miller's observation is supported by studies made by professional family life specialists.[3] Urie Bronfenbrenner, famed Cornell psychologist, found that "absence of the father was more critical than absence of the mother" in personality formation.

Other factors undermining community life in modern society perhaps have even more negative impact on youngsters than family mobility. The result of the population explosion and implosion into great metropolitan areas that has occurred in the past twenty-five years is a case in point. Philip Hauser, noted demographer at the University of Chicago, says: "It is my contention that the confusion and disorder of contemporary life may be better understood and dealt with as frictions in the transition still under way from the little community to the mass society." In talking of the confusion and "chaos" of contemporary life, he mentioned delinquency, crime, alcoholism, drug addiction, mental disorder, and the youthful revolt which in its extreme form has manifested itself in the hippie resolving his problems by dropping out.

The impact on children of the environment of a mass society that is increasingly anonymous has been specifically singled out for critical reports or comments by several behavioral experts in childhood development.

Herbert Wright and associates at the University of Kansas compared the everyday lives of youngsters growing up in a small town with the lives of youngsters living in a modern metropolitan area. They found that the children in the small town got to know *well* a considerably greater number of adults in various walks of life than their urban agemates. And, further, the small-town youngsters were more likely to be *active participants* in the adult settings where they found themselves.[4] (Here again we see a causative factor in the "generation gap.")

Urie Bronfenbrenner is another who is concerned about the impact of the constricted world of "shifting suburbia" on children. He points out:

"Whereas the world in which the child lived before [the small town] consisted of a diversity of people in a diversity of settings, now for millions of American children the neighborhood is nothing but row upon row of buildings inhabited by strangers. One house, or apartment, is much like another, and so are the people. They all have about the same income and the same way of life."[5]

Only a restructuring of urban life to recapture something resembling the socializing environment of small towns would seem to offer much hope of relieving the present constricted environment provided for children in most large urban settings. But specific things, it would seem to me, can be done at schools and within the family to ease at least the negative impact of mobility. At schools, teachers can see that an incoming child gets a little welcoming ceremony. A classmate can be appointed to serve as a buddy to the newcomer in getting him involved with his new classmates. Preferably the buddy would be someone living near the newcomer so that there would also be someone to walk to and from school with.

Several family researchers have offered the opinion that any negative effect of mobility on children can be small if the relationships within the family are solid. This belief was echoed by a number of wives I consulted. A recently arrived mother in Darien observed: "One of the most important things is this: if you have a good family situation —and especially if the father is firm but companionable— that wipes out an awful lot of the headaches of mobility that can come from being transplanted."

Mr. Thomas, principal of the military base school at high-mobile Great Falls, Montana, said: "Parents who have a good home life, open, affectionate, but firm, tend to have few problems." Difficulties develop, he added, if the father is away at a missile base much of the time and the mother unwittingly overcompensates by letting the children have their way.

At the least, it would seem, there is a very real *potential* negative impact in all the uprootedness of modern life upon the children. Another Great Falls educator put this in somber terms by asserting: "There is a hazard to society with all this moving, where children don't have roots and don't have grandmothers they can see fairly regularly."

"Those who remain behind must repair the social fissures that the transients have created."—PHILIP SLATER, BRANDEIS UNIVERSITY SOCIOLOGIST.

19.

People Turnover and Community Demoralization

Transients create fissures in a community. So do the young who leave and don't come back. And so do those who leave in large numbers because of rapid changes in the character of their community. All three types of movement have a disruptive, often disintegrating and demoralizing effect on the community's functioning.

Thus far I have been discussing mainly the impact of uprootedness upon individuals. At many points—such as in Great Falls, Azusa and Darien—it has been evident, however, that uprootedness has significant implications for the communities involved. These deserve a specific assessment.

All the individual transience, I believe, is adding up to an increase in community disruption and turbulence. And for the nation as a whole it is adding up to an ominous trend toward a fragmentation of the whole society.

While a case can often reasonably be made for an individual life pattern of turbulence, it is far more difficult to find anything to cheer about in the impact that such people, in large numbers, have upon the communities they leave behind. A community is a network of social relationships, not just a geographical location. If people come and go at a high rate the physical structure of the community may remain reasonably intact but the community itself falls into disarray.

People of above average talent who live in an area only a couple of years—or whose jobs require a good deal of traveling—have a substantially below-average tendency to become *genuinely* involved in community affairs.

In 1970 the *Wall Street Journal* did a series of articles on how various businessmen lived. One particularly fascinating account was about a family in Charlotte, North Carolina, the city that has become the branch office hub of the Carolinas for many national corporations. The husband had been there a year and a half as branch office head of a national office equipment company. Although the *Journal* identified the family by name, I will modify the name slightly since time has passed, and I imagine the family members must have squirmed when they saw their life style described in cold type. I will call them the Jensens.

The article's headlines included the following: *"The Jensens Like Life in Charlotte, but They Won't Be There Long. . . . As Corporate Gypsies, They Focus Life on Job, Avoid Involvement in the Community."*

Mr. Jensen, it said, was a man on the move and would probably be offered another job in another city within a year or two. For him and his wife, it stated, Charlotte was little more than a way station on the road to business success. "That means they can't ever get to know their neighbors too well, can't become deeply involved in civic affairs, and can't grow too fond of this city or any other. Living far from old friends and relatives, with no reason to believe they will be here long, the Jensens and their friends have few ties to this city and little motive to develop any. . . . Outside of regular church attendance, the Jensens have avoided involvement in community activity."

The analysis added: "Because corporate gypsies like the Jensens identify with neither the old aristocracy in town nor the local Chamber of Commerce types they

limit their social life largely to entertaining each other."
Most of the Jensens' neighbors, like them, came from
other parts of the country.

Modern America has hundreds of thousands of people
like the Jensens. Many of them live in Wilton and Darien,
Connecticut, which are small enough for the results of
their life style to show with some clarity.

In Wilton, town officials have complained that turnover
on the town's boards and commissions is high—and that
the town has been having increasing difficulty persuading
qualified residents to volunteer to serve on boards and
commissions.[1] The chairman of the dominant (Republi-
can) party there stated that when you do finally get a
good man involved in political activity his company transfers him. Some of the men who are transients there or
who travel a lot often do more harm than good if they do
get on a town board, one official said. They don't have
enough time to study up on the problems they must vote
on.

In nearby Darien, in many ways similar to Wilton, a
longtime businessman said of commuters and transients
that the majority "show little interest in local town affairs
unless they are personally affected by an issue, such as
zoning in their neighborhood or a tax that will affect their
pocketbooks. Any contributions made to the town are
made primarily by the wives, not the husbands."

In disheveled Great Falls the Reverend Robert K.
Leland, who has been a leader in the "Forward Great
Falls Movement," told me: "To maintain any continuity
we need people who have been around awhile and have
gotten themselves involved in the community long enough
to help make decisions. People who are here only a year
aren't very effective."

If transients involve themselves at all in local affairs the
most likely area of involvement will be that affecting their
children. The *Wall Street Journal* mentioned that Mrs.
Jensen of Charlotte, mother of two, was active in a church
youth group and helped out at a local children's theater
group. In the bedroom communities of northern Los Angeles such as Granada Hills and Sylmar, the most common

community activity in which residents become involved is the Parent-Teacher Association.

But schools, too, are hampered when so many of a town's more talented residents keep moving on and travel so much. Consider Darien. One school official lamented that his school had just lost a magnificent mother who had forcefully headed the Parents' Council. Within two months after she was elected she and her husband were transferred to New Hampshire, he said. "It slowed down the whole program." A wife in the Newcomers Club there stated: "Many of us are disappointed in the schools, and we don't know if we are going to be here long enough to fight it and as a result we are letting things go by. . . . Husbands should be on school boards but they don't have the time."

School projects in Darien occasionally fall by the wayside because involved parents move. One school had an exchange program with a town in India. The people in the Indian town sent peppercorns in exchange for money raised at the Darien school to help the Indians build a new school. Parents and students in Darien agreed it would be a marvelous idea to use the income from selling the pepper to put a fountain in the lobby of the school. There was a committee of parents to handle projects such as this, but the chairmanship changed three times in less than two years because the chairmen moved away. School officials finally discovered that a fountain had indeed been purchased by a committee member who had since departed. The fountain was discovered gathering dust in a storeroom.

Until a couple of years ago the Darien school system had tried to save money in its school libraries—and encourage community involvement—by using volunteer parents in the libraries. For four years Mrs. Helen Miller sought to coordinate this program and taught a great many bright enthusiastic mothers how to run the libraries. But it was exasperating. After she had trained them and got them started she found that most of them had to resign because their husbands were moving somewhere else. Mrs. Miller persuaded the Board of Education the project was hopeless and the Board agreed to begin hiring regular librarians, with parents used as helpers when available.

Another kind of loss suffered by schools in high-mobile areas is intangible but important: the loss of the sense of pride and achievement that good teachers traditionally have gotten in seeing their pupils grow in wisdom and maturity thanks to their guidance. Mobile youngsters are here today, gone tomorrow.

The volunteer fire department is another community institution badly shaken by all the transients and job travel. Volunteer firemen in America have long furnished living proof that neighbors can depend on one another in times of trouble but they are fading from the scene.

A survey of U.S. firemen found that in suburbs and other fast-growing areas all across the country volunteer fire departments were becoming unworkable.[2] A major reason given was this: "Because of a high mobile society, the number of men available to answer fire alarms during the day has dwindled. More men in metropolitan areas now work at jobs far from the community in which they live." A fireman in fast-growing Lake Barton, Florida, near Orlando, explained: "The whistle would blow and hardly anyone would show up."

A report by Elizabeth Squire on newcomers in Wilton found that management-type transients were unlikely to join the Volunteer Fire Department.[3] Meanwhile their inundation into the town has raised housing prices to the point where the kind of people who have the time and interest to become volunteer firemen often can't afford to live there any more.

Fund raisers for worthy local projects have a hard time obtaining contributions from transients. Why contribute to a new YMCA or community center, no matter how glorious it looks on paper and how badly it is needed, if you will probably be gone by the time it can be built? Or why worry about the local poor and unfortunates, only vaguely known to you, unless you can get some recognition as a fund solicitor? There will be poor and unfortunate people in the next town too. A woman leading a drive to raise funds to expand an existing art center in

Fairfield County said of the prospects of canvassing Darien: "Unfortunately many of the people in Darien who could make real contributions are transients, and are more interested in what they can get than what they can give."

In Great Falls—where about 43 percent of the population move every year—a community leader said: "Fund raising has always been slow here."

Great Falls in fact reflects many of the troubles that beset community projects in high-mobile areas. The Little Leagues have been in trouble because of the difficulty of getting fathers to help out. The fathers not only are likely to be relative newcomers but many travel on the job either to their company's local offices throughout Montana or to do their tours of duty at distant missile sites.

Great Falls chronically has difficulty also in getting enough blood donors to maintain a sufficient blood supply. It gets only about a third of what it needs from donors. A person active in this program attributed much of the difficulty to the in-and-out movement of the city's population.

A British sociologist in a study of blood donation systems in twenty-three countries reported that in America the donating of one's blood is increasingly done on a commercial rather than on a voluntary system. He said that commercialism regresses the expression of altruism and erodes the sense of community.

In general there is, among transients, a relative indifference to, or unawareness of, local problems, a blurred sense of having any responsibility to the community. This is not inevitable but it is a common pattern, except in brand-new communities. In Darien with its many transient managers and professionals, one newcomer acknowledged there is among such people a tendency not to become committed to long-term activities. A man there who had moved many times said he felt that corporate policies impelling or encouraging frequent moving had "contributed largely to the sense of malaise that afflicts our country today. . . . You haven't time to get involved in the community so you don't really *care*. Then you move again.

Somehow the handful of more stable families keep things going for the next group to move in and out again. When we lose touch with our government roots we begin to have that helpless feeling."

A study by Community Research Associates in high-mobile, affluent Birmingham, Michigan, found that relative newcomers do not participate in local affairs to the same extent as the older residents. Specifically it found that during the first two years of residence half of the new-comers don't get much beyond membership in church, unions, or PTA though some plunged into fund raising. But there is a sharp increase in participation in the two to five years after arrival. And maximum participation comes after five years of residence in the community. The study also found that residential mobility depressed the frequency of voting in school elections. Since quality of schooling is of great concern to newcomers, this seemed odd. But as Helen Giammattei, a Birmingham resident and author, explained to me: "Knowing individuals [running for local office] takes a longer time than leaping right into a United Fund Drive collection or what not."

National leaders concerned about getting people to register and to vote have been disturbed by a long-term downtrend in U.S. voter participation (relevant to all types of registering and voting). In the 1970 primaries only about half the U.S. citizenry eligible to participate in politics actually voted, one of the lowest rates of the century. And in the 1968 presidential election, 39 percent of the eligible voters—or 47 million people—didn't vote. In most Western societies the proportion of eligible non-voters rarely rises above 25 percent.

Ramsey Clark, the former U.S. Attorney General, has contended that a major cause of this growing dropout of the electorate in the U.S. is the high mobility of the American society. Transients are unfamiliar with how and where to register even if they want to do so. And up until the early 1970s there were formidable legal barriers to registering or voting. Fifteen states required a year's residency, even to vote in national elections, and many others required a half year. Nearly 10 million potential voters were specifically inhibited from voting by residency requirements. Congressional action and Supreme Court decisions have recently helped ease the way for any adult who has lived in a state thirty days to vote in elections (although voting requirements in local elections have been left to the states). Lowering the voting age to 18 has, in the meantime, made mobile college students a potent factor.

However, Americans new to urban areas find it difficult to understand the complexities of local issues and so by the millions they don't vote even though they could do so. And many more thoughtful transients question in their own minds the ethics of voting on bond issues and other issues involving the expenditure of substantial sums of money when they probably won't be around long enough to help pay for the projects being authorized. This question has also been raised in college towns, with their temporary student populations, where student voting on local problems has become an issue. Local officials in essentially college towns, fearful of a take-over, have frequently ruled that students must register in their parents' home communities. High courts in a number of states, including California and Michigan, have ruled that students may vote in campus towns. Students have been voting in Berkeley, California, Champagne-Urbana, Illinois, Amherst, Massachusetts, and in a number of Texas towns such as Lubbock. But perhaps the students face the same ethical question that high-mobile managers face. Should they properly vote on long-term issues—or only on relatively short-term issues, relevant during their stay in the campus town, such as the election of town officials, proposed changes in law-enforcement procedures, and in local liquor laws?

If transient husbands and wives do vote for local candidates for office they usually lack personal knowledge of the candidates, and are thus more prone to be influenced by image builders and TV hucksters. And if they don't vote because they haven't been around long enough to understand the issues involved they are helping throw the effective control of U.S. society more and more into the hands of professionals.

By opting out of the democratic process they are thereby making the nation more vulnerable to professional elites and even to totalitarianism.

Although commuting managers can, and do, tend to be relatively indifferent to most civic affairs if they live in bedroom towns such as Darien, the situation can be quite different if they live in the same town or middle-sized city where their corporation's facilities or branch stores are located. This is particularly true if the corporation is important to the area's economy and has high visibility and if the managers have responsible positions in the company. In such a situation the high-mobile manager is expected to pitch in and conspicuously become a good corporate citizen. When *Dun's Review* asked its panel of corporate presidents if they expected their subordinates to be active in community affairs the great majority said they did. The report said that participating in private clubs and public charities was not considered so important *to the company* as were "civic and community affairs, where altruism and responsibility, along with more practical motives, are cited." *Management Record* several years ago noted a growing expectation by companies that all their responsible employees take part in civic activities. It cited one company's statement exhorting its personnel to take part in activities in a way that "reflects creditably upon the company's place in the community."

Such an expectation that aspiring managers will actively help enhance the company's image in their spare time, when combined with the increasing transience of such managers, produces an interesting situation. A really dedicated citizen is not a role actor. If our transient manager who is given the cue to plunge into community affairs—which can be immensely challenging—really becomes deeply involved and committed he won't want to move. That could create a threat to the company's basic assumption that it can shift its people wherever and whenever it wants. A leading investment counselor advised me that the presidents of two different companies confided to him that they had transferred good men because the men were developing too many roots in the town where they had been assigned.

So what emerges when the company wants its manager to get involved in his community but also wants him to stay ready to move on? An adaptive technique often takes over. The manager learns to look involved without actually becoming involved. In short he becomes adept at pseudo citizenship. In modern high-mobile America such pseudo citizens can be found busily improving their visibility in hundreds of towns and cities where their companies also have high visibility.

Whether the talented transients are indifferent to local affairs or whether they are briefly engaged in energetic role-playing, they contribute to a decline in authentic and effective ongoing communities. The long-run result for the community at most levels of civic activity is one of discouragement. And in many towns the transients by their ignorance and indifference help keep the old-line hack politicians in office.

Just as serious a demoralization occurs when people-turnover results from rapid changes in the character of the community—or from the fact that young people leave to seek education or jobs elsewhere and don't come back.

A couple of years ago the *New York Post* ran a series of lengthy articles in which reporters went back to the New York City neighborhoods of their youth and reported on the current mood and life style there. At roughly the same time *The New York Times* began presenting—on an occasional basis—reports on the moods, life styles, and problems of different "neighborhoods" of the city. At this writing the *Times'* neighborhood reports still appear from time to time.

I began collecting these neighborhood reports of the two newspapers and just recently read through all those I had collected. They covered a total of sixteen New York neighborhoods (Flatbush, northeast Bronx, Park Slope, Greenwich Village, Park Avenue, Jackson Heights, Kingsbridge, Lower East Side, Ozone Park, the Concourse,

Woodside, Riverside Drive, Corona, Astoria, Maspeth, the Yankee Stadium area).

My primary interest was in the mood of the neighborhood as reflected in comments by residents and in the investigators' assessments. For three neighborhoods the reports seemed relatively neutral or unrevealing as far as mood was concerned. But for the other thirteen the mood was distinctly negative in eight and distinctly positive in five (Maspeth, Astoria, Kingsbridge, Corona, and Woodside).

What was of particular interest to me was that in the neighborhoods where the mood was positive the explanations mainly reflected a satisfaction arising from the ongoing character and stability of the neighborhood. And in the neighborhoods where the mood was negative the explanations reflected frustrations and anxieties arising from changes taking place in the character of the neighborhood and from its instability.

For example, characteristics frequently mentioned regarding those neighborhoods where the over-all tenor of reports reflected a negative mood were:

—A decrease in the number of young people in the area and in the number of children playing in the streets
—Changes in the ethnic mix of the neighborhood
—Conspicuous changes in the physical appearance of the neighborhood
—A disappearance from the area of old friends and a decline in the number of people the residents knew by name in their immediate area
—A new mood of anxiety about personal safety, a wariness about going out after dark (which can contribute greatly to a sense of aloneness), and a new mood of uncertainty about the future of the neighborhood
—A faster turnover of tenants

For those other neighborhoods where the over-all tenor of reports reflected a positive mood, these characteristics were frequently mentioned:

—A great many families who had been there two or three generations

—A high level of home ownership and pride in maintaining neatness of grounds both for owned and rented homes

—Many traditional hangouts or centers where people still gathered; and often a church (especially Catholic) that played a unifying role

—Quite widespread neighborly feelings

—Little concern about crime or personal safety

—A mood that the area was a special place, and apart from New York City as a whole

The report on Maspeth in Queens, bordering Brooklyn, was a good example of one that had an emphatically positive tone.

The *Times* report was entitled "Safe, Proud Maspeth."[4] Crime was low and declining at a time when crime in the borough as a whole was soaring. The residents, mainly middle class or lower middle class, were largely of Polish, Lithuanian, German, and Irish ancestry. Greeks and Jews were also mentioned as residents. There were few complicated locks on doors. Multitudes of children played football or roller-skate hockey on clean, tree-lined streets. Neighbors chatted on the stoops. One wife explained proudly that she was a "real Maspether" because she had been born there. A mother said, "In Maspeth children are kept stricter." There were heavy turnouts for parades. Many residents held jobs at offices or factories right in, or on the edge of, Maspeth. The owner of a butcher shop, John Budzynski, age sixty-three, was quoted as saying: "When the kids go to school in the morning they stick their heads in and say 'Hello!' " To him there was no generation gap.

Not far away in white middle-class Jackson Heights, the *Post* report found a pervading mood of tension. There was a feeling that things were changing too fast. Increasingly, young people were leaving the area. People used to seem happier. There was apprehension, and there were iron gates on stores.

To cite another report, that by the *Times* on the Yankee Stadium neighborhood where there used to be a great deal of neighborliness and of leaving doors open, the investigation found that many people now had triple locks plus security bars on their doors. People declined to be quoted by name. Middle-aged and elderly people were now said to "make up so much of the population" and people didn't go out much after dark. The borough president was quoted as stating: "What we need in the area is more young people." Presumably he meant responsible younger residents who would use their vigor to fight to improve the neighborhood and to keep young prowling hoodlums from preying upon older people.

TO SUM UP

In the past several chapters I have been trying to assess the impact of transience and other causes of social fragmentation on the way people behave. It seems to me that, though we are finding that we can adjust to a rootless style of life, we must not become a society that has learned to be rootless.

Rootlessness seems clearly to be associated with a decline in companionship, a decline in satisfying group activities, a decline in mutual trust, and a decline in psychological security. It encourages a shallowness in personal relationships and a relative indifference to community problems. It produces a loss in one's sense of personal well-being along with an increase in both personal and social malaise. And it contributes to a personal sense of powerlessness and insignificance. Whether for better or worse—and I think worse—it encourages hedonism as a life style.

Under the flag of technological progress—with its unthinking demands for giant institutions, environmental turbulence, urban sprawl, and high mobility—we have been pursuing a depersonalizing course that is dangerously radical for man as a social animal. Desmond Morris, the British zoologist, points out: "As a species we are not biologically equipped to cope with a mass of strangers masquerading as members of our tribe." And this, he suggests, is producing considerable human agony.

Man needs a community; he needs continuity. Being a full-fledged card-carrying member of a community is not incompatible—as some assume—with being a free full-fledged individual. It can be, since the community functions through cooperation, consensus and regulations, but it need not be. The community, by encouraging interaction between people, can contribute greatly to the individual's sense of self-respect and can provide opportunities for self-fulfillment. Both contribute to an individual's sense of identity. John Gardner, of Common Cause and an ardent champion of the individual, disposes of the assumed tension between the individual and the community by making an important distinction. He states:

"In some ways modern society binds the individual too tightly, but in other ways it holds him too loosely—and the latter causes as much pain as the former. He feels constrained by the conformity required in a highly organized society, but he also feels lost and without moorings. And both feelings may be traced to the same cause: the disappearance of the natural human community and its replacement by formula controls that irk and give no sense of security."

We need to focus our most creative thinking on developing ways to rediscover the natural human community. And we must work out—invent if necessary—patterns of living that permit us to enjoy some sense of continuity in our lives, so that we can feel clearly that we have a place in the ongoing stream of life.

I will examine what seem to be promising approaches to achieving continuity and community in the next, and final, section.

PART FOUR

Toward
Reducing
the
Fragmentation

European areas, where it comes to income anyway, the
game—for both status and tax reasons—is to try to have
a large highly cream content and low in skim milk.

"If the modern middle-class man does not know who he is, that is in part because he does not know where he is from."—ANTHONY LEWIS, INTERNATIONAL CORRESPONDENT.

20.

On Recovering Our Sense of Continuity

Knowing, in a deep-down sense, where you are from contributes not only to your sense of identity but to your sense of continuity. Psychologist Abraham Maslow in his famed hierarchy of human needs places among the four main ones the social need to attain a sense of security through belonging, through association, through being accepted, through giving and receiving close friendship.

If one's life has continuity, one can look back upon it in his twilight years and see a "continuous whole," to use the dictionary phrase, rather than a long series of disjointed moves, many barely worth remembering. Some psychiatrists believe that for our well-being and sense of continuity we need to have roots in a specific geographic place, to have a sense of place.

Some people feel that simply *knowing* where you are from is enough. A wife who had moved fifteen times in three decades of marriage was deeply concerned that her children were growing up without such knowledge. She explained:

"Although I can only occasionally return to the town

where I was born, the knowledge that it is there and that my sisters and several of my relatives are there lies inside me like a little, warm, furry thing and is comforting. I can go back there and see the people I grew up with and know *home*. But where will my children go?"

Better than "knowledge" of having a home somewhere is living *now* in the area that you identify with sufficiently to think of it as home. That means, for example, that merchants know you well enough to trust you. They don't ask for identification when you give them a check. Jane Wayne, wife of actor David Wayne, has led an extraordinarily high-mobile life, attending dozens of schools and living in dozens of places. Now for a number of years she and her family have lived in the same house in Fairfield County, Connecticut, despite pressures or temptations to move on. It is going to take something pretty compelling to get her to move again. She explained to me that she had finally achieved a *home* and likes very much the sense of roots it gives. When she calls the plumber about an ailing faucet he will say, "Mrs. Wayne, is that the faucet in the back bathroom you had trouble with three or four years ago?" She thinks such interchanges are marvelous.

American society has an urgent need for remedies that will reduce the feeling of so many people that they are in the midst of relative strangers. Achieving a sense of continuity is one major way to shed feelings of strangeness. But where do we begin to gain more sense of continuity?

Ideally, you begin by finding a reasonably congenial area to live in and making a point of sinking roots there for at least a few years. You can of course occasionally sample different houses or apartments but you should stay within the area of familiarity. An exception should be made for young adults under, say, twenty-six. They are still testing themselves, broadening personal horizons and learning as they respond to the challenges of adapting to new environments. Mobility—but not chronic nomadism—may possibly be helpful to them.

But assuming that we are talking about people who are past twenty-six and who find themselves feeling rootless because of mobility or living in a barren metropolized environment, where do we begin, beyond sending Christmas cards to everyone we can remember? Here are some possibilities.

One obvious place for us to begin is to re-examine the built-in assumption of organizations that they can feel free to shift personnel about the landscape purely on the basis of what seems at the moment to be the most efficient utilization of that personnel. Such shifting—by both business and governmental organizations—is often not only mindless but frequently heartless. The social needs of the individuals involved, and of their families, are viewed as non-economic and therefore irrelevant in the decision-making process. It is just assumed that the jobholder and his or her family will *want* to move if they wish to be known as team players within the system.

Such assumptions, unfortunately, are just one aspect of the rising importance of institutions in American life and the corresponding decrease in the seeming importance of the individual. Institutions have reached such size and power that increasingly they are controlling our lives, dictating where and for how long we should live in any one area, and to a larger extent controlling our way of life.

Corporations have been making assumptions about employee movability just as casually as they have assumed that communities where they have plants will be happy to put up with the polluting practices at the plants since the plants provide jobs in the area.

Recently corporations have been getting some warnings and admonitions to proceed more thoughtfully in their transfer policies. Urie Bronfenbrenner, the child psychologist, in a report to the White House Conference on Children recently urged business to cut back on both job travel and job transfers. The National Industrial Conference Board found in a survey that reluctance of managers to move was becoming a nationwide phenomenon. The reluctance was undoubtedly intensified by the increased difficulties transferees began to have in the early 1970s in selling the old house and raising mortgage money to buy a house at the new location. A survey by Louis

Harris & Associates on attitudes of young people asked: "Would you like a job that involves being transferred to different places?" Sixty-three percent said no. And a nationwide firm that helps transferred executives locate homes finds that more and more of them are stating that their current moves are absolutely their last. A spokesman told me, "They have moved so many times that they are putting their feet down and saying that their children have to have some successive years in a town to build up a foundation. They are worried not only about the hardships of moving but about the fact that they don't seem to have time to develop roots."

Some companies are listening. And meanwhile they have been adding up the dollar costs to themselves of their own increasingly liberal policies designed to reassure nervous transferees that any move would not create an undue financial hardship for the transferee and his family. A number have been cutting back on transfers.

One company that has been listening to the rumbles of protests and caution is International Business Machines, whose initials, as indicated, had come to mean "I've Been Moved" to many of the company's families. First the company made some surveys of employee attitudes toward moving. These revealed that, though most employees still wanted the *option* of making a move if a really good opportunity presented itself, employees in general were concerned about not only the costs of moving but the effects upon their families. The latter concern was particularly prevalent among families with school-age children.

Out of the rethinking at IBM has come a specific program designed to force both the company and its employees to be more cautious about transfers. Orders have gone out throughout the company that a relocation should be considered only when really necessary and when it is in the best interests of the employee's career development. Will the new post give him "room to grow"? An employee is to be given more time to think things over before he accepts a relocation. He and his wife are now allowed to visit the new location at company expense *before* deciding whether or not they want to move.

To assure that division managers are taking a conservative approach to transfers, the company now asks each division to estimate the number of transfers that will be necessary during the coming year. A company spokesman advised me that as a result of the new policies "our divisions have informed us that the number of relocations is down and employee concern over moving has subsided."

IBM has also been giving thought to the impact on communities of any large-scale moves of personnel and facilities it is considering. As a result of its thinking, the spokesman said, IBM now tries "to avoid any abrupt turnover in community population."

Boeing, the aerospace firm, is another giant company that is taking a much closer look at a man and his family before moving him. It became concerned by reports that frequent moves were creating an "aerospace syndrome" (see Chapter 17).

Another approach to improving a family's sense of continuity is to work near home. This applies not only to the father but to the mother if she works. Children whose parents work near home have a better understanding of who their parents are—and thus who they themselves are. Their own sense of place will be reinforced.

It is often not economically feasible, however, in today's society to do this. The place of work may be located in an expensive area. Corporations, if they are to be socially responsible, should show more resolve than they have heretofore to locate facilities only in areas that can provide homes for the total range of their employees. And town and city planners should also bear this consideration in mind when encouraging or discouraging companies that want to build facilities in their areas. In many parts of the United States considerable sentiment is building up to force such a viewpoint upon planners.

If a family leads a relatively rootless existence much of the time, because of mobility or because it is surrounded by urban strangers, it still can enjoy some sense of continuity by having a fixed second home to which it can always return. This can be a summer seaside or lakeside cottage, a mountain chalet, a once abandoned farmhouse in the country, a rural townhouse, or a place in a vacation community. Interstate highway systems make such places reasonably accessible if they are within five hundred miles. Approximately two million Americans now have second homes.[1]

The futuristic architect and thinker Buckminster Fuller, who has a professorship in Illinois, is a globe-hopper who scorns national boundaries and applauds today's youth as being "wonderfully uprooted." Yet, as writer Barry Farrell has noted, Mr. Fuller admits there is one place he retreats to that he confesses does give him a deep feeling of belonging. It is an island off the Maine coast that his family has owned for almost seventy years.

I suspect that one reason the island of Martha's Vineyard, Massachusetts, commands such intense loyalty from its summer residents is that the Vineyard has become a substitute—or real—home for many high-mobile or metropolized Americans. Thousands of summer people there maintain year-round subscriptions to the *Vineyard Gazette* even though they get to the Vineyard only for a few summer weeks or months, and perhaps for Thanksgiving or Christmas holidays. I find that my off-island acquaintances who subscribe read each issue intently during the winter. My family, now scattered, gets back together for a while every summer on the Vineyard, where we have been going for twenty-two years, while renting our Connecticut house. Almost all of our neighbors in the part of the Vineyard where we stay have been coming there for at least fifteen years; yet many of them have lived in several parts of the country or world during the same fifteen years. To many, the Vineyard is their real home. There they have come to know their druggist, the hardware clerks, and the First Selectman better than they do the equivalent in the mainland towns or cities where they currently reside. And many seem to feel more intensely about Vineyard issues than they do about issues of their official areas of residence. My wife Virginia was chatting with a fairly new girl at the checkout counter of the A&P when

the girl startled her by asking, "How is your mother?"
Virginia's mother had broken her hip while visiting us a
couple of months earlier. As they continued chatting the
girl said, "Did you know Mrs. K——— broke her hip
too yesterday?" Mrs. K——— is a friend but this was the
first Virginia had heard about the accident.

In our increasingly estranged, uprooted world such
small talk—and such a neighborly grapevine—can be very
gratifying.

Still another promising approach to promoting continuity would be to greatly encourage the present trend toward developing really good four-year community colleges
within commuting distance of every talented young person
in the land. This would reduce the "brain drain" felt by
many communities and tend to keep young people closer
to their families, friends, and geographical roots.

If achieving a geographic sense of place is an impossible
dream because of one's career pattern, one may still
achieve some sense of continuity that is unrelated to
geographic locations.

It is possible to maintain ties to a network of widely
separated friends or colleagues. Family life specialists—a
breed I have observed—are located on campuses or in offices or clinics all across the country, yet many know one
another better than they know their neighbors. They get
together several times a year at conferences, they invite
one another to be guest lecturers at their own places of
employment, they correspond, and they argue with one
another in the pages of their journals. These colleagues
may make contact ten or twenty times a year.

A lawyer I know who for years has been involved in
causes related to civil liberties and women's rights happens
to have roots geographically in New York City but she
also flies off to meetings in various parts of the globe
several times a month and is on the phone to distant colleagues many times a week. Her colleagues probably
mean more to her in terms of a sense of continuity in her
life than do her social friends where she lives and relaxes,
although she and her husband do attach great importance

to having a weekend retreat in the country and get there despite blizzards.

Even enthusiasts can form networks that become meaningful to them over the years though the network members live hundreds of miles apart. Skiing enthusiasts get together for reunions at resorts on many weekends during the winter months, and such networks can remain substantially intact over many years.

From the typical American's viewpoint, however, such networks are exceptional. Often they can be sustained only by the expenditure of a great deal of energy and money.

A strong family solidarity can also help provide one with a sense of meaningful continuity when the world about you is changing. This includes strong ties to spouse, children, and one's parents, brothers, sisters, and close relatives. Much of our geographic and psychological rootlessness is caused by the malfunctioning or breakup of marriages. If there is a breakup—and half of all marriages now do result in divorce, separation, desertion, or annulment—geographic rootlessness often occurs as the wife and children move elsewhere.

In these rootless times marriages are increasingly held together by emotional rather than functional bonds. Many people today feel an urgent need for warmth and stability. One important role of the wife-mother in a mobile family is, in the words of sociologist Warren Bennis, "to provide continuity, the portable roots." It is becoming urgent that we as a society move to place a higher value on family solidarity. One simple way to begin doing so is to require that couples applying for a marriage license wait for a month in order to reflect upon their decision before the license is actually issued. This would greatly reduce the proportion of impulsive or ill-considered unions.

Perhaps the greatest and most challenging possibility of helping a great many people achieve a sense of roots and continuity is to bring more stability to the neighborhoods of large metropolitan areas.

This means slowing the upheaval and obsolescence of

neighborhoods. It means checking the flow of urban sprawl. It means ending the drawing of mean boundaries which only create pressure points that burst and cause fear and pandemonium.

It is inherent in man's nature to be nervous about strangers. The more different they look from us the warier we are. I recall as a farm boy in Pennsylvania hearing about the terrible creatures who were said to maintain a reign of terror in Pittston, Pennsylvania, a coal-mining town a few dozen miles away. The creatures I heard about were said to be bearded, dark-complected Dagos who, I gathered, all carried knives in their teeth and molested decent women. Later my travels took me through Pittston. I was fearful but all I saw were amiable Italian immigrants with somewhat deeper tans than the natives.

People who have a different skin pigmentation than the viewer's are especially likely to be regarded as strangers. And in this regard the 12 or so percent of Americans who are "black" have encountered the most wariness from the "white" majority, especially since the abolition of job opportunities in rural areas by the invention of mechanical crop pickers induced millions of blacks to settle in large urban areas.

We might as well face the fact that the main cat on the back of urban America is these blacks. The way white dwellers have responded to them—by trying to draw tight boundaries around them—contributes greatly to keeping urbanites of all hues and national origins jumping.

The persistence of white urbanites in resisting open housing for anyone who can afford to buy at a fair price is forcing a great amount of upheaval in urban areas. When pressure points break there is an instant scrambling that not only transforms neighborhoods where this breakthrough has occurred but has reverberating effects for miles around. The failure of many Americans to accept the principle of open housing is creating a vast amount of unnecessary rootlessness.

Suburbanites conjure up images of being inundated if they let down the bars even a little bit. The truth is that, if people in an entire metropolitan area would genuinely accept the principle that anyone can buy or rent any home for sale or rent that he can afford at a fair price, that would make it impossible for resisters to flee to new suburban sanctuaries—and urban upheaval would calm down considerably.

If blacks dispersed themselves evenly throughout a large metropolitan area, then at most any neighborhood's population would be somewhere between 10 and 25 percent non-white. As a practical matter, if open housing became a reality so that blacks had freedom of choice as to where they lived and were made to feel welcome, and if suburbs had housing available for all income groups, the proportion of blacks settling in any suburb still would rarely rise above 10 to 15 percent. Many blacks would prefer to remain in inner-city neighborhoods that have become familiar to them. They only resent—and justly— being hemmed in.

Until open housing comes—and it will—blockbusting by realtors eager to generate house turnover by scare tactics should be treated and enforced as a crime against the whole city. All cities should set up and implement the legal machinery which permits residents who are besieged by unwanted solicitations from realtors to force the solicitors into court.

Meanwhile another reality must be faced by responsible blacks. They have a moral duty to condemn and help to combat predatory and vengeful attitudes that a small but conspicuous segment of blacks have toward whites in the cities where they live. The achieving blacks have the task of being leaders of their people rather than, as often has been the case, shunning unruly elements or shrugging off their anti-social behavior. This would go far toward convincing the white majority that they can welcome blacks into white areas without having to assume the entry will be accompanied by an increase in belligerence, violence, or crime. Such increases have *not* occurred in many successfully integrated areas, usually middle- or upper-middle-class. A significant change in the past decade, I believe, is that urban U.S. middle- and upper-class whites are showing a new willingness to accept at least middle- and upper-class blacks as neighbors. Although this is a qualified change it still will loom as a notable development in the world's history of black-white relations.

But in less clearly middle- or upper-class areas, increases in violence or crime have occurred frequently enough with the entry of blacks to make the receiving whites in such areas, who are already in an anxious mood, understandably wary.

Urban turbulence will subside considerably when ethnic groups stop shoving each other around and start cooperating to achieve neighborhood stability. In March 1972 a nationwide gathering of 1,600 representatives of white, black, and Spanish-speaking ethnic groups from fifty American cities held a meeting in Chicago that would have been inconceivable even two years earlier. Spokesmen for Polish, Italian, black, Puerto Rican, and many other ethnic communities felt they had a common cause in fighting the forces promoting urban upheaval.[2] Mrs. Gale Cincotta, a conference leader who wore a big "I'm Staying" button on her blouse to indicate her determination to stay in her central city, summed up a common sentiment by saying:

"What for so long has been considered a natural phenomenon—change in neighborhoods, deteriorating cities—is not natural. It's a plan and somebody's making a lot of money out of changing neighborhoods."

Much of the anger of the conferees was focused upon profiteering by real estate interests in cities that encourage neighborhood deterioration, get the neighborhood abandoned, then after a cosmetics job on the dwellings, obtain inflated mortgage guarantees from the U.S. Federal Housing Administration and maneuver a financial windfall. Whatever the provocation, the fact that urban ethnics are finding common cause and conferring is exciting news indeed.

Three specific steps could be taken to help all lower-income people to remain, and maintain roots, in familiar places. These would all involve government actions.

1. Enact a comprehensive federal guaranteed minimum income program for families that would be geared to regional living costs. This allowance for regional differences would be a force for stability because it would reduce some of the migration of workers in search of higher-paying jobs, or because of temporary layoffs.

2. Help more low-income people develop the pride and stability frequently associated with home ownership. For several years the U.S. Department of Housing and Redevelopment has been experimenting with this concept, under the program known as Turnkey III. It works like ordinary public housing except that the federal payments go toward helping the recipient make payments on a home, usually a single-family house or a townhouse type. The recipient not only has to help out by cash payments but by the "sweat" of maintaining the home. One original objective of the program was to reduce vandalism and irresponsibility among public housing dwellers, which it has. But a more important effect, it turns out, is that it gives people a stake in living where they are. Many "owners" at their own expense are adding terraces and patios. At a project in Raleigh, North Carolina, new owners of the Turnkey homes have formed their own homeowners' association to set curfew rules, standards of maintenance, etc.[3] The non-profit Urban America, Inc., with foundation and church help, has set out to develop broad support for the Turnkey concept among non-profit housing sponsors.

Although to date only about 20,000 public housing dwellers are affected by the concept, there is no reason why this program couldn't in this decade come to involve at least half of all such housing.

3. In making moves that will generate economic activity, both corporations and government agencies should devote far more thought to establishing their installations in salutary areas where possible employees already *are*, such as in the rural South. This offers far more hope for reducing people-turbulence than the present common practice of assuming that needy job-seekers will gladly migrate

to wherever the decision-makers choose to place the installations.

A final important step the people of the United States should take to promote stability and a personal sense of continuity is to stop glorifying growth for growth's sake. At the top of my hometown newspaper is the slogan "Grow or Go." The town has doubled in size in twenty years. Happily the slogan is now in very small type. The grow-or-go philosophy long cherished by Chamber of Commerce boosters is at the heart of much of our urban turmoil. It has encouraged rapid, sprawling growth which is overwhelming established communities and recreational facilities.

City and state planners are starting to become wary of uncontrolled growth. They used to assume that more people meant more prosperity and more tax revenues. But now they are finding that as they get many more people those people tend to demand more services than they pay for. One of the fastest-growing regions in the U.S., Santa Clara County, California, down the peninsula from San Francisco, is near bankruptcy.[4] And the county, once made up of visible small towns and cities, has become a sad example of urban sprawl.

The first step to getting uncontrolled growth in hand is to stabilize the nation's population by taking advantage of conception control techniques now readily available. Until population stabilization is achieved Americans should think in terms of establishing viable communities—both by starting fresh and by developing them within existing metropolitan areas.

It is this monumental challenge of developing really authentic, workable, scaled-to-man communities that I will explore in the remaining chapters.

"The quest for community will not be denied, for it springs from some of the powerful needs of human nature—need for a clear sense of cultural purpose, membership, status and continuity. Without these, no amount of mere material welfare will serve to arrest the developing sense of alienation in our society. . . ."
—ROBERT A. NISBET, SOCIOLOGIST, UNIVERSITY OF CALIFORNIA, RIVERSIDE.

21.

New Approaches to a Sense of Community

If the yearning for community is long frustrated the quest for it can become dangerous to a democratic society, Dr. Nisbet stated. He is a leading scholar in the area of the individual's relation to community.

When environmental turbulence or strangeness blocks meaningful association within a democratic group, the individual may seek his identity in some unit of a totalitarian government, such as a local unit of the Communist Party or the Hitler Youth. "The greatest appeal of the totalitarian party, Marxist or other," Nisbet contends, "lies in the capacity to provide a sense of moral coherence and communal membership to those who have become . . . victims of the sense of exclusion from the ordinary channels of belonging in a society."[1]

In a free, well-conceived society, Nisbet emphasized, a person ordinarily finds community through social groups "small enough to infuse the individual's life with a sense of membership in society and meaning of the basic moral values."

This stress on size or scale emerged too in a study covering several countries and cultures that UNESCO sponsored some years ago.[2] The study developed four criteria for a healthy society:

1. The important social groupings are small.

2. All aspects of life are closely integrated. Work, for instance, is not something apart and distinct.

3. Social belonging is automatic.

4. Changes occur relatively slowly, and their purpose and direction are apparent.

Those are excellent criteria to keep in mind as we examine a number of the contemporary efforts to recapture a sense of community.

Some of our planners, I believe, get their priorities mixed. During 1968 a special task force set up by the American Institute of Planners issued a report entitled "New Communities: Challenge for Today." In the report the task force listed thirteen objectives for "new communities"; and not a one of the thirteen said anything about enabling dwellers to achieve a sense of community, unless you consider one vague reference to providing people with "greater social and economic opportunities, especially in the areas of housing, employment and education."

On the other hand urban affairs expert Patrick Moynihan, in talking about how to save U.S. cities a few months later, got (I thought) near to the heart of the problem, in discussing public buildings. He called for "a public architecture of intimacy, one that brings people together in an experience of confidence and trust . . . and restores to American public life the sense of shared experience, trust and common purpose that seems to be draining out of it."

The "sense of shared experience" he calls for—and the UNESCO criterion that "social belonging is automatic"—both assume that the individual can still have a say in neighborhood matters that vitally concern him or her. But what are the realities? A woman who lives part of each week in her house in a Manhattan skyscraper and part of it in a small town in a semirural area of Long Island feels the difference in "having a say" at the two locations is enormous. In the small town she is in several community projects and she plunges into battles over garbage collection and/or whether the lounge of the new school should have a marble fireplace. In New York she knows few of her neighbors and confines her "say" pretty much to professional colleagues.

Recapturing this right of the individual to have a say about matters that clearly affect him is one of the most formidable cultural challenges of modern urban life.

Ken Patton, Economic Development Director for New York City, was in a Brooklyn living room discussing this challenge in concrete terms.

"Take the guy sitting in Sheepshead Bay shaking his fist at airplanes that are coming in over his house to land at Kennedy Airport. The air traffic patterns for the planes are controlled by the Federal Aviation Administration, which is located out in Suffolk County, and it is obeying rules that are established in Washington. This man shaking his fist feels there is nothing he can do about it." Or consider the planning for a subway that may or may not place a stop near his neighborhood. Plans for the subway are in the hands of a regional tri-state planning board. "Everything is getting further from him. He has lost any sense of being anything," Mr. Patton continued.

The frustrations of the man in Sheepshead Bay and of other New Yorkers is aggravated by the mindless overlapping of service districts: New York City has 30 health districts, 57 sanitation districts, 31 school districts, and 75 police precincts. Mayor John Lindsay confessed that all this is contributing to the "fragmentation of citizen involvement."

Mr. Patton expressed a conviction that ways can be found for people like the man in Sheepshead Bay to get his views heard and acted upon. Authentic communities within cities must be developed to give amplification to the ordinary citizen's grievances and yearnings.

Many thousands of Americans, especially younger

middle-class, college-educated ones, are seeking escape from the feelings of helplessness and meaninglessness by retreating into what they hope will be more congenial communal settings. Author Wright Morris once said of such moves: "It is a pattern of flight from a world that will not stand still." Many are going into traditional villages such as are found in southern Vermont. Dozens of new families in the towns and villages in Windham County are escapees from metropolitan life. They have developed new—usually less financially rewarding—livelihoods in exchange for immersion in community living.

A great many others have been joining together in communes. In the four years starting in 1968 literally thousands of communes developed in the U.S. Some simply involved several people living together in a city apartment building or cluster of row houses. They share costs and sometimes physical intimacy in varying degrees. The sharing of physical intimacy—though publicized—may not exist, or may be a minor attraction. Some people, women especially, just like the idea of having people around them when they get up in the morning: or the presence of other adults who can share in baby-sitting.

Hundreds of more ambitious groups have sought a joint return to nature and to small-community living by setting up communes in rural areas of southern Oregon, New Mexico, or Appalachia, to mention just three of the more popular places. These are often based to some extent on communes of earlier America. One "family" of 270 persons traveled all the way from San Francisco to a rustic hollow in Tennessee. They were trying to slow down the pace of life. Although the group involved more than a dozen four-person marriages, the "family" was received in friendly fashion by local residents because of the members' obvious seriousness of purpose and because they held a view of the world somewhat compatible with fundamentalist religious beliefs common in the area. Then too there are dozens of communes of young monastic religious mystics.

Even though the yearning for community is very real the people involved in many of the new communes do not necessarily live happily forever after. A psychiatric social worker in the New York area advised me that many appeals to her association were made by people in communes who were having problems involving jealousy or children. Also, many of the more alienated young Americans who are attracted to communal life have led such transient, angry, emotionally constricted lives that when they join a commune, seeking escape, they are not really ready to stabilize their lives or to accept involvement and long-term interaction with others. Restlessness and aloofness are too deeply ingrained in their personalities.

The progress of those communes that prove durable should be followed with keen analytical interest by behavioral scientists and community planners for insights that may have applicability in the present surge of interest in community development. Thus far, however, the communes must be viewed primarily as symptomatic of the national problem.

For solutions applicable to the tens of millions of ordinary, lonely, uprooted Americans a broad-scale search must be undertaken that will harness the most creative thinking of not only architects, planners, and government officials but psychiatrists, psychologists, philosophers, sociologists, and especially specialists in child development and family living and concerned citizens whatever their background.

The search will focus primarily on two challenges:

1. To find ways to bring metropolitan areas back into scale with man by establishing within them networks of communities so that every resident can sense that he is a part of an ongoing community in which he can participate and have a say.

2. To start afresh and establish brand-new towns and cities outside the present spread of megalopolis that are designed for man rather than for automobiles or corporate plants.

Let us now explore the first, seemingly more formidable challenge—that of humanizing the metropolis.

A good place to start is New York City and environs, America's greatest concentration of jam-packed people. By conservative count Greater New York City encompasses somewhere between 11 and 16 million people, depending on how you count. That is more than the total population of at least nine Western states (Oregon, Colorado, Montana, Idaho, Wyoming, New Mexico, Arizona, Utah, and Nevada).

As we noted in Chapter 19, New York is not quite the hopeless sprawl of people that one might assume in looking at it from the air. There are still some robustly viable neighborhoods such as Maspeth. Some New Yorkers have even found community in high-rise apartment building areas.

An important lesson in community-building within a large city has emerged from the Park Slope area of Brooklyn near Prospect Park.

The area contains thousands of seventy-five-year-old brownstone row houses once owned by prosperous Brooklynites. The brownstone areas began to run down, especially after World War II, as owners moved to the suburbs instead of trying to cope with coal-burning stoves, gaslight fixtures, ailing toilets, jungles of lead pipe in the cellar, and peeling wallpaper. The homes became mainly rooming houses with old people and transients as their new occupants. There were almost no children, and young people were moving out in droves. The area was deteriorating so rapidly that slumdom seemed only a few years away.

Several younger people with roots in the neighborhood decided to make a fight to try to revive it. One of their leaders was a handsome soft-spoken young Brooklyn youth worker named Joe Ferris. They set up a Park Slope Betterment Committee and began trying to persuade friends and acquaintances that these dilapidated old four-story houses with pinnacles, mahogany paneling, numerous fireplaces, stained-glass windows, and twelve-foot ceilings were basically solid and if renovated could be a great bargain for families tired of paying high rents for cramped apartments. In the beginning such houses could be bought for as little as $12,000. And a park, a museum, a library, and a zoo were nearby. These young residents invited potential buyers to tours of some of the homes.

The first several dozen "settlers" were understandably

nervous and plunged into the renovations with enormous energy. Like those to follow, they themselves did much of the work such as painting, stripping walls, staining beams, and building flowerboxes for geraniums outside the windows. The splendid results they achieved in terms of spacious, livable homes inspired others to buy, and the dozens of settlers soon became first hundreds, then thousands. Many of the old brownstones within a 144-square-block area have been "settled" by newcomers. Block by block the "new people" blended into an ethnically mixed neighborhood. Many of them were middle-class teachers, editors, lawyers, and business people.

In their renovating the couples sought counsel from each other on problems of plumbing, electricity, wallpaper, fireplaces. Soon there was a great deal of conferring and helping each other, and this led to coffee parties and then cocktail and dinner parties. And these led to many discussions over larger, community-type problems they all faced.

Since many of the wives had careers there was an urgently felt need for day care of small children. No acceptable nursery was nearby so a number of the parents decided to set up a cooperative one and persuaded a neighborhood church to make two rooms available. Parents who were interested painted the rooms and made or procured creative equipment for the rooms. All this involved a vast amount of telephoning and holding of meetings. Another problem was cleaning up the typically littered streets in that part of Brooklyn. The need to cooperate regarding litter helped lead to the formation of block associations. These brought newcomers and old residents together to arrange Saturday morning street sweeps. Everybody got out with brooms and the Sanitation Department was glad to cooperate by flushing the streets after the sweep and by making bulk pickups of neatly piled debris.

Still another problem was that, though Prospect Park was nearby, the park was alleged to be too dangerous for children to play in because of roving bands of young hellraisers. So the fathers got some footballs and they and their children began having touch football games in the park every Saturday when weather permitted. They still do.

Thus, what started as a thousand or so families seeking a "buy" in a home became—in the process of conferring and working together to make their homes and area livable —a true community of interacting neighbors. The block organizations or other groups now have gala cookouts with each neighbor contributing a native dish. There are champagne breakfasts in the park in the spring and block festivals for young and old.

The block associations are planting trees and many residents have—for the first time in their lives—become intensely active on political issues that involve civic improvement. Hundreds of close friendships have emerged. Everywhere—in the stores, in the streets, in the park— you now see people chatting, where people rarely chatted before. And everywhere there are children playing.

One woman told me that the nearby Brooklyn Museum "is always fighting for its life and we work for it, and we work for the Brooklyn Academy of Music, because we believe we have to sustain and maintain it." Then she added, "I don't know why but I never worked for a thing before in my life."

Another said: "I have a sister who lives in a very typical suburb of Syracuse and she talks about how isolated she feels, especially when it comes to emergencies or getting away. Here we take care of each other's babies, borrow things, and rely on each other in very personal ways. It makes living very rich and has created a really incredible sense of community." And her husband added: "There are a lot of people we often talk to and yet feel no obligation to invite them into our home when we're having a party; and they feel the same way. There is no forced sociability. We can still enjoy our privacy."

Park Slope is not unique in New York. The "brownstoners" have recently been creating authentic communities out of rundown areas on the Upper West Side, in Chelsea on the Lower East Side in Manhattan, and at Cobble Hill, Boerum Hill, and Fort Greene in Brooklyn.

In literally hundreds of areas of New York City, in fact, the yearning for community in that vast, shifting, depersonalized megalopolis is bursting out in concrete actions. The progress made in gaining more neighborhood control of schools is simply symbolic of a broader striving.

Ten years ago block parties had virtually disappeared in New York. By 1970, the city received more than 2,500 requests to close off streets so that block residents could stage a sweep-up or have a party—usually both.[3] Sometimes they plant trees or clear up a vest-pocket park. And sometimes they have carnivals or flower festivals. But mainly they have found a way to know—and not just nod to—people living next door to them. The absence of cars when the streets are closed off gives a new dimension to their street that helps them feel the street now belongs to them. One city official told me, "When we began closing off streets to traffic people just poured out into them. They wanted to get back together again."

The striving for community in New York is not confined to occasional block parties. A few years ago sixty-two specific "communities" were recognized by the city and each was given a Community Planning Board. The members of each were appointed by the president of the borough containing the community. At first the Boards were not taken very seriously by anyone. They were advisory, and met once a month and had no real power. But in the early 1970s—with the dramatic surge of interest in bringing a say in government to the neighborhoods—these Boards took on new life. A 1969 law began requiring the City Planning Commission to consult with a community's Board before making any decisions that would importantly affect that area, such as granting a variance to zoning laws or undertaking major construction.

The Boards discovered that most city agencies were reluctant to override a Community Board when it clearly reflecting the sentiments of most of the residents. For ple the Community Board representing the Yorkville of Manhattan has won zoning battles and forced s or changes in plans on controversial projects rang-om high-rise buildings to subway construction in

Central Park.[4] And the Board in Greenwich Village was influential in getting the city government to promise to demolish the tall, grim, noisy Women's House of Detention on Village Square. Within just two years the boards have gained impressively not only in power but in popularity. Where it was once difficult to get anyone to serve, some Manhattan Community Boards have a waiting list of more than a hundred and fifty people seeking to serve on them.

At this writing the mayor, along with several other top city officials, is moving to make these Community Boards the basic unit of "government" for their neighborhoods, with a "Community Hall" for each neighborhood. It is planned that a full-time "Community Director" will be selected from a list of five recommended by each Community Board. The present crazy-quilt boundaries of fire, police, sanitation, etc., districts will be made to conform as closely as possible to Community Board lines. Some memberships on each Board will become automatic, such as a representative from the area's School Board. And ultimately most members to the Community Boards will be elected by the people of the area at a "Community Election Day" that will be held throughout the city.

The aim, in the mayor's words, is to make "city agencies more responsive and accountable at the neighborhood level and to reduce the alienation and distance that citizens feel toward a remote city government." Even when the Boards take on a more imposing structure, their decisions will still be advisory. New Yorkers as they move toward their avowed goal of "decentralization" will have to decide by analysis what functions and policies affecting communities really demand city-wide uniformity or central planning (with advice from the communities affected). Air pollution controls, for example, may require city-wide policies. And at the same time New Yorkers must decide what functions and policies can be determined primarily by the voice of the people at the community level. It may well be that they will decide that issues involving recreation, education, and fire protection, for example, can be almost fully resolved at the community level.

Although the people of New York are starting to reach out for community they have a long way to go to equal the sense of community that prevails in the comparably vast megalopolis of Greater London. Despite its great size, most of London is a collection of townlike neighborhoods such as Islington and Carlyle Square. Nearly a decade ago the Royal Commission on Local Government in Greater London concluded: "As many local functions as possible should be given to local authorities of the smallest practical size. Local authorities should be small enough to maintain and promote a sense of community in local affairs."

London is dotted with verdant small parks where people can walk or play without fear and with squares that frequently serve as centers for the many neighborhoods. Unlike American cities, London has for the most part refused to permit itself to be strangled—and its neighborhoods to be slashed—by skyways and expressways. Likewise, it has strongly resisted skyscrapers and other high-rise buildings. But more important, London seems to be a far more neighborly city than New York. I have heard several reports similar to that of a New York City professor who, with his wife, took a flat in South Kensington for several months. Within two days there was a formal note through the mail slot from a Mrs. W———— who lived nearby. It said she would appreciate their company at an informal party three days hence. Most of the people on the street were there. The professor and his wife also received notes from the lady who lived above them and from the girls who lived in the basement flat, each inviting them to drop by at a certain hour. Within two weeks they felt very much settled in and subsequently developed several warm and lasting friendships on that street.

If communities are to survive and thrive in American cities, it should become national, state, and city policy to put expressways that go through cities largely underground, as they do in Guanajuato, Mexico. Such expressways could be covered with playgrounds and small parks. Engineers will cry that it is much more expensive to put them underground, but such a nationwide policy would be considerably less expensive than exploring the moon, and considerably less expensive than conducting a protracted war 10,000 miles away in Southeast Asia. Outcries from residents have already forced the expressway builders to go at least partially underground in planned or future construction in Philadelphia, San Francisco, and Boston.

Since apartment living seems to be the wave of the future in urban America and Europe too—in both the urbs and the suburbs—schools of architecture and urban planning should start requiring their students to live a year in a typical high-rise apartment complex as part of their apprenticeship. The students should be required to prepare papers on how some high-rise dwellers have succeeded in humanizing their environment and why others have failed. They should develop concepts on how to humanize life in apartment buildings.

They might, incidentally, gain an understanding of this challenge by considering the experiment of a photographer in Munich, Germany. He was so outraged by the cold, depersonalized appearance and arrangement of a new nine-story apartment building that he proposed to take pictures of the inhabitants and exhibit the photos, poster size, in the windows of their apartments as an experiment. Most liked the idea and suddenly the façade of the entire building blossomed with faces. Almost overnight the anonymous prisonlike atmosphere of the building melted. Dwellers recognized and began hailing their neighbors in the corridors and on the street.[5]

An obvious approach to bringing apartment living into scale with man would be to lower the profiles of apartment buildings down to two- or three-story garden apartments or townhouse-type structures. If many apartments are involved they should be oriented inward—as toward a court that contains benches, greenery, recreational facilities for children, and perhaps a pool—to promote more spontaneous sociability. The typical high mobility of apartment renters which has frequent unfortunate consequences for both individuals and society could be reduced by public policy, such as by providing tax incentives that would encourage people to invest in cooperatives or condominiums, and thus develop a stake in their community.

Where large high-rise apartment houses are inevitable, public policy—as expressed perhaps through zoning regulations—should encourage builders to devise structures in which every fifth floor is left open. The open area would be a "neighborhood" center. It would have shrubs, swings, lounge chairs, and a nook—manned or automated —where residents on nearby floors could purchase soft drinks, newspapers, stamps, and staple items such as bread and coffee. Stairs on escalators would lead to each open deck-type floor so that every resident would be within two easy flights of an open area. Such an arrangement would promote a more relaxed, neighborly atmosphere for those who chose to enjoy it.

In suburbs where single-family dwellings are still practical, public policy—as expressed perhaps by zoning officials—should discourage the developers' present common practice of using all the land available to build several hundred substantially identical residential houses on one-third-acre plots, and instead encourage cluster housing. This would make it economically feasible to require that a third of the total acreage remain as open, landscaped land available to all residents. It would contain places to lounge and an area where children might wish to play. There would be pathways but no roads. In short, it would be designed to promote casual neighborliness.

Finally, public policy should encourage—by zoning regulations if necessary—the big shopping plazas, which increasingly are filling a vacuum and becoming pseudo downtowns, to become authentic downtowns with provision for public areas and facilities that belong to the community, not to the developer.

By such moves, perhaps we can halt the drift toward a mass society of feebly rooted people and achieve settings small enough in scale to meet people's needs for social interaction and a sense of significant citizenship.

22.

Are One-Layer Communities the Answer?

In exploring new approaches to creating a sense of community, we must decide what to make of a phenomenon quite new to the American scene—the emergence of many hundreds of essentially one-layer communities. There are not only communities consisting overwhelmingly of people in one income group or ethnic category but also, most recently, many communities containing people who overwhelmingly come from one age bracket. These one-layer communities are found not only in metropolitan areas but outside them as well.

The mass producers of housing who have emerged so prominently since World War II—with their vast tracts and "planned communities"—are partly responsible for the phenomenon. They tend to become specialists in catering to one particular market for housing. And they have learned they can often move houses faster by appealing to one type of prospect. Of course they employ status appeals but they also attract buyers by playing to the very real tendency for human birds of a feather to flock together—and to try to draw territorial lines around their nesting places. Even the new communes are pretty much age-graded.

This surge to one-layer communities raises some hard questions. Should public policy seek to discourage or encourage a trend that obviously is both profitable and at the moment at least apparently popular?

Traditional towns such as Glens Falls, New York, in contrast, are small functioning worlds, microcosms. There are usually streets where the rich tend to congregate or where certain ethnics settle or where older or poor people predominate. But such communities are small enough in scale so that all groups see each other and cooperate on projects. Children see men with lunch buckets, live near the firemen they envy, and know people of all ages. There is a sense of wholeness.

Possibly most startling is the trend toward age-layered communities. There are, most obviously, the new "retirement communities" (see Chapter 8) where the sight of a child is a rarity. Some specify you have to be fifty to move in. Managements of some of these communities boast of their age segregation as an asset. Del E. Webb, founder of the chain of Sun City retirement communities, recently proclaimed: "In the average community there certainly is no way of controlling the age bracket of our neighbors or the number of their children. This we can control, thus avoiding the problem of mixing conflicting living patterns and, in many cases, forcing social contacts that actually constitute for our senior citizens an invasion of privacy."

It is not only senior citizens who are being layered out by age. At many suburban tract "communities" built around shopping plazas or golf courses, all the available housing falls within a narrow price range so that the tracts tend to get families with, say, preschool children or with high school children. And there are now developments where children's age is specified as a factor carefully weighed in considering applicants. The Ring Brothers, developers in Los Angeles, have one large complex of units that is designed for families with children under the age of eight and another designed for adults without children.

Still another variant of age layering is the growth of large apartment "communities" for singles only. These are appearing in several U.S. cities. Perhaps the most ambitious is the chain of South Bay Clubs, based on garden apartment complexes with clubhouse and recreational facilities, that started in Los Angeles. Now it is spreading to other parts of the country. There are about a dozen in California alone. Each has an average of approximately one thousand residents. Applicants must be single and in their twenties or thirties. The manager of one club said of his clientele: "They're all strangers in some way." A friend of mine who checked the "action" at three South Bay Clubs before he married said of them: "I've been struck by the relative absence of the type of people I would call swingers, and think of the residents more in terms of the large number of divorced, socially inept, and foreign people who live there. Nearly 40 percent come directly to the clubs from out of state."

It is the current popularity of retirement communities that is most in conflict with our preconceptions of American life patterns.

I described in Chapter 8 the massive trend of older people toward segregating themselves from society at large and some of the reasons for it. Considering the givens of modern society, the bargain they have struck is understandable. Hundreds of thousands find living even in thin-walled metal boxes that are packed a dozen to an acre in a mobile park a thousand miles from "home" offers a more congenial setting for retirement than the last neighborhood they lived in before retirement.

That is what is happening, but can we settle for it? What is it doing to those older people involved? What is it doing to society?

Though it is certainly not intentional, the self-segregating older folks are copping out. In the study of 521 men who had retired to Arizona, cited earlier, the retirees were asked:

"Do you personally think that retired persons should take part in some type of community or public service, or

*do you think they deserve the right to relax and should
feel free to avoid activities of this type?"*

Only a fourth of the respondents felt it was best if older
people remained active in some form of service-oriented
or community activity. Most felt they deserved to feel
free to avoid such activities since they had earned the
right to a life of leisure and thus had no obligation to become involved in anything but purely social or recreational
activities.

In short most had fully embraced a hedonistic life
style. Any busyness was leisure-oriented. How would such
people expect to achieve a sense of self-fulfillment, which
psychologists have found to be so vital to well-being? Take
up a hobby? Psychiatrist Robert Weiss is dubious. He
states: "For the retired, activities that clearly benefit
others, or display competence in an important or valued
way, may substitute for employment; but a make-work
task, a hobby, or just keeping busy will not."

A minister in a west Florida retirement town said that
a number of retirees have told him they want to be members of his church but that they don't want to be involved
in church activities because they are retired. He could not
resist telling one such retiree: "I don't remember seeing
anything in the Bible about retired Christians."

Some people in retirement communities might also be
charged with dropping out on responsible citizenship.
There is evidence that where people in retirement centers
have the right to vote in local affairs their reluctance to
approve bond issues—as for schools—which might affect
their property tax is conspicuous. The small town of
Woodburn, Oregon, on the fertile plain south of Portland,
found itself with a Woodburn Senior Estates containing
about 1,200 retired couples from thirty-six states in its
midst. They live in many rows of neat small houses built
around a recreational area. Many residents ride big tricycles. A large sign by this Senior Estates area, when I
saw it, proclaimed: "This is a Happy Place." But the town
of Woodburn was not happy. The senior citizens were a
major reason why in 1969 it took four different ballotings
by the town's voters to get a school budget approved, and

then only after the increase that town officials had requested was slashed in half.

Further, older people are tending, perhaps out of discouragement, to neglect their responsibilities to nurture others and share their wisdom. Mental health experts Leo Levy and Harold Visotsky state, "The grandparent-child relationship has always been a special one and in our view a constructive one for both parties." They are concerned that many psychiatric casualties among older people occur because they have been living outside any family context.

Many older people have become so imbued with the value of independence that they are failing to play their needed roles in generational interdependence. Anthropologist Margaret Mead believes that "one of the reasons we have as bad a generation gap today as we do is that grandparents have copped out." She states: "Young people are being deprived of the thing they need most—perspective, to know why their parents behave so peculiarly and why their grandparents say the things they do." The present generation of grandparents, she added, has seen the most change of any generation in history, and young people need to know about the change, and about the past, before they can really understand the present or reasonably chart their own future. While fostering independence for older people, we need to find a style of aging, she feels, that will encourage older people "to think in terms of what they can do for someone else."

Anthropologist Sula Benet of Hunter College came up with some fascinating observations about the importance of age-mingling in her study of the Abkhasians, who live in the part of Russia between the Black Sea and the Caucasus Mountains.[2] The Abkhasians are a life-loving people who have attracted considerable scientific attention because of their extraordinary longevity. Many villages have a number of people between ninety and a hundred and ten years old. An Abkhasian's chance of living past 90 are about six times as great as that of an American.

In searching for explanations for their longevity Professor Benet was impressed particularly by their sense of group identity, which "gives each individual an unshaken feeling of personal security and continuity." She was also deeply impressed by their attitude toward aging. They do not have a phrase for "old people"; those over a hundred are called long-living people. Even the very old people are never seen sitting around in chairs for long periods, like vegetables. They have no fear of becoming "dependents" and they never "retire." They continue all their lives working at tasks geared to their energy levels, and with increased age their status increases rather than decreases. In a culture which places such a high value on continuity in its traditions the elders are indispensable in their transmission. Professor Benet feels mobile Americans can and should learn something from the Abkhasian view of long-living people.

To sum up, the emergence of one-layer "communities" based upon age may be economically attractive to entrepreneurs, and they may seem attractive to some residents, by filling a kind of vacuum in offering a way people can quickly ease feelings of loneliness. But in my view they are misguided, socially corrosive institutions. Only a badly confused society would have spawned them. A wiser society in its pursuit of community will abort them.

Now we turn to one-layer communities of another broad type: those that cluster people together by income levels or ethnic categories. I take them up together rather than separately because income layers often define ethnic layers. A suburb that offers few houses for sale at less than $40,000—or which permit only single-family dwellings on one-acre plots—may be creating a one-layer town not only economically but also ethnically. No one with an annual income under $20,000 could afford a $40,000-plus house in such a town. Intentionally or unintentionally, WASPs and/or Jews would probably be greatly overrepresented in such a town while people of east or south European ancestry would be underrepresented. And there would usually be, at best, relatively few black Americans.

Both types of layering abound in today's larger metropolitan areas. When it comes to income layering, the game—for both status and tax reasons—is to try to have a layer high in cream content and low in skim milk.

A good example of a one-income-layer community that went after the cream is Smoke Rise, New Jersey. Before you can buy a house in Smoke Rise, which is near Butler in the north central part of the state, you have to be screened for membership in this "club community." The gates are guarded and the many hundreds of residents must have Smoke Rise stickers on their windshields.

The management boasts: "Corporate executives predominate among the heads of families living here." The new houses available to people who are accepted by the club for membership are mainly in the $60,000 to $90,000 range. Not really posh. It's not a chairman-of-the-board kind of community. But the houses have relatively handsome settings. Smoke Rise has a special appeal to families of transferred executives, and the management promotes this by providing an "Executive Transfer Plan" under which you can defer payment on your new house until you unload the house back at your former place of residence.

Smoke Rise's special appeal to certain types of reticent or insecure executive transferees and their families is that upon being accepted by the organization to live there all further anxieties about winning social acceptance are minimal. There are no pains of being on a tennis or beach club waiting list. All become available upon acceptance. A coordinator of social activities will see that you get a chance to go on theater parties or get into the dancing groups or into the Round Robin Bridge for Women of Smoke Rise if you wish.

Another interesting approach to creating one-layer communities is at Mission Viajo in the hills south of Los Angeles. The management has built five distinct neighborhoods on the hillsides that stretch for thousands of acres along the Santa Ana Freeway. Each neighborhood aims at a different income layer. When I was there, houses in the Coronado neighborhood cost around $22,000 . . . those in the Eldorado neighborhood about $28,000 . . . those in the LaPaz neighborhood ran roughly from $30,000 to $40,000 . . . those in the Granada neighborhood, many with fairway views, were somewhat higher . . . and the houses in the most elite Mission Ridge neighborhood "at the very top of Mission Viajo" were priced in the $55,000 to $65,000 range.

Altogether there are in five-layered Mission Viajo many thousands of slightly separated homes with Spanish touches. Residents can belong to the recreational center by paying a membership fee and annual dues. The management also provides churches, tree-shaded shopping areas, and has arranged for a fire department and for schools up through two years of college. There is a nearby golf course.

The arguments in favor of having a house in any kind of thriving one-layer community boil down to two: (1) the birds-of-a-feather one and (2) the fact that realtors tend to place a higher value on houses in a homogeneous setting. The realtors feel more secure. They become confused and worried when they have to set a price in a "mixed" neighborhood, whether the mixture is in the kinds of houses or in the kinds of people. They tend to become cautious.

But that is about the end of the pro arguments.

A "community"—if it is to be an authentic one—needs balance. It should offer reasonable living facilities for all the people needed to make the community function. Its schoolteachers, clerks, policemen, craftsmen, custodians, and blue-collar workers should not have to commute. In predominantly middle-class Mahwah, New Jersey (pop. 11,000), which has been aggressive in attracting new industries, less than 5 percent of the thousands of workers employed there can afford to live there. The rest must commute, mainly from New York and Newark at an annual cost of more than $1,000 a year for each working family, not to mention the hundreds of hours of traveling time. The town has prohibited new apartment construction and enforced one and two acre zoning. Mahwah's residents enjoy a tax bonanza—with enormous tax revenues from corporations and with few social services to support. In Japan such an arrangement would be unthinkable. Japanese companies feel a responsibility to assure employees of adequate housing in the localities where they establish facilities. Any major U.S. hiring organization should, in establishing new facilities, make sure that reasonable living facilities are available to all employees within six or seven miles.

As American companies move toward "cleanness" in their facilities, as at sophisticated electronic plants, they are increasingly welcomed by suburbs eager to ease property taxes. This has contributed to the fact that today about 80 percent of all new job opportunities are opening up in the suburbs.[3] Yet the U.S. Census Bureau finds that only 5 percent of all American suburbanites are black Americans. If the rest want jobs in the suburbs they are expected to commute from inner cities, which can be a heavy burden. Partly they don't live in the suburbs because of exclusion. But even with open housing laws, they, and members of many other ethnic groups, frequently just can't afford to obtain living accommodations in the suburbs. The building industry—complemented by building codes and union rules—has permitted decent housing costs to become preposterously high.

This growing inability of many people of modest means to live where they can find work is generating class and race tensions of serious proportions. And it is aggravating feelings of uprootedness. One of the hottest political issues of the early 1970s is going to center on the legal and other efforts being made to provide homes in suburbs for people of moderate and modest incomes seeking to fill job opportunities in those areas. These efforts involve, for example, proposals to devise a broad new taxing arrangement for financing public schools (rather than depending entirely on local property taxes). This dependence on local property taxes creates gross inequities in the quality of education available to children in the same area, and encourages towns to keep out people who would not pay their "share" of property taxes. Within Illinois, for example, some school districts spend nearly four times as much per child as others do. In Texas a federal court has held that school taxes tied to property are discriminatory and unconstitutional.

The efforts also involve developing county rules to require big developers to produce at least 15 percent of their units for moderate- and low-income families. They involve proposals that no federal installations can go into communities that refuse to provide housing for the workers who will work at the installations.

Providing appropriately priced homes for all the people who are required to make a community function seems like a minimum goal for a democratic society that can put men on the moon.

But even without the factor of social obligation, there are excellent reasons why Americans should view their multitudes of one-layer "communities" as poor answers to their mounting need for functioning communities. This is true whether the layering is by income, ethnic group, or age.

A community that does not have both older people and children, that does not have working people as well as bosses, that does not have town characters as well as conventional types, isn't really a community at all. I would agree with sociologist Philip Slater that such a place, rather, "is the same kind of truncated and deformed monstrosity that most people inhabit today."

Children who are exposed year after year to only one kind of people who think and act pretty much the same grow up crippled in their understanding of the world. And if they see few older people they grow up missing the sense of continuity so essential to well-being.

People, especially older people, who take refuge in vast mobile home parks are crippling themselves not only by being separated from many kinds of people but by being isolated from the challenges of a real community. W. Scott Ditch, who has long studied the problem of how to make a new community work, comments: "Our retreat to mobile home parks is a travesty of our whole industrial system. If you are in a mobile home park you are forced to give up many aspects of community life except the very artificial ones such as gathering at the recreational centers." The opportunities for service and the chance to help effect meaningful improvements in your environment are greatly reduced.

In Chapter 21 I described the extraordinarily high level of community spirit and neighborliness that prevailed in the rejuvenated area of the Park Slope, Brooklyn. Some characteristics of the people of this neighborhood are pertinent. The new settlers—mainly younger professional and business families with children—blended in with older long-time residents and became friends. Natives and newcomers worked together. Of the first four presidents of the Park Slope council, three were natives. One settler explained: "We wanted to get back to a place where all kinds of people, all kinds of income groups lived." I was sitting in a living room on a block called St. John's Place when he made that statement. Someone commented that within that one block not only WASPs, Catholics, and Jews lived side by side in neighborly harmony but specifically there were Koreans, American blacks, Haitians, Spaniards, Jamaicans, Australians, and U.S. Southerners. The settlers are convinced that Park Slope has a better chance than most New York neighborhoods to be normally integrated on a long-term basis. And most are pleased at the prospect.

Some social stratification (by income and ethnic background) is probably inevitable in any complex society. But we miss much of life's richness if we fail to take affirmative action against the current trend among developers to layer us all out with "our own kind" of people. This would be a misguided approach in the current widespread search for community.

"When we lived in Washington I spoke my mind and nobody heard. Here I speak my mind and it gets onto the front page of the local newspapers."—S. ZEKE OR-LINSKY, A LAWYER WHO WITH HIS WIFE GAVE UP THEIR JOBS IN WASHINGTON SO THAT THEY COULD MOVE TO THE "NEW TOWN" OF COLUMBIA, MARYLAND.

23.

New Towns—
and
a Bold Test
of
Neighborliness

The quest for community and the quest for ways to avoid becoming an anthill society because of continued urban population growth have recently produced a remarkable rise in interest in the concept of the New Town.

A New Town offers planners a chance to make a fresh start. That is very appealing. Planners don't have to wrestle with the rigidities built into central cities that were started in another era, or with the fragmentation produced by current peripheral sprawl. They can try out new concepts of how people want to live. They have greater freedom of choice than in the past in locating their New Towns. With our new economy increasingly devoted to services and to light industry, and to new modes of transportation, it is no longer critical to locate towns or cities on waterways or along railroad trunk lines or near food-production areas.

Many of the New Towns, if properly conceived, can grow into New Cities. Furthermore, many of the lessons being learned from these laboratory-type situations in New Towns—and from one in particular in Maryland—can be applied *inside* existing cities to promote neighborliness and a sense of community. In fact they already are being applied.

The planners and settlers of New Towns sometimes refer to themselves as being on a frontier—but without the Indians.

Much of the earliest pioneering—and the trying and erring—of New Towns took place in Europe. Great Britain alone has created more than thirty New Towns.

The English were striving to build New Towns (they were called "garden cities" then) as early as the turn of the century. A first attempt was Letchworth, north of London. Although it was plagued with money problems, it tried bold new ideas such as cul-de-sac streets and the use of plenty of open space. A fine spirit of neighborliness prevailed even though the planners neglected to include a single pub in initially creating the town.

In the 1920s Welwyn, also north of London, became much talked about as a true garden city. The emphasis then was on greenery everywhere, including a lawn-covered central mall. The national government took over the direction of Welwyn after World War II and gave priority in housing to people actually working in Welwyn.

An explosion of interest in New Towns in Great Britain occurred after the New Towns Act of 1946 was passed. More than a dozen New Towns were begun. The government established a development corporation for each New Town and gave each the power to acquire land by eminent domain. A second burst of growth of New Towns occurred in the 1960s. Altogether, these British New Towns now house more than a million people, and most are still growing inside their greenbelts. To get a government-subsidized house in one of them you must have a job in the town.

Many of these New Towns were designed specifically to take the pressure off nearby major cities and are not especially innovative in terms of community-building.

The most celebrated of them is Cumbernauld, which

won many rave comments from visiting architects. Perched on a ridge northeast of Scotland's grimy Glasgow, it is scenically spectacular, providing fine views. At the core is a multilevel concrete shopping center which has caused some to liken it to a battleship. The town (pop. about 30,000) has been praised for its many footpaths that wind through buildings and under highways. But, over all, it is a pretty grim place and some critics call it anti-human.

Norman Whitefield, a Briton with long experience in building and studying New Towns, told me: "Some of the plans for these paradises had no concept of community." In his view Britain's best contribution to date, in terms of building a community, is at Hemel Hempstead, a small city northwest of London. It puts stress on neighborhoods, has a broad spectrum of social mix, and is relatively self-sufficient.

West Germany has created a number of new satellite towns outside cities, such as Nordwestadt near Frankfurt and Kippekausen near Nuremberg. And there is at least one self-sufficient New Town at Wolfsburg, a one-company community based in the Volkswagen plants. A number of these German towns have brilliantly engineered buildings, improvised walkways, parks, and spacious shopping areas. Yet the Germans are starting to rethink their efforts and are placing more weight on human interest in future planning. Sociologists in Wolfsburg found that the average family had no more than two close acquaintances in town.[1] And psychologists working with the Urban Planning Institute at Nuremberg found from studying children's paintings that children in New Towns near there considered them oppressively orderly and lacking in exciting ways to have fun.

France got off to a bad start in the creation of New Towns, I was advised by Lucien Karpik of the National Center of Scientific Research in Paris. One of the first, Sarcelles, near Paris, involved little planning beyond getting housing up in a hurry, and it attracted a high proportion of rootless people. Juvenile delinquency became a problem. Since then French architects and sociologists have been analyzing at considerable length the kinds of social relationships they want to create in New Towns. Their thinking is now going into the creation of a number of new cities near Paris, Marseilles, Toulouse, and Le Havre.

Scandinavia's ventures into New Towns tend to be more visually exciting than those in the rest of Europe. Sweden's Farsta, a kind of bedroom town to Stockholm, has many pleasant walkways and malls, and uses colors ingeniously. On the other hand a more recent New Town outside Stockholm, Skarholmen, is an architectural hodgepodge. It has been criticized for putting too much emphasis on shopping areas and not enough on providing ways for people to get together naturally. One of its interesting innovations is a four-level parking garage capable of handling 4,000 cars. Each level is connected to a different access route.

Beyond question, the world's most visually delightful New Town is Tapiola, near Helsinki, Finland. It is dispersed amid a substantially undisturbed forest of evergreens and birches bordering the Gulf of Finland. The "downtown" is an elevated, tree-shaded mall that you approach up seventy-foot-wide terraced steps. The mall is surrounded on two sides by an architecturally appealing two-story building that has shops on the first floor and professional offices on the second. On part of the third side is a towering building that houses the town's administration, and on its top a restaurant with a magnificent view. Factories are hidden in the forest. Winding through the forest are footpaths, bicycle paths and—quite apart— paved paths for autos. Neighborhoods in the forest were planned so that no woman with a baby would have to push a baby carriage more than 250 yards to obtain ordinary necessities such as bread or soap.[2]

In the past dozen years several hundred American urbanists and developers have visited Europe's experimental New Towns and have returned home sometimes admiring, sometimes critical, but usually filled with ideas they would like to try themselves.

Most of Europe's experiments in New Town creations have occurred as projects of their national governments. In the United States the national government, after tentative moves (first during the Depression and then in the late sixties), only came seriously into the picture of helping develop entire communities in 1970 with the passage of Title VII of the 1970 Housing Act. It guarantees loans to both private and public new community developers and offers direct loans and grants to help in the planning and provision of public services to the new communities. Altogether nearly a billion dollars was put on the line. Requests are pouring in.

Meanwhile the government has provided, from earlier appropriations, seed money for starting new communities in such places as Jonathan, southwest of Minneapolis; Park Forest South, near Chicago; Flower Mound between Dallas and Fort Worth, Texas; and Maumelle near Little Rock, Arkansas. New York State, the first state to have its own Urban Development Corporation, has started New Towns near Syracuse and Buffalo.

But the American "New Towns" far enough along to inspect as possible answers to the need for community are mostly private ventures, mostly privately financed, that did their planning before substantial government help was available.

Some that pass as New Towns are little more than oversized highly glossed real estate developments. Two of the very handsome New Towns that might fit this description have appeared on the fringes of Greater Los Angeles. One is at Westlake, which is rising on the old Russell Cattle Ranch in a valley of the mountains northwest of Los Angeles; and the other is University Park, which is rising in the more barren hills of the old, vast Irvine Ranch southeast of Los Angeles. Both adopted the sensible idea of clustering houses either together as townhouses or on small lots and have surrounded them with common lawns or water. Westlake has a vast bulldozer-created lake that has fingers reaching into many backyards. University Park uses open space made available by small-lot planning to create a kind of campus, laced with walkways and spotted with children's play areas, behind its tightly packed houses. Both places heavily emphasize recreational facilities. And both emphasize strict architectural controls. They frown on the gaudier or distracting aspects of typical developments. Westlake, for example, bans billboards, neon lights, and exposed power lines.

Both have established industrial parks nearby but there is little evidence in either case that the people who live in the towns work in the local industrial park or vice versa. Neither has much to offer for families with less than a $12,000 income. Most Westlake breadwinners commute about 35 miles to Los Angeles. I was visiting Westlake on a Sunday and while being gassed up at a posh Westlake station I asked the attendant if there were any churches in town. At that point I still hadn't seen any. He replied: "I don't know. I don't live here."

Southern California's biggest, most robust, most well-rounded New Town—despite its layering of neighborhoods —is Mission Viajo, which is several miles south of University Park. I described it in the last chapter. It incorporates most of the innovative features of Westlake and University Park, and seems somewhat more self-sufficient and has a somewhat broader range in the types of people it attracts.

A far more serious (and saddening) attempt by venture capital to create a real New Town has occurred at Reston, Virginia. This attracted worldwide attention in the early sixties. It was to be America's answer to Finland's Tapiola. There was an abundance of woods and water, a handsome plaza, walkways, clustered houses, townhouses and apartment buildings available at a fairly broad range of prices. And in the beginning there was the concept that it would grow big not by sprawl but as a series of villages.

Reston fell into difficulty, partly because it was underfinanced for such a vast undertaking . . . partly because so much of the emphasis was on dazzling, severely modern architecture . . . and partly because commuting to downtown Washington was difficult. A hoped-for access onto a federal freeway that passed right through Reston's acres was not granted. Reston fell into the hands of a corporate creditor which has switched to a more conventional approach to marketing houses.

America, however, does have one extraordinary success story in New Town creation. That is Columbia, Maryland, not far from Baltimore in the Washington-Baltimore corridor. While growing rapidly, it has kept its eye on the individual and his quest for community. It is dedicated to keeping everything it introduces to human scale. In terms of the challenges being explored in this book, Columbia is by far the most fascinating and innovative experiment in new creation that I have encountered.

It is the creation, primarily, of James Rouse, who has already bet $100 million (through his Rouse Company) that he can build a whole city of 100,000 people based on neighborhoods. It began about a decade ago when he managed, within ten months of very quiet dickering, to purchase a tract of rolling terrain of Maryland farmland and woodland about the size of Manhattan Island. More than a hundred and fifty separate negotiations were involved.

Mr. Rouse is a mortgage banker who branched into real estate development and prospered in the pioneering of enclosed shopping malls.

A bald, owlish-looking man who usually wears an amiable or perplexed look on his face, he is an astute businessman who knows how to borrow by the tens of millions. He also happens to be an idealist with a missionary's zeal for combating the depersonalization of modern urban life. He was a small-town boy from the Eastern Shore of Maryland.

A major influence on his thinking was his wife, a remarkably appealing, thoughtful woman. He acknowledged to me that over the decades her needling and questioning played a big role in getting him actively committed to trying to make communities more livable. She recalls that she went on their first date with some reluctance because she couldn't imagine anyone in the mortgage business being interesting. But they got to talking, on that first date, about the advantages of country and city living and they've been doing it ever since. Almost every week, after their marriage, they would go into a different section of Baltimore, talk to people, and ponder why some areas seemed to exude a strong sense of community while other areas nearby did not. Clear, visible boundaries seemed to make a difference.

They also went and looked at the New Towns and the grand old cities—so satisfying to most of their inhabitants —of Europe. Mrs. Rouse said to me: "If we don't learn to create real communities inside American cities and get them in scale that man can relate to, the historians are going to say: 'America was a highly technological society that failed for human reasons.'"

At Columbia the Rouses are trying to combine the advantages of small-town life with the excitement and amenities of city living. But how do you go about it? Rouse explains his approach this way: "If you want to plan out from the needs and yearnings of the people the kind of community that will best serve and nourish their growth . . . where do you go? Whom do you ask? Architects, engineers, planners, bankers, and developers are not the people who work intimately with people. Why not go to teachers and ministers and doctors, to psychiatrists, psychologists, and social scientists to plan a city?"

And that is what he did. He assembled a group of consultants that included a woman sociologist, an expert on human relations, an expert on urban sociology, a recreational expert, an expert on the ways people develop lines of communication, an expert on local governments, a psychologist, an educator, an expert on people's medical needs. In round-table talks, these and other experts were pumped for two hundred hours. Out of the pumping came many of the basic ideas that are shaping Columbia. The most important conclusion was that a good physical plan can actually encourage social activities and individual growth.

Today Columbia is approaching 25,000 in population and by 1976, it is expected, will be approaching 75,000. But there are not now, and never will be if Mr. Rouse can help it, any of the familiar signs of urban sprawl. This is because of the master plan. The plan calls for the center of the city to be separated by open greenery and water from the seven villages where people will live. And each village is being separated from its neighboring village by water, woodland, or a greenbelt. Four villages are already full or partially built. Columbia, incidentally, does not permit billboards or utility poles to mar its landscape.

But the heart of the plan is that each village consists of approximately three neighborhoods built around the village center. The "neighborhood" is the basic building block of Columbia. It consists of from 800 to 1,200 families whose townhouses, detached houses, or apartments are oriented to a neighborhood center. Most of the homes are on cul-de-sac roads which are credited, among other things, with producing a low burglary rate.

At each neighborhood center is an elementary school. It is within easy walking distance of most children in the neighborhood. Older children go to village schools within reasonable walking distance for them. Also at the neighborhood center is a convenience store, a snack bar, a park, a playground, a swimming pool, and a meeting room. Some neighborhoods also have day care centers. This kind of neighborhood is what James Rouse means when he talks about getting cities down to human scale.

A pathway system and roads lead to the village centers. Some of the paths have underpasses under roads. The pathway system allows children, older people, or mothers with baby carriages to reach the large village center on foot. One nine-year-old girl told me she not only walks to school but to her ballet classes, her religious class, and her flute lessons. "Mom doesn't have to drive me anywhere," she said. The village centers are walking malls. No cars can get in. The villages vary but most have restaurants, larger more specialized stores, religious centers, big pools. There are art exhibits and sidewalk cafés. At least two already have centers largely created by teen-agers. One is called the Orange Propeller.

At the core of Columbia is the "downtown" area of the city, which overlooks Lake Kittamaqundl and has fine statuary on a lawn and plaza facing the lake. This has become more of a public gathering place than even most New England towns can offer. By the lake there are administration buildings and a gourmet restaurant. An outdoor 5,000-seat symphony hall is in the woods nearby. In the downtown area also is the first phase of what will become the world's largest enclosed shopping mall, including a cinema, bookstore, fine clothing stores, department stores. Columbia is apparently America's first city to have an enclosed shopping mall as the retail core of its downtown. Most malls are out in the urban sprawl. There is also near the city's center a dinner-theater in the round where residents can bring their own bottles and where actors and actresses double as food servers. A museum, art galleries, and a central library are planned for the downtown area but at this writing are still to be installed.

About one fourth of Columbia—or about six hundred acres—will remain as permanent open space if present plans are followed. This includes woodland, three lakes, greenbelts, golf courses open to any resident for a relatively modest fee, tennis courts, and parks.

Some of the more remarkable innovations of Columbia are things you may not see. For example:

The famed Johns Hopkins Medical School has set up a comprehensive medical system, complete with clinic, that any Columbia resident can join. A new family moving in doesn't have the common worry of getting pediatricians and other doctors to accept them as patients. A member pays no doctor bills, just a monthly fee, which runs lower than annual medical bills of the average American family.

There is a network of child care centers where children of working mothers can be left, or where any busy wife can park a child for seventy-five cents an hour. There are village play areas where children can be left while Mother shops. And there are after-school, supervised play areas for six- to twelve-year-olds who have working mothers.

Columbia has a revolutionary approach to elementary education based on a Ford Foundation study. The first thing you notice is that the children seem happy as they study. There are few walls, no classrooms, and team teaching. Children often sit in circles on the floor and study as teams, not classes. Teachers are viewed more as resource persons than disciplinarians. Many mothers were helping out in the media room (broader in concept than a library) and by doing office work at the school I visited.

A ten-year-old girl named Liz explained to me: "You can go to any teacher for help if your teacher is busy. And you can choose the teachers you like to work with best."

The major religious faiths are using Columbia as a base for experimenting with pooled religious facilities. Every village has plans for a religious center with movable religious symbols. One has been built in Wilde Lake. Spaces are allotted to the major faiths. Religious leaders are suggesting that the ecumenical ministries and interfaith cooperation evolving at Columbia may turn out to be revolutionary models of the future.

Theoretically Columbia will soon have enough jobs to keep all its residents employed. It already has several dozen industries; and General Electric is building on the edge of Columbia a $250,000,000 appliance park. Columbia's goal is to have houses and apartments available for sale or rent that anyone working in Columbia can afford, whether he is a corporate executive or a janitor. As a practical matter it is not clear yet how self-sufficient Columbia will become. Many of the earlier settlers had jobs in Baltimore or Washington. The chief of long-range planning said that in 1970 about 40 percent of all the people living in Columbia work in Columbia or in its immediate area. But at least the potential for evolving toward a relatively self-sufficient city is there.

Well, that briefly is how the physical plan for this brand-new kind of city is emerging. How is it actually working out as far as the people are concerned? Some people say they experienced a letdown from overexpectation due in part perhaps to certain overly exuberant promises. But in general, as far as developing a sense of community is concerned, the results (gathered from many conversations) seem to be most encouraging.

The way newcomers are welcomed and made to feel at home undoubtedly plays a part in creating the encouraging results. In the early planning days Mr. Rouse concluded that the amount of trauma some people might feel in moving to a strange area would be related to the time it took before they were made to feel welcome.

So Mr. Rouse arranged for the Columbia Association to have trained welcomers make almost instant contact with newcomers. The welcomers bring along a 40-page manual that offers ready-reference answers to hundreds of questions the newcomer may wonder about—whether it concerns trash collection or dog licenses. The welcomer also asks newcomers what specific questions are on their minds and tries to give them advice. And the welcomer gives the newcomer the Columbia Association's phone number in case further questions arise.

Simultaneously a more personalized community service organization swings into action. This is the non-profit Friendship Exchange, Inc., whose members—volunteer residents of Columbia—also call on the newcomers with cookies and candy. The caller from the Exchange explains to the newcomer that the Exchange has 400 members, some in the immediate neighborhood, who are on instant call to offer help if the newcomer has emergencies or problems. The Exchange answering service, the newcomer is assured, operates twenty-four hours each day and will send volunteers to help with problems if help is needed. The Exchange, for example, will have people on the spot if a husband calls after midnight to say his wife is having a baby and he needs someone to stay with the children. One new arrival was helped when he had an urgent need for cash. The moving company would not unload the family's furniture until cash, not a check, was forthcoming. In many instances the Exchange arranges for people to call every day on shut-ins who are lonely and would like to talk with someone.

Newcomers to Columbia also receive flyers with information on clubs and organizations which residents themselves have created. There are already literally hundreds of such organizations from modern dance classes to volleyball clubs. The Columbia Association makes a mimeograph machine available for printing the flyers; and all it takes is ten signatures for residents to use the machine and start any organization they want.

People have come to Columbia from more than forty states. Many are looking for a utopia. As a result, perhaps, the city has an above-average attraction for people who were having troubles where they came from and are seeking a fresh start. Some do not succeed in shedding their old problems—such as an ailing marriage, for instance—when they get to Columbia. This may help account for the fact that Columbia is believed to have a higher-than-average rate of divorce and separation. On the other hand it also attracts an above-average number of people who were lonely where they were. It is hard to stay lonely, unless it is an interior type of loneliness, in Columbia. The city also, at least in its early years, has attracted a large proportion of idealists questing for community and they are given an inviting place to seek actualization of their ideals.

For those fed up with the drabness of living in one-layer communities, Columbia immerses them in a substantial diversity of people. At least they can see a variety of types at school meetings or at the neighborhood park.

Although the residents are predominantly white, college-educated younger marrieds with family incomes of about $17,000, there is a considerable variety as to age, income, and ethnic type. For example there is an association of retired people. Some older people prefer to live in one of the few buildings set aside as "all adult" (over twenty-one) but most are interspersed. One well-to-do man with a $70,000 house told me that when his mother came from California to be near his family they had no difficulty finding a low-priced place for her a few hundred yards away. A Columbia official said there were no special arrangements for getting young and old together. "It all comes naturally" from the layout, he said. And he added, "Here you at least have the option of living out your whole life in the same community and going from stage to stage."

The range in prices for housing at Columbia is close to $25,000 for a townhouse to $75,000. However, for poorer families, there are several hundred federally subsidized units that rent for $100 a month and up and more are being built. Ten percent of all housing in Columbia will be for low-income families.

People coming to Columbia know beforehand that it is an open city. It's so stated in the advertising. A glance at the "C's" in the directory shows that, though there are many people with names such as Campbell, Cavanaugh, Clay, and Calson, there are also residents named Capriano, Capik, Chao, Cohen, and Csanyi.

About one in six residents of Columbia is non-white. A black merchant runs a cleaning establishment in the village of Harpers Choice. A black person has recently been in charge of the Columbia Association's welcoming services. There have been several situations in which a black house hunter has selected a home and later found that he would be living next to a black family, whereupon he complained that that was not why he came to Columbia and asked to be relocated.

One black woman I consulted, the wife of a church official, said she had been living in the village of Harpers Choice for nine months and liked her street very much because people were so friendly. She has white neighbors. She recalled that the day she and her husband came to close the purchase a white neighboring family offered to take care of their children while they went to the office to complete the transaction. She said one of her friends (black) in the neighborhood complained at a group discussion that only two people on the street had come to call after she moved in; but a white woman said that no one on her street called on her in any formal way either. It was agreed, she explained to me, that though there is relatively little formal calling, people quickly get to know one another *automatically* through the activities in the neighborhood. I sense from a number of comments by whites in Columbia that they were glad they had knowingly chosen an "open" city. That way they would never be under any pressure from neighbors or blockbusters to run away the first time a dark-toned person appeared on their street. There certainly has been little or no panic selling. A townhouse bought in 1969 had increased in value nearly 50 percent when it was sold in 1971.

The people of Columbia have had their problems, some of them aggravating. Considering its location between Washington and Baltimore, it probably never could expect to escape people-problems associated with America's big old cities. There has been some racial tension especially among youngsters at the early teen period. This probably was heightened by the general nationwide confrontation orientations of many young whites and blacks in the past few years. The city has also had its share of young drug users.

Another problem is that most of the residential areas have been developed, under the Rouse Company's over-all guidelines, by a dozen different builders. Some of these builders are less concerned than Rouse is about preserving trees or maintaining high-quality workmanship. When groups of residents have gotten up in arms it has sometimes been hard to convince them that their grievance is with the builders, not with the Rouse Company.

One of the expectations early settlers had that the Rouse Company has not been able to fill was a system of minibuses running on their own roadways throughout the city. This would have eliminated the need of many residents for a second car. Partly, this minibus plan was defeated by the well-known preference of Americans to hop in the car instead of a bus. The Rouse Company soon found there wasn't enough traffic to justify paying the salaries of all the minibus drivers needed to make the promise a reality. The bus schedules were cut back and finally dropped. A radio-dispatched Call-a-Ride system has been replacing most of the minibuses, and that too has had its troubles. Meanwhile the Rouse Company, with federal help, is exploring the possibility of an automated, elevated transit system.

But perhaps the most puzzling problem—and the one most frustrating to community-minded residents—is Columbia's political structure.

A city being built by a private entrepreneur—even so enlightened a one as Jim Rouse—probably cannot have a mayor and City Council elected by the city's residents. At least not until it is fairly well built. The first settlers could raise havoc with a master plan that had cost millions to develop. Still, it is frustrating to live in a "city" that is not democratically run. This is a dilemma that all New Towns —at least those financed by private enterprise—will face.

Technically the only government in Columbia is that of Howard County, in which the city is situated. The Columbia Association, which makes all major policy decisions affecting services and environment for the city, is dominated by Rouse Company officials. However, provision is made that residents will get a member on the Association's ruling board every time the city grows by 4,000 dwellings. Thus residents now have one elected fellow resident as a member of the controlling board. Before the end of the 1970s they should have a majority of seats in the Association. Meanwhile they elect their own village boards, which are advisory. Many dozens of residents have been campaigning in elections for positions on the technically toothless village boards; and residents have been showing intense interest in their village elections and problems. A great many residents skipped work one day to make a mass demand that a builder stop bulldozing trees.

One insurgent who has served on the Wilde Lake Village Board is an amiable lawyer-editor, S. Zeke Orlinsky. He explained the real power structure to me in these terms:

"There is absolutely nothing we have control over. But we do have the power of persuasion and harassment. In controversies involving trees and fences where residents showed considerable concern the Columbia Association has sided with residents against the builder in several instances. We are learning to get leverage through counteraction and bad publicity. That's the one thing they don't want, and that's their Achilles' heel."

As thousands of Columbians have been speaking their minds Mr. Rouse has gradually granted more power. Now village representatives are allowed to work directly with the Columbia Association's financial director and use their persuasion to influence how the citizens' money is spent to develop their community.

Although Mr. Orlinsky was viewed as a political insurgent in Columbia, he was glad he was living there instead of Washington, where his family had formerly lived. He explained: "The focus on the villages really does enhance a sense of community. You tend to see more people and have more shared interests. We personally have found a lot of close friends here just within a couple of years. We met people we would never have met in Washington. I think in Washington you tend to know people you meet on the job or in an organization you belong to. Here there are a lot of reasons you can meet other people."

In prowling about Columbia I met a good many residents and a number gave me, I believe, candid reactions to Columbia. Robert Waller, an environmental engineer, left a job in Wilmington, Delaware, to take a job near the Columbia home they bought. Mrs. Waller commented:

"The most important thing that's going on here is the development of a sense of community. I hope it can be maintained." Her husband said that for exercise he bought a basketball and began shooting baskets at the three different play yards within walking distance of his house. This Ph.D. added: "Often I find myself playing basketball with the kids."

A Westinghouse engineer, Bob Gorrie, was explaining that in signing up to live at Columbia he had expected a better bus system and more walkways than exist in his particular neighborhood. But he added: "Don't get me wrong. Their concept of the village has worked out. Marcia and I are both deeply involved in village projects. Most of our best friends now are from this village [Wilde Lake]. We hope we can stay here for a long time. We think of it as our home." He said they had previously lived in Arlington, Virginia, which he called a vast amorphous place where you never quite knew where the center was, and where people all around you kept moving.

One couple I questioned insisted that they not be quoted. From that I assumed they had negative views.

They were from Pikesville, a part of the overflow of Baltimore. Both said that they had somehow imagined there would be more open space in Columbia than they found as their village developed. But then they indicated that they knew all their neighbors. The wife explained: "There is no social pressure but if you want to you can enjoy a real sense of neighborliness. A lot of people know me here. Everything is so much closer. I think of the seven years we lived in Pikesville. Except for the neighbors on each side of us I never got to know many people in the town. Here I know so many people. My circle of friends is tremendous here. And it was not in Pikesville. Yet I am the same person!" She added that she felt she had grown intellectually, socially, and in self-confidence in the Columbia environment.

Mr. Rouse is not content to devote himself just to building a full-sized city in Columbia. He and his colleagues are mapping a second New Town on the order of Columbia. And they are trying out some of the insights they have achieved in Columbia to improve the quality of community living inside existing cities. For example experts in his Urban Division have been seeking in Hartford, Connecticut, to get the many government officials there whose actions are affecting the lives of Hartford citizens to develop closer "linkages" through better communication and to stop the working at cross-purposes that frequently befuddles bureaucracy and bewilders citizens. His urban experts also have been developing for New York City a proposal to create a new town of 10,000 acres within South Richmond on Staten Island.

A college educator in Columbia who has a pretty hard-boiled view of the world said that there is a "desperate sense of rootlessness everywhere, especially among the young." He added: "One of the things I like about officials of the Rouse Company is that even if they don't solve problems they are concerned and they listen. Jim Rouse listens. And he is serious about what he hopes can be achieved at Columbia." From now on, whatever is achieved will increasingly be the achievement of the residents themselves.

All citizens who are concerned about the state of the American life style and environment should, like Mr. Rouse, be listening, thinking, and acting. The people of America have no more urgent problem today, I believe, than to combat the uprootedness and unconnectedness which are producing so much social fragmentation. Most can start in their own towns and urban neighborhoods.

We have seen in this exploration, I believe, that in many areas the natural human community is endangered. In much of America it is beset by environment turbulence, the onrush of relatively anonymous living, the breakdown of blood ties, the widespread rootlessness of people.

Technological progress is no bargain if we lose the natural human community in the process. This seems a fair warning for many societies outside the U.S.A., as well as for Americans.

But we are also seeing that individuals by the millions are fighting back. There is a new groping and searching, a reaching out for community. We are gradually learning what we have to do to recapture something resembling the natural human community. For example we now realize that:

—The natural human community is one that is small enough to be in scale to man.
—It provides a natural way for people to come together if they wish to do so.
—It offers a natural setting for individuals to achieve personal recognition, to share experience, to find assurance of emotional and other support, and to develop some enduring friendships.
—Its stability and diversity provide a sense of wholeness and coherence to a participant's life, a sense that what is happening today is part of an ongoing process.
—It provides people with a sense that they have some control over events about to happen that can affect their lives.
—And it offers people a special group and a special place that they can think of as their own. They

have a living environment they can seek to improve and one in which they can come to feel a proprietary pride.

All these taken together can provide man with a setting that offers him some reasonable chance for achieving some degree of personal serenity.

Appendices

Appendix A

EVIDENCES OF
WORLDWIDE INCREASES IN MOBILITY

In other parts of the world, especially Europe, people are increasingly on the move. The rate of movement—and uprooting—has been increasing, and this is especially conspicuous in the movement across national borders of businessmen and people seeking jobs. The surging of people across borders has not been matched since the convulsion of the Second World War. And in several countries, including Germany, Sweden, the Netherlands, and Italy, movement within the countries is reported to be increasing.

The English are so clearly on the move that professional welcoming services have been set up to welcome newcomers in a number of English towns and cities. The British behaviorial science journal *New Society* reports that in some parts of England migratory movements are "nothing less than frenetic." It cites the fact that in some areas in and around London a fifth of all residents live in their homes less than a year. Many apparently are young apartment dwellers paying ordinary rent. It should be noted that many English apartment dwellers who might be inclined to move frequently are impeded—more than in the U.S.A.—by the fact that they must buy a lease for a specified number of years. *New Society* also reports that new house owners expect to move many more times than their parents.

Although migration within Germany is increasing the more drastic change is the influx of a half million immigrants each year from southern Europe seeking jobs in Germany's economy, which has been booming during most of the past decade. Altogether Germany has a million and a half foreign workers.

In small but prosperous Switzerland, which has a population of only six million, the hottest political issue in a quarter century is the fact that it has 600,000 foreign workers, mostly Italians. In addition it has 400,000 other foreign residents. During mid-1970 a proposal to expel half of the employed foreigners was put to a popular vote and was narrowly defeated.

France, too, has a very high number of foreign workers. There are nearly two million. Mostly they are Algerians, Italians, Spaniards, and Portuguese. Professor Lucien Karpik, sociologist at the National Center of Scientific Research in Paris, advised me these immigrants were, until recently, a political problem, but that the situation has eased and there is now considerable social integration. In French industry there is relatively little mobility of managers, though, in contrast with the recent past, the bigger companies now find that it can be helpful for a person to have some previous experience with other companies. And within the companies there is a moderate amount of transfers to branch plants within the country.

In general, however, the French just don't like to move. The farmers, who are in surplus, are so attached to their particular *terre* that the European Common Market in 1971 began offering them special incentives to move to the cities. Frenchmen in general resist moving more than 20 miles for a better job. And as for Paris, residents are so attached to it that they not only resist moving to other cities, but influential Parisians resist moving to the city's suburbs.

Italians on the other hand are not only highly mobile in immigrating to northern countries but are quite mobile within their country. Business managers and executives are becoming so much more mobile that newspapers carry large sections of classified ads announcing their availability. Some companies are insisting upon contracts specifying a long "notice of departure." The great source of mobility in Italy, however, is the recent renewal of the great migrations of poor southerners to the more prosperous northern cities, especially to booming Milan. In 1970 Milan's population grew 50,000 in three months. There is considerable hostility among rank and file Milanese toward the southerners; and reports of bank robberies, holdups, and knifings have been soaring. If the culprits are from the south the newspapers usually make a point of mentioning it.

The northbound surge of job-seeking people from many of the Mediterranean countries reaches to Denmark and Sweden. And Scandinavians by the tens of thousands go to Mediterranean seacoast towns for long vacations. Even the Turks of Europe and Asia Minor who, as indicated earlier, have traditionally been appalled by the idea of leaving their home areas, are migrating in great numbers, at least from their cities, to northern countries. Author Alvin Toffler, in investigating recent European migration patterns, discovered that 1,000 Turks leave Istanbul by train each weekend. So many disembark at Munich, Germany, he found that Munich now has a Turkish-language newspaper.

In other parts of the world we have the swarming about of vast numbers of refugees.

A good example is in African countries such as Kenya, Uganda, and Ghana. Millions of African refugees have been created as the people sort themselves out after the elimination of the white colonial rulers who created arbitrarily drawn borders; and as the new black governments harass Asians who were encouraged to come to Africa as merchants, clerks, etc., under colonial rule. Uganda and Kenya have been returning one another's immigrants in order to open more job opportunities for their own citizens.

And then there is South Vietnam. The American military, in the process of helping defend the country, contributed greatly to the creation of five million refugees. That is a fourth of the entire population.

In China we are seeing the reverse of the mass movement from farm to city so conspicuous in America and Western Europe. In 1969 there were news reports that 25 million Chinese—or 15 percent of the urban population—were being sent into the countryside to do manual labor.

Finally we have Japan, traditionally the most socially rigid of the advanced societies in the world. In the past there was almost no mobility in the Japanese world of business. The employer was assumed to be the master of the employee, and the employee should expect to spend his life with that firm. The young Japanese who aspired to get a responsible job in a major company, furthermore, had to go to a specific school, the University of Tokyo. And he had to be accepted by the firm he aspired to join within one year after graduation.

Today these rigidities are loosening with great velocity. The incredible growth of the Japanese economy has created so much demand for talented personnel that many of the better middle-sized companies are raiding smaller companies. The huge companies, while still trying to maintain the traditional anti-mobility line, have felt free to raid the government to procure talented personnel.

And to help all this mobility along, enterprising Japanese businessmen have created firms which recruit—often furtively—managers and professionals for companies. One night only eight years ago I was dining in Tokyo with several industrialists who questioned me about business practices in America. The traditional taboos against movement then still prevailed in almost all Japanese industries. The industrialists seemed only politely attentive to my remarks until I mentioned a new institution in America, the executive recruiting firm. Suddenly they were all talking excitedly. They had never heard of such a thing. They questioned me intently and several got out notebooks and made notes. Although fascinated, they seemed mainly horrified that such a disruptive institution had been created. Obviously it was not appropriate for Japan and should never be permitted to take root there. Today at least six such firms are flourishing there.

That is a pretty good indication of how fast attitudes toward mobility are changing in most industrialized countries of the world.

Appendix B

HIGH MOBILITY STATES

Here are the most stable and most volatile states as reflected in the percentages of main residential telephones in the Bell System that were disconnected during 1971:

MOST STABLE			MOST VOLATILE	
Pennsylvania	16	percent	Nevada	41 percent
New York	17	percent	Arizona	38 percent
New Jersey	18	percent	Colorado	37 percent
West Virginia	19	percent	Texas	37 percent
Massachusetts	19	percent		(approx.)
New Hampshire	19.6	percent	New Mexico	37 percent
Rhode Island	19.9	percent	Wyoming	36 percent
			Oregon	36 percent
			California	35 percent

Appendix C

POPULATION INFLOW

The 1970 Census shows that the big population gainers during the decade of the 1960s were:

Nevada	69 percent gain
Florida	35 percent gain
Arizona	35 percent gain
Alaska	30 percent gain
California	25 percent gain
Colorado	25 percent gain
Maryland	22 percent gain
Delaware	21 percent gain

The few states actually losing population during the decade despite a general upsurge in the U.S. population were:

West Virginia	8 percent loss
South Dakota	3.4 percent loss
North Dakota	3.3 percent loss

| Mississippi | 1 | percent loss |
| Wyoming | .5 | percent loss |

While the population of Pennsylvania and Kentucky did not fall, because of the general population upsurge, they both had heavy losses of residents moving to other states. In sheer numbers Pennsylvania lost more people in the 1960s through net out-migration than any other state: 375,000. However this was an improvement over the 1950s when it lost 475,000.

In 1969 the U.S. Census Bureau made an estimate of the change in population that would occur in 164 major urban areas between 1965 and 1975. It predicted gains for more than nine out of ten. Of the 25 fastest growing, all but two are either west of the Mississippi or in the South. The two exceptions are Madison, Wisconsin, and Brockton, Massachusetts. Of 164 cities, only 13 were expected to see a population decline—and 6 of these were in Pennsylvania. The Census Bureau, interestingly, began to recognize the fact that many cities are starting to bump into each other. It did this by lumping two or three cities under one hyphenated label. Thus its metropolitan areas now have labels such as these: San Bernardino-Riverside-Ontario, California; Bridgeport-Stamford-Norwalk, Connecticut; and Los Angeles-Long Beach, California.

Notes

PERSONAL NOTE

1. John B. Lansing and Eva Mueller, *The Geographic Mobility of Labor* (Ann Arbor, Michigan: Institute for Social Research, University of Michigan, 1967), p. 29.

CHAPTER 1

1. Larry H. Long, "On Measuring Geographic Mobility," *Journal of the American Statistical Association*, September 1970.
2. "Population: Internal Migration 1935 to 1940: Social Characteristics of Migrants," U.S. Bureau of the Census (Washington: U.S. Government Printing Office, 1946). And, "1960 Census: Population: Mobility for States and State Economic Areas," also prepared by the U.S. Bureau of the Census.

CHAPTER 6

1. Pierre de Vise, "Chicago's Widening Color Gap," Report #2, Interuniversity Social Research Committee, December 1967, p. 113.

CHAPTER 7

1. Timothy D. Schellhardt, "Town vs. Gown," *Wall Street Journal,* January 12, 1971.

2. Douglas H. Heath, "Not Just Intellectual Growth," *Contemporary Psychology,* Vol. 14, No. 5, 1969.

3. David G. Brown, *The Mobile Professors* (Washington, D.C.: The American Council on Education, 1967), pp. 25–26.

CHAPTER 8

1. Gordon L. Bultena and Vivian Wood, "The American Retirement Community: Bane or Blessing," *Journal of Gerontology,* April 1969.

2. James S. Honneh, William I. A. Eteng, Douglas G. Marshall, "Retirement and Migration in the North Central States: Comparative Socioeconomic Analyses—Wisconsin and Florida" (mimeograph), July 1969. (Funded by the U.S. Administration on Aging, Department of Health, Education and Welfare.)

CHAPTER 9

1. Philip M. Hauser, "The Chaotic Society: Product of the Social Morphological Revolution." *American Sociological Review,* Vol. 34, No. 6, February 1969, p. 6.

2. Christopher Alexander, "The City as a Mechanism for Sustaining Human Contact" (see especially footnote 39 on families living at high-density levels), from William R. Ewald, *Environment of Man* (Bloomington, Ind.: Indiana University Press, 1966), p. 81.

3. See Harvey Choldin, "The Response to Migrants of the Receiving Community," from *Family Mobility in Our Dynamic Society,* Iowa State University Center for Agricultural and Economic Development (Ames, Iowa: Iowa State University Press, 1965), p. 176.

4. Pierre de Vise, "Persistence of the Hyphenated Americans: Chicago's Ethnic Communities in 1969," an address

before the Chicago Consultation on Ethnicity at the Chicago
Circle Center, University of Illinois, November 17, 1969.

5. Louis Wirth, *The Ghetto* (Chicago: University of Chicago Press, 1928), pp. 226–28.

6. Pierre de Vise, "Chicago's Widening Color Gap," pp. 29–30.

7. Ibid., footnote 4.

8. Chicago Regional Hospital Study, "The Economic Ranks of Chicago's Suburban Municipalities in 1970," Chicago Association of Commerce and Industry, September 1971.

CHAPTER 10

1. John Herbers, "The Outer City: Uneasiness over the Future," *New York Times,* June 2, 1971.

2. Jack H. Morris, "Meet Me at the Mall; Suburbs' Life Often Centers on Shopping Centers," *Wall Street Journal,* February 20, 1969.

3. Ibid.

4. Ibid.

5. Seth H. King, "Supermarkets: Hub of Suburbs," *New York Times,* February 7, 1971.

CHAPTER 11

1. K. K. White, "Reimbursing Personnel for Transfer and Relocation Costs," *American Management Association,* Study #67, 1964.

2. Philip Slater, *The Pursuit of Loneliness* (Boston: Beacon Press, 1970), p. 112.

3. "The Doctor is Busy," *Wall Street Journal,* March 4, 1969.

CHAPTER 12

1. Elizabeth Squire, "Newcomers" series, *The Wilton Bulletin,* March 11, 1970.

2. Ibid.

CHAPTER 13

1. Jack Long, "School for Business Ambassadors," *The Lamp*, Fall 1965.

2. For a fuller description of these organizations see Vance Packard, *The Naked Society* (New York: David McKay Company, 1964).

3. *New Yorker*, June 14, 1969.

4. Dave Bittan and Charles MacNamara, "The Sociology of Talk Radio," *Philadelphia Magazine*, July 1969.

CHAPTER 14

1. See Eugene Litwak, "Geographic Mobility and Extended Family Cohesion," *American Sociological Review*, June 1960, pp. 385–394; Phillip Fellin and Eugene Litwak, "Neighborhood Cohesion Under Conditions of Mobility," *American Sociological Review*, Vol. 28, 1963, pp. 364–378; Eugene Litwak and Joan Szelenyi, "Primary Group Structures and Their Functions: Kin, Neighbors and Friends," *American Sociological Review*, August 1969, p. 465 et seq.

CHAPTER 15

1. "Suing the Doctor," *Newsweek*, January 19, 1970, p. 93.

2. Steven V. Roberts, "Divorce, California Style, Called a Reflection of the Restless West," *New York Times*, January 1, 1970.

3. Elizabeth Squire, op. cit., February 25, 1970.

4. Alvin Toffler, *Future Shock* (New York: Random House, 1970), p. 76.

5. Arthur Schlesinger, Jr., "A Skeptical Democrat Looks at President Nixon," *New York Times Magazine*, November 17, 1968.

CHAPTER 16

1. Robert S. Weiss, "The Fund of Sociability." *Trans-Action*, July/August 1969.

2. *Sales Management* defines "effective buying power per household" as the cash or non-cash income that all members of the family have left after they have paid their taxes. Total average incomes per household *before* taxes in Azusa and Glens Falls would have run a couple of thousand dollars higher.

3. In each town the first 100 questionnaires returned were obtained on the door-to-door basis, as indicated, within a predetermined six-block area. Then in each town a few additional responses were obtained by sampling known high- or low-mobile areas elsewhere in order that each total sample would also reflect quite precisely the town's over-all mobility rate as indicated by telephone records.

CHAPTER 17

1. One of the major studies was supported by a grant from the National Institute for Mental Health. It was conducted by the Center for Community Studies created by the Massachusetts General Hospital and Harvard Medical School, under the direction of Erich Lindemann, psychiatrist, and Marc Fried, clinical psychologist.

For reports on several of the major studies made of the West End displacement of people, see especially Erich Lindemann, "Urban Renewal and Mental Health," a Research Project Summary, National Institute for Mental Health, December 1963; Herbert J. Gans, "The Human Implications of Current Redevelopment and Relocation Planning," *Journal of the American Institute of Planners*, Vol 25, No. 1, February 1959; Ellen Fitzgerald, "Evaluation of Mental Health Services During the Relocation Crisis" (mimeograph), by the Family Relocation Center of the Boston University Medical School; Marc Fried, "Grieving for a Lost Home," Leonard J. Duhl, ed., in *The Urban Condition* (New York: Basic Books, 1963); Chester W. Hartmann, "Other Papers: Social Values and Housing Orientations," *Journal of Social Issues*, Vol XI, No. 2, 1963; Marc Fried, "Effects of Social Change on Mental Health," *American Journal of Orthopsychiatry*, Vol. XXXIV, No. 1, January 1964.

2. See Benjamin Malzberg, "Internal Migration and Mental

Disease Among the White Population of New York, 1960–61," *International Journal of Social Psychiatry*, 1967, pp. 184–91; Everett S. Lee, "Socio-Economic and Migration Differentials in Mental Disease, New York State, 1949–51," *Milbank Fund Quarterly*, July 1963; Leo Levy and Harold M. Visotsky, "The Quality of Urban Life," in "Urban America: Goals and Problems," issued by Subcommittee on Urban Affairs, 90th Congress 1st Session, August 1967; Mildred Kantor, *Mobility and Mental Health* (Springfield, Ill.: Charles C. Thomas, 1965); Seymour Parker et al., "Migration and Mental Illness—Some Reconsiderations and Suggestions for Further Analysis," *Social Science and Medicine*, Vol. 3 (Oxford, England: Pergamon Press, 1969); Christopher Bagley, "Migration, Race and Mental Health: A Review of Some Recent Research," *Race*, Vol. 3, 1968; Benjamin Malzberg and Everett S. Lee, *Migration and Mental Disease* (New York: Social Science Research Council, 1956); Marc Fried, "Effects of Social Change on Mental Health," *The American Journal of Orthopsychiatry*, Vol. XXXIV, no. 1, January 1964.

3. See "The Aerospace Malaise," *Newsweek*, April 8, 1968. (*Time*, in another report based on interviews with different people, came up with several of the same evidences of aerospace life style; see "Life in the Space Age," July 4, 1969.)

4. See Richard D. Lamm, "Urban Growing Pains—Is Bigger Also Better?" *New Republic*, June 5, 1971. Mr. Lamm is a member of the Colorado House of Representatives.

5. Philip G. Zimbardo, "The Human Choice: Individuation, Reason and Order *versus* Deindividuation, Impulse and Chaos," in W. J. Arnold and D. Levine, eds., *1969 Nebraska Symposium on Motivation* (Lincoln, Nebraska: University of Nebraska Press, 1970), pp. 237–307.

6. Neil Morgan, *The California Syndrome* (Englewood Cliffs, N.J.: Prentice-Hall, 1969), p. 80.

7. See Dorothy C. Disney, "The Trials of Families on the Move," *Ladies' Home Journal*, May 1969.

8. Alvin L. Schorr, "Mobile Family Living," *Social Casework*, April 1956.

9. "Doomsday in the Golden State," *Time*, April 11, 1969.

10. Talk by Martin Goldberg at Biennial Conference of the Travelers Aid Association of America in San Juan, Puerto Rico, May 10, 1966.

11. Martin Goldberg, "The Runaway Americans—A Report on the findings of a study of the mental health of people in flight," *Mental Hygiene,* January 1972.

12. Nat Hentoff, "The Cold Society," *Playboy,* September 1966.

13. George C. Homans, *The Human Group* (New York: Harcourt, Brace and Company, 1950), p. 457.

14. C. Tietze, P. Lemkau, M. Cooper, "Personality Disorder and Spatial Mobility," *American Journal of Sociology,* 1, 1942.

15. Robert A. Nisbet, *Community and Power* (London: Oxford University Press, 1962), p. 18.

16. Toffler, op. cit., pp. 291–96.

17. "Who Gets Cancer?" *Newsweek,* April 19, 1971.

18. Alton Blakeslee and Jeremiah Stamler, *Your Heart Has Nine Lives* (New York: Pocket Books Inc., 1971), p. 139.

CHAPTER 18

1. "Executives on the go," *Newsweek,* November 21, 1966.

2. See "The Effect of Pupil Mobility Upon Academic Achievement," *National Elementary Principal,* April 1966; C. H. Gilliland, "The Relationship to Achievement of Mobility in the Elementary School," University Microfilms, Inc., Ann Arbor, Michigan, 1959; E. D. Tetreau and J. V. Fuller, "Some Factors Associated with School Achievement in Migrant Families," *Elementary School Journal,* 42:6, 1942; Carla Fitch and Josephine Hoffer, "Geographic Mobility and Academic Achievement of a Group of Junior High Students," *Journal of Home Economics,* May 1964; and Frank Farmer, "The Effect of School Change on the Achievement of Military Dependent Children," paper presented to the California Education Research Association, Palo Alto, California, March 3–4, 1961.

3. See Vance Packard, *The Sexual Wilderness* (New York: David McKay Company, 1968), Chapter 23.

4. See Urie Bronfenbrenner, "The Split-Level American Family," *Saturday Review,* October 7, 1967.

5. Ibid.

CHAPTER 19

1. Elizabeth Squire, op. cit., March 11, 1970.

2. Jon Nordheimer, "Modern Society Perils the Role of the Fading Volunteer Fireman," *New York Times,* January 2, 1971.

3. Elizabeth Squire, op. cit., March 11, 1970.

4. Murray Schumach, "Neighborhoods: Safe, Proud Maspeth," *New York Times,* October 20, 1971.

CHAPTER 20

1. Bill Kovach, "New Industry: Building That Home Away from Home," *New York Times,* April 6, 1971.

2. John Herbers, "1600 from Ethnic Groups Organize Protest Against Institutions They Say Are Destroying Central Cities," *New York Times,* March 20, 1972.

3. Jonathan Spivak, "Pride of Ownership," *Wall Street Journal,* October 23, 1970.

4. Steven V. Roberts, "Some Areas Seek to Halt Growth," *New York Times,* March 14, 1971.

CHAPTER 21

1. Robert A. Nisbet, op. cit., p. 73.

2. See Daniel Yankelovich, "The Young Adult in an Age of Complexity," address at annual meeting of the Institute of Life Insurance, New York, December 7, 1965.

3. Clyde Haberman, "The Neighborly Thing to Do," *New York Post,* May 29, 1971.

4. Edward C. Burks, "Board in Yorkville Fights Planners," *New York Times,* February 19, 1971.

5. *Life,* October 16, 1970.

CHAPTER 22

1. Linda Greenhouse, "Suburb of a Suburb Has an Identity Problem," *New York Times,* May 11, 1971.

2. Sula Benet, "Why They Live to Be 100, or Even Older, in Abkhasia," *New York Times Magazine,* December 26, 1971.

3. "Can't the Suburbs Be Opened?" *Time,* April 6, 1970.

CHAPTER 23

1. Gurney Breckenfeld, *Columbia and the New Cities* (New York: Ives Washburn, Inc., 1971), p. 101.

2. Ibid., p. 97.

Index